# REACHING FOR DRIFTWOOD

"When you're in the process of manifesting, the Universe will show you all kinds of subtle, smaller signs that what you want is on the way. They're what Abraham-Hicks calls "driftwood." Often, we simply don't notice this guidance, or we dismiss it as just a coincidence.

Driftwood can be so subtle that the signs can be easily missed. The problem with driftwood is that it is often overlooked, not recognized for the beauty and the value it holds. We are so busy looking for the big extravaganza. The big lottery win, the out-of-the-blue-offer-of-the-perfect-job, our perfect soulmate unexpectedly ringing our doorbell. We overlook the small signs that show us that change is, indeed, happening.

Noticing driftwood requires us to be aware of and mindful of what is happening in the moment, and not worried about what the future holds. Noticing driftwood also requires us to be able to appreciate the small things in our life, to express gratitude for the nanoscale, minute-by-minute routines of everyday life. This is where the magic lies. In the minuscule, nanoscale, quantum bits and pieces of our lives. In the single tiny moments that string together to become our days, our weeks, our years. And in the driftwood that seems to appear from nowhere but signals that better things are coming.

We are so busy looking for the big extravaganza—the big lottery win, the out-of-the-blue-offer-of-the-perfect-job, our perfect soulmate unexpectedly ringing our doorbell—that we overlook the small signs that show us that change is, indeed, happening."

– Anne Bolender,
*Seeing Driftwood As a Sign of Success*

# Author's Note

This is a memoir. Which means, yes, these stories are in fact true. Some of the names have been changed to protect the identity of the people I have written about. My intention is not to ruin anyone's life by writing about them. I'm just a woman that heals through writing and transmuting her pain into art.

As a disclaimer, some of these stories are explicit and visceral in nature. Please consider this as a warning in advance, as well as a request to remember that I am merely a woman on her never-ending healing journey. I am human. Humans make mistakes and sometimes growth is messy and embarrassing.

This is my story, my truth, and my life. Please consider reading these contents with an open mind and open heart. Please be kind. Thank you for being and supporting my work.

I love you.

*Brittany Bacinski*

# REACHING FOR DRIFTWOOD

*A Memoir*

BRITTANY BACINSKI

Copyright © 2024 Brittany Bacinski
Print Edition

All rights reserved. No part of this publication may be reproduced, distributed, or transmitted in any form or by any means, including photocopying, recording, or other electronic or mechanical methods, without the prior written permission of the publisher, except in the case of brief quotations embodied in critical reviews and certain other noncommercial uses permitted by copyright law.

To my mother, for being my haven, my home,
and my lighthouse.

Thank you for holding me through it all. I love you.

# Table of Contents

| | |
|---|---|
| If this book was a song | xvii |
| Atlas: Terms often used in RFD and their meaning | xix |
| Introduction | xxi |
| 1. Reaching for the Life Raft | 1 |
| 2. She Filed for Divorce, Ya'll | 8 |
| 3. Clutching My First Life Raft | 10 |
| 4. To Keep Me from Drowning Again | 13 |
| 5. The Solo Hike That Changed Everything | 18 |
| 6. The Whole Foods Hottie | 22 |
| 7. Mom is Taking Stripper Classes? | 53 |
| 8. Dating App Disasters | 54 |
| 9. Everything is Bigger in Texas (Objects in Mirror Appear Larger Than They Are) | 60 |
| 10. Blinded by the Light (And Other Obvious Things) | 70 |
| 11. Becoming a Sex God | 73 |
| 12. Perfect on Paper | 75 |
| 13. Light Out, Hearts Out | 78 |
| 14. Valentine's Day is for the Girls | 85 |
| 15. New Home, New Life | 91 |
| 16. All Tied and Tangled Up | 95 |
| 17. Lessons from a Fiddle Fig | 100 |
| 18. This Isn't Good Night, It's Goodbye | 103 |
| 19. If the Devil Can't Reach You, He'll Send You an Aquarius | 107 |

| | |
|---|---|
| 20. Meeting Your Life Partner | 112 |
| 21. Falling Over Facetime | 114 |
| 22. The Messy Middle | 125 |
| 23. It's Not Always What's There, Sometimes It's in What's Not | 126 |
| 24. That French Guy | 128 |
| 25. Yin Yoga Lesson on the Art of Stillness | 132 |
| 26. Navigation with Your Inner Compass | 135 |
| 27. Sail, Don't Row | 137 |
| 28. Fourteen Lives in a Day | 142 |
| 29. Let Yourself Eat Cake | 151 |
| 30. On His Way Back to Me | 153 |
| 31. A Ride in the Jaguar | 156 |
| 32. Whole Foods Man and the Plot | 158 |
| 33. Summer Fling before the Ring | 169 |
| 34. Every Moment is a Movie | 179 |
| 35. Take Two? Take Three? | 183 |
| 36. Maryland, Motorcycles, Man Buns and Mountains, Oh My! | 188 |
| 37. What Goes up, Must Come… Back Again? | 196 |
| 38. Like a Kid with a Kite | 201 |
| 39. The Counterfeit Always Comes before the Blessing | 203 |
| 40. Facing My Own Emotional Unavailability | 206 |
| 41. A Fated Lesson in Surrender | 210 |
| 42. Sedona Awakenings | 220 |
| 43. Never Settle | 225 |
| 44. Distance Makes the Heart Stop | 227 |
| 45. An Open Love Letter to Men | 233 |

| | |
|---|---|
| 46. One Year of Will | 237 |
| 47. Three for Three | 267 |
| 48. A Love Like Oxygen | 272 |
| 49. Brewed Bonds | 274 |
| 50. The Secret to Letting Go | 283 |
| 51. Screw It All, We Ball | 285 |
| 52. New Year, New Chapter, New Us? | 289 |
| 53. The Seashell Theory | 296 |
| 54. Arriving to Shore | 300 |
| 55. Leap Year | 303 |
| 56. The American Nightmare | 305 |
| 57. The End Is Just a New Beginning in Disguise | 307 |
| | |
| Acknowledgments | 309 |

*When you are not fed love on a silver spoon,*
*you learn to lick it off knives.*

– Lauren Eden

# If this book was a song

## Coldplay - Fix You

**When you try your best, but you don't succeed**
**When you get what you want, but not what you need**
When you feel so tired, but you can't sleep
Stuck in reverse
And the tears come streaming down your face
When you lose something you can't replace
**When you love someone, but it goes to waste**
**Could it be worse?**
Lights will guide you home
And ignite your bones
And I will try to fix you
And high up above, or down below
**When you're too in love to let it go**
**But if you never try, you'll never know**
Just what you're worth
Lights will guide you home
And ignite your bones
And I will try to fix you
Tears stream down your face
**When you lose something you cannot replace**
Tears stream down your face, and I
Tears stream down your face
**I promise you I will learn from my mistakes**
Tears stream down your face, and I

**Lights will guide you home**
And ignite your bones
**And I will try to fix you**

The rest of the *Reaching For Driftwood* playlist can be found on Spotify. Search "Reaching For Driftwood"

## Atlas: Terms often used in **RFD** and their meaning

### Driftwood:
When you're in the process of manifesting, The Universe will show many subtle, smaller signs that what you want is on the way. They're what Abraham-Hicks calls "driftwood." Often, we simply don't notice this guidance, or we dismiss it as just a cool little coincidence. Driftwood is your clue that your desire is almost there.

What does driftwood symbolize spiritually? It symbolizes the Eternal relationship between wood and water, between forest and sea, between life and death.

### Life Raft:
A life raft serves as a person who offers safety while moving you closer to your goal or targeted outcome and farther away from what ails you. A life raft is often temporary, but helpful.

### Port:
A person who you temporarily and quickly pass through, usually to teach you a lesson or offer a unique perspective or set of experiences.

### Lighthouse:
An immovable object strong enough to meet an unstoppable

force. A lighthouse is a person who guides you home. It's a safe person that can weather any storm with you. A lighthouse is someone who offers unconditional love. A lighthouse is a person who stays. They are meant to be in your life for the long haul.

**Your Big Shell:**
The one big thing in life you know you are meant for.

# Introduction

Say what you will about Taylor Swift, but the girl knows what's up. Whether you like her music or not, she has done something powerful for us women that we can't deny. She wears her heart on her sleeve unabashedly, gets her heart repeatedly broken, all while turning her pain into purpose by savagely writing a song about the men who did her wrong. It's honest, it's vulnerable, and she doesn't care if she looks like a fool to the world—she will be brave enough to put her heart on the line once more, fall in love all over again, risking another painful heartbreak that seems inevitable to recover from, all while documenting the story, capturing its luminosity and its darkness in real time. She reminds us of what it is to be human and what it is to be hopelessly romantic in the pursuit of love. Her work has garnered a huge following of fans that deeply resonate with her, and it's no wonder. Taylor uses her voice to help others to feel seen. Her fans are called "Swifties." They are the ones making friendship bracelets and swapping them at concerts. They build community and connection through her art. As a female artist myself, I find this part to be wildly inspiring. To know that something you've created has also built unity, compassion for the self and for others, with the goal of sharing love and making an impact.

I didn't write this book with Taylor Swift in mind at all. In fact, she wasn't an inspiration until the book was nearly finished. It hit me that someday, the words within this book could have a similar response within women. I hope they feel seen, I hope they feel validated by their big tender loving hearts that likely haven't been handled with the care they deserve. I hope this book and my story inspires the masses to feel strength within their own authentic journey, through love, loss and beginning again. To feel the courage within themselves to lead a life that feels like it was truly meant for them while remaining open to all the signs and synchronicities along the way. Maybe I'm silly for this, but I imagine these people to be called "Drifties." A Driftie, like a Swiftie, is a person who might appear to others as lost and alone. But they're not. A Driftie is simply a person who is on their way. They're making the journey towards calmer waters and higher shores, weathering every storm along the way.

To my future Drifties, with this book in your hand, I see you, I know you, I am you. You aren't lost. You're on your way. In the famous words of Taylor Swift, "I don't know if you know who you are until you lose who you are." And in the words of my therapist Tina, "Something is missing, go find it."

I can't wait to see what you leave behind to make space for the new journey filled with what you deserve.

I hope you lose everything until you find it.

*BB*

# Reaching for the Life Raft

I PROMISED I'D never spend another dollar on a psychic. I swore I was done with that shit. Nothing ever came of them anyway, except that one time when a psychic woman in a wheelchair told me I'd give birth to two boys back-to-back and was right. The rest of them? Debatable at best. But my friend Amber said this woman was a psychic *medium* and it was different because she could speak to dead people, though they also somehow knew about the future. She swore up and down this woman bestowed otherworldly wisdom on her, that no one else would know, after her dad passed away. It was an expensive thing to splurge on, but I figured it was almost my birthday, I was turning 31, and I had tripled my business income the month before. If anyone deserved to spend over two hundred dollars to talk with her dead ex-boyfriend about what was happening in her life, it was gonna be me. I had so many questions, especially the burning one that had been festering in my gut for years: *Was I getting a divorce?*

I sent the woman a message on Instagram. Right away, we tried to set an appointment, but she was booked out for over a month. It was a good sign that she was legit, and I wasn't going to be lighting two hundred dollars on fire. Or maybe I was, but at this point I was all in. I started crying as I began booking and something in me asked if she had any spots for that very day. She said that she didn't but did say my spirit guides were nudging an urgent message. To my surprise, we planned a virtual call to connect that evening.

"Take a deep breath while I connect to your energy," she said. "And think quietly about who you want to connect with and what message you're hoping to hear today."

I closed my eyes and saw his face when I did.

"Okay." I said, exhaling my anxiety.

"I have to tell you. I have had a huge nudge since I saw your name pop up from someone on the other side that this was urgent."

"Really?"

"I do want to talk about this male coming through. I am getting a male presence. Younger male that feels like he's from your generation, close to your age. Is this resonating so far?"

*It's him.*

"Do you know who this is?" she asked.

Tears choked my throat. Right away, my dead ex-boyfriend, my first love, the person I wanted to hear from. He came through.

"Yes." I mutter. And the tears begin to fall.

"I saw his face as soon as I saw your name and in fact, he told me you needed this. And I wasn't going to, but he told me 'Nope, she needs this. She needs this,'" the medium said. "And he is right there beside you, he wants you to know that."

I close my eyes and picture him next to me. I wish he was still here more than anything.

"His first big message is that you're afraid to feel. So you distract yourself. Because if you feel, you're afraid you'll never stop."

"Yeah." I swallow hard. "That's me."

"And second, he says you can't run from everything. And that you're holding responsibility for something that you shouldn't."

Tears stream down my face as my voice trembles. "His death."

"I'm getting the sense that he had something to do with his death in some way."

He did, but it was an accident. "Yes."

"He takes full responsibility, and he doesn't want you to own that," she said. "And you feel smothered in your life so much that you can't breathe. He's telling you to focus on you and what you need, because you're on the verge of breaking through."

As my friend stated, it was uncanny. How did she know all these details? At first, he was telling me things about my day to day… and then we talked about my big question, and it came up before I could even ask. *He knew.*

"Are you planning on moving in the next six months?" she asked me. "Because I'm seeing moving boxes." I swallowed another lump in my throat and shook my head.

"No, I don't really see that happening." I had just bought this big, beautiful home with my husband a couple years ago, a few short miles from our swim club. It was meant to be our forever home with a big garden in the back that deer loved to steal vegetables from, and big, beautiful daisies and cosmos I had planted on my hands and knees with my mother-in-law in the sun that very spring. Surely, this was where I'd always be. How could it not? Our life was just getting started, finally getting easier. My boys were now three and five. After the whirlwind of life with toddlers, I was, at last, sleeping through the night. Us moving? I couldn't see it. It was impossible.

Unless—it hit me. The truth is, I was thinking about separating from my husband. I just hadn't told many people, other than my closest friends, and my husband that I was thinking about it. There is no way she could have known.

"I definitely see you moving," she affirmed.

"Really? Moving?" My voice shook a little and chills covered my skin.

"Don't be afraid that life will be different. Because he promises it will be different. But it will be a life on your terms. Your life isn't blowing up, it's about to blow open."

A week later I woke up in our big king bed, looked directly at my husband and said, "I want a divorce."

She was right. I was going to leave. Up until that moment, I didn't think I would ever have the strength to do it, but it was like a switch went off one night as I was sleeping, and I woke up an entirely different person. If you're a religious or spiritual person like I am, it has been said that when that switch goes off, that's God. The truth is, I had been contemplating a divorce for years and I knew the exact day I left him in my mind, heart, and soul.

The day I checked out of my marriage, I was in labor with my second son. My first love, Wil, had passed away two days beforehand, and the stress of his loss sent my blood pressure through the roof. I wasn't due for two more weeks, but I had to be induced into labor. In the hospital, with a heavy grieving heart, I was preparing to meet my new child. And more than anything, I needed my husband. Not only physically in that moment, but emotionally. When I reached for his hand during a painful contraction, he pulled it away. I knew then it was over. When I asked him to stay up with me and hold me through my pain, he said, "I really need to get some sleep." I knew he was not my person. I knew. My soulmate would never leave me to go to war alone. My soulmate is the man that suits up for battle and goes to war with me. In that moment, I realized I had been fighting these battles alone.

I was a lonely, wounded soldier on the field. I knew I couldn't fight to the end alone; I needed another person to go to war with, a true partner on every level. Because you're not supposed to do this thing called life alone. And when I realized I felt more alone with him than without him, I knew I couldn't stay any longer. But leaving is no easy task. I wish I could tell you that I left soon after that day in the hospital. I wish I could tell you that was the first time I had experienced pain in my marriage that felt unbearable. But it wasn't the first and it wasn't the last. It progressively got worse. The battles got harder, and I was so wounded and beat down that it was manifesting in physical wounds and illness.

Shortly after my son was born, I was diagnosed with Crohn's disease. The symptoms were excruciating and debilitating to the point it interfered with my daily life. I couldn't leave the house without living in fear of vomiting or simply not digesting a single thing I ate. My body couldn't keep food down and I was losing weight rapidly, just like my mother did when she was diagnosed with the same genetic illness. My mouth and stomach were full of ulcers and I had stomach pains that were so violent, they would send me in the fetal position in tears on our bedroom floor. And when I looked up at my husband from the ground while my health had hit rock bottom, he would look right through me. As if I wasn't there at all. *I knew.*

Getting sick was the catalyst of a journey towards healing myself emotionally that I had been avoiding. Because Wil was right, I was afraid to feel it. But as I've painfully learned so far, feeling it is the only way to heal it.

All of which lead me here.

A FEW WEEKS after I told him I was done, I threw my wedding ring into the thick of the pine trees next to the shed. More lies came to surface and of course, after being repeatedly gaslit, psychologically, and emotionally abused, it was all just nails in the coffin. I cared less about the junky thing anyway—it was a "shut up ring" that he made sure that I didn't like. I know this because he purposely bought me the exact opposite of what I wanted. I'll never fully understand why a narcissist does what he does, but now it doesn't even bother me anymore to care. It's all as good as gone. And that ring? It forever lives in the dirt with the earthworms where it belongs. Call me bitter, call me petty, or call me his ex-wife. They all fit the same now.

I am officially done.

Being done looked like taking my therapist's advice even further and checking myself into an online support group for women of abuse. Every week, I sat there on a virtual Zoom appointment full of strong women being beat down by weak men. Initially, it came as a shock to me, though it shouldn't have. They were bold, powerful, stunningly attractive women and I wanted so badly to shake them and just shout at the top of my lungs, *OH MY GOD GIRL, JUST LEAVE HIM ALREADY! YOU DESERVE SO MUCH BETTER!* Until I realized, "Oh, shit. I am one of them. I am that girl." It was a humbling moment in time, staring at my own reflection in the faces of these women. In our group therapy sessions, I saw myself in each of these ladies and it was a painful reminder of where I was and how much work I had to do to change the outcome of my life, in hopes to one day find and build healthy relationships in the future. This chapter of my healing journey had just begun, but it's not where it started.

Growing up, all I knew was abuse in some form. I knew "love" to be tumultuous, dangerous, scary, and violent. From a young age I'd seen my mother survive as a victim of every form of abuse a woman can endure. At just six years old, I saved her from a blow to the face from my father's drunken fist. Many holes from his whiskey rage (that had surprisingly missed one of our bodies that night) remained hidden in our home behind picture frames on walls and closed doors. Love was a father that went missing often for days and weeks. Love was thumbing through phone books as a child, calling every bar and hotel in town to see if they saw the face of my father that I hadn't seen in days. Love was a state of constant fear and terror. It was checking to see if he was still breathing when he passed out on the floor. Love was saving my mom from getting shot in the head when he pulled out a gun, pressed it against her temple and told me, *step away*, as he slurred his words, but I refused to move. I was young, but I was my mother's warrior. If he was trying to take her out, he'd have to go through me first. Love was being scared shitless until it forced me to be brave. At the age of 17 I left my home into the arms of my older boyfriend, whom I married at 23. Love as I knew it was deeply painful and deeply traumatic. It wasn't until I was a 31-year-old woman that I learned in the corner of my therapist's office that love is not what I have been experiencing most of my life. Love isn't supposed to hurt. Love is safe. Love is gentle. Love is kind. Love doesn't make you feel the way my husband was making me feel, either. That just because the abuse didn't always strike my body or was worn visible on my skin, it was still abuse.

It took me some time to learn and unlearn why I fell into similar trauma bonds and patterns with men who resembled my father in one way or another, through their absence or avoidance, narcissistic tendencies, hatred, and misogyny towards women, providing hostile, violent and unsafe environments (emotionally, psychologically, mentally, physically, or spiritually) or because that's what I was used to. But it is never too late to make a run for it. You just might save your life and inspire others to find the courage to do the same.

Maybe that psychic was right. Maybe my world was just blowing open.

## She Filed for Divorce, Ya'll

TELL ME YOU'RE entering a mid-life crisis without telling me. I'll go first.

I got myself a shamanic drum and a divorce for my 31$^{st}$ birthday. I was on my emotional and spiritual journey, after all. Breathwork, EFT, sound and somatic healing were a few modalities I was dabbling with as I attempted to move forward and heal. I was willing to try anything to feel better, because numbing wasn't working anymore.

To some, that was a blazing red flag signaling a mid-life crisis.

Here's the thing about that "mid-life crisis," though.

It's not a crisis at all. It's an awakening. A remembering of who you really are. Who you've always been and a reminder of who you are meant to become. And the reason it has those negative connotations around it is because it triggers the people who are still sleeping. The people who are not awake to their own wishes, dreams, and desires. They project their own shame and self-disapproval onto those who have freed themselves from their own chains. That person in their forties leaving their marriage, getting a wrist tattoo, dying their hair pink and quitting their nine-to-five knows more about who they really are than the person still safely coloring in the lines and doing what everyone else expects of them.

So yeah, maybe everyone around me, like my ex-husband and his family, were questioning my sanity. And sure, maybe I've been labeled as "the crazy ex-wife." I guess it is crazy to listen to your heart, to follow in the direction of your soul, to leave a man that made you feel like you would wither away into nothingness without him. In this world, that is crazy. And if that makes me crazy, I don't ever want to be sane.

But the real ones? The ones who knew the truth? Who heard conversations and witnessed what no one else did? The ones who believed me. They didn't question a thing. In fact, they danced right along with me to the beat of my brand-new drum.

# Clutching My First Life Raft

YOU MIGHT NOT realize how close you are to drowning, how badly you've been flailing around, how exhausted your body and arms are, until you feel the peace of hanging onto a life raft. My life raft showed up the summer that I filed for divorce. He showed up in the form of a hot pro-baseball player that gave me the perfect amount of attention.

His name was "Ben." He sent his number in my TikTok DM's. And every night, like some sort of schoolgirl, I'd lay out on the lawn under the stars and talk to Ben for hours. This was my first crush after my divorce. I almost forgot what a crush felt like until that first call.

**Me:** Let's play truth or dare

**Ben:** Okay haha You go first

**Me:** Truth or dare?

**Ben:** Dare

**Me:** I dare you to tell me what you're thinking right now

**Him:** I'm listening to Coldplay and I'm thinking about lying next to you

**Me:** Just laying? That's it?

**Him:** Yes, I promise. Just laying.

**Me:** I think you're a romantic. I have the feeling.

**Him:** You might be right…

From here, we'd talk daily. He'd voice text me from the dugout and I'd receive his messages while strapping my kids into their car seats or chasing them down at the park. It was a new feeling, but one I was enjoying. I had a crush for the first time in years and it felt... surreal. This gorgeous, bearded athlete was talking to *me?* A single mom of two? My husband would often tell me no one would want me if I left him.

"You're a mom. You don't have a career. You have nothing left to offer. Maybe some fat, old man would take you, but it wouldn't be anyone nearly as good looking or as great of a catch as me," he'd say, laughing as it left his tongue.

For a long while, I believed him. That fear of never finding anyone kept me stuck by his side. But quickly, after letting him go, I realized it was quite the opposite, like perhaps all along he didn't want me to know the truth. That I could meet interested men. That I was still valuable. And now, I had this athlete messaging me, reminding me that all hope of someone finding me attractive was not lost. I was not doomed. In fact, it showed me what I was able to attract. I was not only still desirable, but I was valuable.

This life raft showed up, just to prove it to me. It was then that I knew that I could do better than my ex-husband. It was at this moment that I knew a "fat old man" was not my destiny, but rather it was my husband who feared me leaving him. Because if a successful, attractive man who was not my husband could see my value, I knew I was on the right track to something better.

Sadly, this was not my person to keep. Ben had been traveling with baseball for years and wouldn't be back in the States for a long time. Potentially years. However, Ben and I became quick and close friends. We are still friends to this day.

Recently he texted me out of the blue.

**Ben:** *You know, maybe if we're both still available when I make* *it back to the States and travel baseball ends, we could give us a shot.*

**Me:** *It might be our only option, B. Maybe it's us in the end...*

**Ben:** *Maybe you're right. Regardless, I hope for nothing but the absolute best for you. I'm always rooting for you and your dreams.*

**Me:** *I'm rooting for you, too, Ben.*

Ben probably doesn't know the role he played in my life or how he saved it. But I will forever be grateful. He was the first life raft on my journey swimming away from my old life. And he likely wasn't going to be my last. By now I know that every connection serves a purpose whether I realize it at that moment or not. Some people are life rafts.

## To Keep Me from Drowning Again

WHAT DO YOU do when your high school ex-boyfriend calls you once he finds out you're getting divorced, talks to you on the phone for three hours and doesn't want to hang up? *Is there still something here?* I wondered.

Things with the baseball player weren't shaking out as I thought it would. I don't know what I expected, really. To be honest, I just wanted an escape from the throes of my divorce, and I was hoping some hot bearded man in a baseball uniform would be my knight in shining armor. As it turns out, I was just beginning to embark on a much bigger journey to becoming my own knight in shining armor. I would be learning how to be both the princess and the knight. I was learning how to build my own castle and my own kingdom from scratch.

During our phone call, it was hard not to wonder if maybe Derek was my person. I was pacing back and forth on my parents' big front porch, just like I did when we were kids. Ironically, when he called, I was in our hometown hosting a leadership event in town that weekend. Nostalgia flooded back quickly. There I was again, barefoot in the summertime smiling and restless over the same boy I met at space camp, bonding over taking our inhalers like a couple of fated-to-meet dweebs all those years ago.

The connection and bond we have is strong. There's no denying this is one of those connections you never forget about. Derek knows me better than most. And he knows the real me. He knows my humble beginnings and he liked me then, anyway. I wasn't the girl with a lot of money. I lived in a mobile home and my family was rough around the edges. My home life was never what it could've or should've been, and he knew. He liked me for me—flaws and all. As I grew older, I became more established, more successful, and I had grown into myself and into my body. I don't know how else to say it humbly, but I was fit and active, and my body reflected all the hard work and dedication I had poured into it. I was confident, and I earned it. At 31, it was about time I finally started to love myself. I wasn't the troubled, nerdy teen with braces, a band tee-shirt and dirty converse anymore. I was a woman who worked hard to build a life, a name, and a career for herself. I was the girl everyone in our hometown never thought I'd be. Because yes, I had a bit of a rebellious streak in high school. I did what a lot of teenagers do, except I had the audacity to do it in a small conservative town, living out loud, smoking cigarettes, skipping class, staying out past curfew. I became an expert at kissing frogs. I was a rebel with a cause. And that cause was a broken home and trauma that kept me awake most nights.

I was just a teen and I didn't know what to do with all that trauma. So, I acted out. As a result, his parents forbid him from pursuing a relationship with me. He wasn't allowed to date me, so he didn't.

That didn't stop us from attempting, and it didn't stop me from taking his virginity in the front seat of his car.

Derek was another "close enough, but far enough away" love that I had encountered. If you read my novel *On His Way Back to Me*, it loosely follows the Romeo and Juliet style forbidden love story of my first love, someone before Derek. A love that was so close, but just out of reach. It wasn't "right person, wrong time." It was the right person, the wrong circumstances. The wrong set of obstacles and challenges. It was us against the world. Neither my first love, nor Derek all those years ago, were ready, willing, or able to go to war with me or for me. So, we went our separate directions. Whether we still had feelings or not. That's just what it was.

So, if Ben was a life raft, why was Derek coming back into my life? If fifteen years couldn't change this man's feelings for me, what could? Well, it could be the girlfriend he's had for nine years. The one he didn't marry, because he said he was never sure about her. But on the phone with me, he said, "I would've married you. I could see it with you. I'd marry you, Brittany." But, as we know, I married someone else. Similar to my first love, he still had feelings for me and had been sitting on them all these years. To his defense, I was with my ex-husband for almost fifteen years. There was no other time for him to tell me how he felt until my divorce. Until now.

Derek was the guy that burned me romantic cd's, wrote me letters and made me laugh until my stomach hurt. He understood me deeply and truly, on an emotional and spiritual level. He just "got me" and I got him. Two nerdy weirdos with the same sort of outlook on life. If they say to marry your best friend, I knew for sure that this was mine. And I was curious, after a failed marriage, if maybe this was it. Maybe it was always supposed to be us. Maybe now was our time. Enter, the long-distance relationship we would have to endure and him ending his current long-term relationship to be with me.

It just sort of happened.

Once we started talking, we couldn't stop. We talked for months on the phone, and he had made many promises to meet up with me, yet never followed through. I just wanted to see him. I was single, he wasn't married, and we both agreed cheating was not in alignment with our values, though one could argue that he was having an emotional affair with me. I wanted to know if the feelings were still there. What better way than to meet up and see for ourselves.

"I miss you, Brittany." Derek said, his voice pained. This time I was in my driveway, pacing outside, while my ex-husband and two children slept in the house that I still lived in.

"I miss you, too. I want to see you…what about tomorrow? Can we meet halfway?"

"I don't just want to see you tomorrow, Brittany. I want to see you every day. Forever," he said. The words in this moment felt like warm honey pouring over the jagged cracks of my heart.

"It took me some time to realize, a long time ago. But I always cared about you. Wanting you to achieve your writing dreams, to be happy…" he said. "Maybe the reason I can't stay away from you is because I'm supposed to be with you. You drive me wild in the best way, and I'm never not thinking about you."

Yet, there were months of empty and broken promises, including a trip to the Pacific Northwest that we wanted to take together. I ended up taking that trip alone and was starting to realize this man could not be the one for me. He still belonged to someone else, and regardless of what he was saying to me, he was doing nothing about it. He stayed with her, even when he told me he had feelings for me, wanted to be with me, wanted to move near me, and yes, even said he wanted to marry me. In my head, I thought my life and my new beginning was about to start with a man I never thought I'd end up with. But quickly I realized it was the start to another ending on my journey that sent me further on my quest to leave behind what's not meant for me.

Even if it was so painful that I sobbed into the carpet for weeks, even if I knew our connection was beyond special, even if I knew he likely did mean the things he said to me. I had reached a place within myself to no longer accept anything less than what I deserved. And I deserved a man whose words aligned with his actions, who was able to mean what he said and say what he meant. Who could make a promise and keep it. After the final broken promise and his inability to hold himself accountable for roping me into this emotional tornado in the first place, I knew that I had to pull myself out and away. Before more than just me got hurt. I needed to save myself all over again.

Derek was and is not my person. He was just another lesson in the importance of letting go, another life raft showing up to help me know my worth and choose myself. I will never know if this man is happier with her than with me. It has been almost two years since we've spoken. I will never know what was real and what wasn't. All I know is that I can't look to the past to build the kind of future I desire and deserve. I have big dreams, and my dreams will always come before belonging to a man. In this new season of life, I am no longer looking to be a man's helpmeet, his accessory, or his possession. I am looking for a man to grow with, build with and that begins with the man that chooses me. Love is a choice. And because he didn't, even when he said he would, he's not the one.

And so, with another patch sewn to my worn and tattered heart, I was ready to brave the journey and go to war. Even if that meant I was going to war alone.

## The Solo Hike That Changed Everything

ON THE TRIP that Derek promised he would go on with me, I booked the most beautiful, scenic, and romantic cottage on the channel in Washington. Every time, broken promise after broken promise, I waited for him to make a move towards me. Hopeful and believing like a little kid. When he didn't show up, when the promises kept arriving empty and unanswered, I knew I had two choices. Cancel the trip or go alone. My friend Elizabeth called me from her solo trip in Italy and said, "Sister, go alone. You CAN do this."

So, to get started on my new journey as a divorcee, I took that solo hiking trip two thousand miles away from home. It scared the life out of me, even if I almost canceled it five times and cried the night before. I talked myself out of it more than I talked myself into it. And that's why I knew I had to do it. I had no internet, no cell service, no electronics—just me, Mother Nature, and the higher power. If you're looking for answers in life, you'll find them in a forest somewhere, I can almost guarantee it.

BEFORE I LEFT, my ex-husband made sure to sow seeds of doubt. He'd say things like, "If you get lost or hurt, don't call me. If you need anything, I won't be there. You can't do this. And I will laugh so hard when it all goes wrong for you." More than my safety, he wanted me hurt. Because being hurt would prove to him that I couldn't do it without him. More than anything, he wanted me to continue to need him.

My first night at the cottage, I was so fatigued from the hustle and bustle of travel and the time change that I called it an early night. I felt too tired to be scared to explore. Too occupied and distracted with planning routes through the mountains to worry or think about anything else. Maybe on a subconscious level that's why I'm here. To run away from everything. And one thing I know about myself is that if I'm going to be lost, I want to be lost in the mountains alone. The trip had many purposes, including the biggest reason I booked it in the first place. I had plans to visit the real *Phone of Wind*, the very phone I wrote about in my book *On His Way Back To Me*. Of course, in my novel, I added a few fictitious paranormal elements that couldn't exist in this reality. But, nevertheless, was it the same rotary phone attached to a towering pine tree in the middle of a misty forest used for the grieving to talk to the dead? Yes. The only difference is the connection in my book goes through. In real life, it was merely a meditative prayer whispered to the wind. With my pack on my back, and after several winding loops of getting lost on the trail. I found it. And when I did, I fell to my knees. I had so much to say to him, my first love that passed away, but *I miss you, I love you* and *you were right* were first on the list. It was the cathartic release I never knew I needed, and it was like doing ten years of therapy in ten minutes. It felt like closure, peace, acceptance, and a sense of relief that I didn't expect but desperately craved. And though that was incredible, I still had several more days on that mountain. Alone.

ONE OF THE days, my friend Abby who lived nearby in Washington planned on joining me on Mount Rainier. Abby and I used to wait tables together in Michigan when I was in college, and it had been years since I had seen her last. Abby arrived at my dreamy romantic lakefront cottage in the mountains carrying a large paper bag full of fresh, organic farmer's market ingredients with the intention to make me the tastiest meal I'd ever had. She knew I was heartbroken and healing by taking one look at me. Unwashed face, puffy eyes and a head full of hair that hadn't seen a brush in days. Abby rolled up her sleeves, ordered me to the couch to rest and insisted on making me dinner. I did not oblige. I had been eating oatmeal, granola bars and fruit leather. I didn't have the energy or emotional bandwidth to make anything better for myself. And something I remember about Abby from our restaurant days, is how great of a cook she is. She not only used the best ingredients, but she also cooked for the soul, from the soul. Abby whipped up a sweet and spicy Thai green curry with organic basil, veggies. Mushrooms, and man, did it hit the spot. With an act of kindness and a full belly, I went from crying all alone in a pit of grief, loneliness, and despair, to suddenly feeling loved, held, and supported. That night, she let me cry in her arms, wiped my tears and she took care of me. And that night, I took my armor off, and I let her. After dinner, we watched the sea otters play around in the channel while fishermen peacefully cast their final line before sunset.

The rest of the solo trip was beautiful and painful and yet it still taught me many things, but the most important lesson I learned in that short window of time was that I could be alone; I could do this. It would be hard and even scary at times, but it was possible. More than that, it might even be pretty damn enjoyable. I might surprise myself with just how independent and capable I am. I might even like being in my own company. I might look around and find the helpers. It might not be as bad as I thought. It might be better than ever.

MY EX THOUGHT I'd die out there without him. A part of him seemed like he was hoping I would. But boy, was he wrong. And very much like the story of *The Little Engine that Could*, I thought I could. And I did.

Who knew, other than the psychic of course, that this would be the year I walked away from everything and everyone that was no longer serving my highest good. Most days, if I was honest, I didn't feel as brave as I had hoped. Most days, I felt like I was torturing myself by doing these hard things I knew I had to do. However, every time I felt like giving up and walking back to the comfort zone that was slowly killing me, one therapy session continued to play on loop and stand out in my brain.

My therapist said, "Brittany, I don't know if you realize this or not, but every session has one recurring theme. Do you know what that is?"

I shook my head. I didn't know.

"Something is missing. Go find it."

Her words echoed through me. I left that session forever changed, knowing that I had to say goodbye to the only life I ever knew to call in and make space for the life that truly belonged to me. I had to stop living a lie. It was finally time to honor myself, my heart, my soul.

In my mind, the big heavy lifting began in those woods. I hiked. I watched sunsets melt into orange ripples every night. I romanced myself. I grieved the men who failed me, and I let them all go. One by one. I was ready and finally okay with being alone.

# The Whole Foods Hottie

THE IRONIC PART about arriving at this place mentally and emotionally? I always run into someone after. It's right when I swear off men, when I'm finally comfortable and happy alone, that's when he finds me.

I didn't always go to the grocery store dressed like a homeless woman, but when I did, I ended up seeing the most beautiful man in the produce aisle. There was something about him that made me sweat a little and my heart flutter three times too fast. Maybe it was the fact that he was wearing a fitted flannel jacket or the way he walked with confidence. It was unclear why I couldn't take my eyes off him. I hadn't felt that feeling in a while, so naturally, I panic and push my shopping cart in the opposite direction hoping to not see him again. Every turn I take, there he is. So much so that I laugh a little as I shift in another direction down another aisle. Even though my mind was saying no, my body was screaming *yes*.

The pull towards him was as inexplicable as the tide. Something inside of me needed to know who this man in Whole Foods was. And it needed to know right now. So, what did I do? Panic and leave the store immediately, of course. For whatever reason, I turn into a shy hermit when I see a man I'm attracted to. I get quiet and awkward, and I hate that about myself. It was happening; fear took over my body quickly and I couldn't stop it. I ran as fast as I could in the exact opposite direction. I felt the fight or flight response kick in and I fled. Until I heard a voice in my head that begged me to go back into the store. To which I replied *absolutely not. No way. No way am I turning back around.* I ignored the voice until I reached the second red stop light on my way home. Then, something else took over. Something came over me and made me pull a U-turn, placing me right back around in the very direction of Whole Foods. As I was driving back it felt like driving against a strong current. I didn't want to, I was terrified, I had never done this before, but something, I have no idea what, made me.

I circled the parking lot four different times. FOUR. TIMES. *There's no point in going in now, there's no way he's still in there. He probably left by now.* I tried talking myself out of it. Yet still, the voice made me park, march into the store in my sweatpants, baggy winter coat and all, looking every bit of homeless. When I cleared the front doors, he was right there, standing at the checkout in plain sight. Of course he was. My heart was pounding out of my chest and the most dizzying sensation took over me. If I didn't pass out it'll be a miracle.

He's there. Holy shit. He's still there, looking every bit sexy and now I had to walk up to him and say something? Why did this voice pick me to do this today of all days, without a shred of makeup on? In fact, I had cried my entire way to the store that very afternoon. I was sure my eyes were pink and swollen to some degree and remembering that in this moment only made me want to run in the opposite direction all over again.

*Fuck it.* I made it this far, there's no looking back. What's the worst thing that could happen? I took a deep breath in and beelined straight to his checkout lane.

"Hi," I said entirely too fast. My body was a bit wobbly standing this close to him, but I hadn't collapsed yet.

He looked at me confused. "Hi," he said.

"I know this is awkward, but I felt—something, I don't know—a vibe when I saw you and I would regret it if I didn't say anything to you." I was talking so fast, why was I like this? What was wrong with me? "Sorry—umm." I laughed a little at myself. I didn't know what to say and suddenly I panicked wondering if he had a girlfriend and I was about to face rejection anyway. How could he not have had a girlfriend? Look at him. Stylish, great shoes. Something about a man with a good shoe game.

"Are you single?" I asked next.

"Yes, I am," he says and smiles, giving me that look that he knows I'm nervous. It made me want to jump in front of a moving vehicle. Eight years of a marriage had made me rusty, I definitely did not feel as smooth as I once was.

"Can I get your number?" I asked him. *Jesus. Who the hell am I? A Teenager? Why am I doing this again? This feels ridiculous.*

He pulled his phone from his flannel jacket and handed it to me to put my number into his phone. Probably to delete it as soon as I left is my guess.

"What's your name? You want to walk out with me?" he asked. He was as confident as he looked.

"Brittany. Yes, I'd like that." Walking still felt wobbly, but I was uncertain if I would pass out. It felt as if it could have happened.

"What's yours?"

"Will," he says.

A familiar pang of grief hit me in the chest when I heard his name. It was the same name of my dead ex-boyfriend who passed away. I hadn't met anyone with that name since him and when I took a closer look, oh my god, he sort of resembled him too. I couldn't tell from far away, but now I saw it. He had the same build, same body type. Similar height, strong athletic features.

What kind of weird parallel universe type shit was this? And while I was studying him closer, I noticed something else that gave me a sinking feeling. He looked—young. Not a wrinkle, not a gray hair, not a single line on his face. Smooth, glowing, well-rested, healthy skin. I almost forgot what a face like that looked like on a man. My ex-husband had salt and pepper hair, was thirty-five with deep tired bags under his eyes and often looked older than his age. Two kids under five and a skewed world view can do that to a person.

"I'm sorry," I covered my mouth. "You look a bit on the younger side. How old are you?" I asked inquisitively, almost afraid to know the answer.

"I'm twenty-three."

My cheeks flush. I cover my mouth again and my eyes widen. I can't help it. He is so much younger than me, good god. "I'm sorry. I didn't realize," I said, still laughing, putting my arm around his shoulder to squeeze it playfully. The beard really threw me off. "Never mind then."

"How old are you?" he asked.

"Too old for you. I'm thirty-one." The whole thirties-are-the-new-twenties thing felt like a scam at this moment. Because no. No, they fucking are not. Thirty is clearly thirty. Twenty is clearly twenty.

"Wait. Come on," he said, touching my arm. "Age is just a number."

"Is that so?" I laughed. "Well, what's your zodiac sign? This could be the real deal breaker."

"Gemini," he said.

I laughed again and shook my head. "Oh, this will never work. Especially now."

We laughed together and I walked towards my car, certain he would never text me or see me ever again. He was eight years my junior. There was no way he'd be into an older homeless looking woman in her thirties. I don't know why I did it, but I gave him a hug goodbye. I also can't explain why that was the least awkward part of the whole interaction.

WHEN I PULLED into the driveway, a text lit up my phone.

*It's Will. The Gemini.*

Not only did he text me, but he also texted me within the hour. Which could only mean one thing. He was actually interested in me. I responded quickly and the playful banter continued. The next morning, I was surprised to see he asked me out on a date.

Like a full-on date at a restaurant with his undivided attention. My ex-husband hadn't taken me on a date in over a year. I hadn't dated anyone new since seventeen. And this was not just any ordinary date he had up his sleeve, he wanted to impress me. He wanted to take me out in Birmingham, also known as the fancy side of town.

I gushed to my friends, who were knee deep in diapers and toddler tantrums. They gobbled up my daily soap opera life like it was a delicacy. Naturally, they were all for it. They would kill to have this sort of adventure and were living through me. Doing this for me meant I was also doing it for them. I was taking one for the team, so I could come back and reinvigorate their morning routine with a rowdy "Hey, guess what happened last night?" phone call as they spoonfed mashed avocado into their babies' mouths and picked Legos off the floor. It wasn't that long ago where that was me in that exact scene. Why watch Keeping up with the Kardashians or Real Housewives when your best friend has a juicy newly divorced life happening in real time?

Even if they couldn't experience this with me, I was determined to bring them along for the ride in a way they could.

**Claire:** *Are you going?! You have to go!*
**Audri:** *You deserve this. YESSSSSS! GO!*
**Natalia:** *Lol Wait. How old is he again?*

Yes, he was twenty-three and I was still going. Honestly, I was already impressed.

**Will:** *Wednesday night it is. How does 6 sound?*
**Me:** *That should work. Let's do it. Tomorrow night, I'm all yours.*

That sounded sexual. Was I going to sleep with him?!

**Will:** *Mm so submissive of you*

Okay. It got steamy quick. My heart was beating a little faster, and I found myself pacing the living room back and forth. I didn't know what I was expecting, but it wasn't this. Not exactly. What was the harm in flirting back? I was just having a little fun.

**Me:** *I think you're trouble, mister…*
**Will:** *Who doesn't love a little trouble?*

You couldn't have wiped the smirk on my face if you paid me a million dollars. This milf of two bagged a hottie from Whole Foods.

**Me:** *See you soon, Will*

On a serious note, what would I even wear on a date with a man, a young man, from an entirely different generation? He was Gen Z. I'm a Millennial. How would this look out in public? Would it be obvious he's a fresh college graduate, a former frat boy attempting to jump in bed with a milf? Would I look like a cougar? Wait. Did this make me a cougar? Oh god. Was I a cougar? *Jesus*. I didn't want to know the answers to these questions. I'd never been a cougar before. I'd never even once developed a particular attraction to men younger than me. This was—new. All of it. What a vulnerable experience it was already.

I had less than twenty-four hours before my date with Will. Panic set in. I had never wanted to set my closet on fire before today, but now I wanted to burn everything inside of it and start over. Thumbing through hangers full of clothes I either never wear, hadn't worn in years or were definitely not in style, on trend or suitable for a date. I was fucked. I didn't even own more than a single thong. Why would I? I had left the bar hopping and glam scene behind after I had babies. I never went out and I certainly didn't have a husband that cared about my underwear. What would I even wear if we *did* have sex? I'd need a new outfit and new underwear immediately. I drove myself to Nordstrom Rack, and with a baby on my hip, I shopped for an outfit that made me look eight years younger. I decided on black combat boots, a form fitting black crop top, stacked necklaces, and the most flattering black jeans I could find. I wore a darker lip and kept the rest of the make-up light. The hair was giving Carrie Bradshaw—big, wild and wavy.

Will and I decided on a trendy place with health-conscious options. I was already impressed. Had I said that? I guess I was under the impression that all young men in their twenties were likely living in their parents' basements eating pizza rolls and playing video games. But this one showed up in a nice fitted black bomber jacket, clean cut, with a perfect smile, smelling every bit like a man, and a beard that made me want to kiss him almost immediately. When he saw me, his first reaction was to open his arms and hug me. It felt so natural, like I had waited lifetimes for this hug, but also like I have had this hug for centuries. It felt easy with him. He brushed his arm on my tan wool pea coat. "This is nice," he said as he looked into my eyes. "You look nice, too."

"Thank you." I blushed. His voice, deep and gentle. He did not sound twenty-three, either.

We sat down at the bar as we waited for a table to open.

He looked at me, confident. "You nervous?" he said.

I look at him then, hesitant to be honest. "A little. Yeah." I was actually very nervous. My hands were holding in the shakes, I was seconds away from trembling. I could hardly look at him or speak to him without my words catching. This is how I knew I was in trouble. The last time this happened, I ended up marrying that man. And oddly enough, I was the one to approach my ex-husband first as well. I was having a weird sort of Déjà vu about the whole thing. I knew all these feelings; I'd had them before. But I didn't expect them to show up like this, and not for this person, especially knowing his age. I tried my best to be present and not overthink any of the specifics. If I did, I'd run right out the door.

"What are you getting to drink?" he asked.

"I don't really drink. I'm not sure." I said, scanning the drink menu. I was nearly two years sober-curious. Not entirely sober but living a very sober-conscious lifestyle.

He looked at me and turned his head. "Really? Me either."

"You don't?" I asked, doubt hung over my voice. How could he not drink when he was so young? That's what young people did. They drink and make mistakes. Live and learn.

"No. It always stresses people out because I don't drink." He laughed. "I'm always the weird responsible one."

"Oh my god, I know! Same."

There it was. Our first similarity. Something we had in common outside of shopping at Whole Foods.

Still, I had my nerves. "It's a special occasion, so I will get just one. To celebrate."

"Yeah? What's the special occasion?"

"This." I said, smiling as I looked into his eyes. "Us." I was already regretting staring into them as long as I did. Those brown eyes pulled in me almost immediately and I couldn't find my way out of them if I tried. I didn't want dinner anymore. I wanted to be in his mouth. The chemistry was heating up quickly and without any control. Just then, the waitress announced our table was ready.

We finally got a seat and sat at a table for two. It was a date. A real date. My first date in forever and my first date as a newly single woman. I couldn't believe it. As we sat across from one another, the conversation flowed naturally from there. Like we were two old friends playing catch up. Finally, it came up. He had after all asked to be my friend on Instagram. So, if he did any digging or sleuthing at all, he knew.

"Do you wanna tell me about it or not?" he asked. In a direct yet indirect way. We both knew it was time to address the elephant in the room.

"My divorce or my kids?" I said, taking a sip of my drink.

"Both, I guess."

"Well, I'm divorced, and I have two kids." I mean, how else would I sum that up? It was pretty cut and dry.

He took a bite of his food, unphased. He finished chewing and looked at me blankly.

I looked at him expecting a freaked-out, child-like or animated reaction. Because I had kids and he was... young. Wasn't that scary to him? He said nothing, so my anxiety pulled words from under my tongue to fill the silence.

"Does that bother you?" I asked, convinced he would run out

the door any minute. Besides, my ex-husband had told me nobody would want me. To him, I was a divorced mom of two with nothing to offer and no one except maybe an old, overweight man would have any real interest in me.

Instead, Will leaned in a little and said, "If you think that you being a mom is going to stop me, it's not." He wiped his face with his napkin. "I will say, though. I have never gone on a date with a woman like you before. Older, established, successful. Or a divorced mom of two. This is new for me." He smiled then, reassuringly, that all was well and he was totally comfortable with me and my baggage.

"Really? I'm your first?" I joked, of course I was.

"You are." He said. "And it's quite refreshing. It's—real."

"Refreshing." I affirmed. In a way, I was refreshed too. Here he was, beautiful and baggage-free. Just a hot young man looking for a good time. And honestly, that's all I was here for, too.

The sexual tension was so intense at this point I had to make a joke about it. I picked up my butter knife, twirled it side-to-side as I locked his eyes, and said, "You feel that? You could cut this sexual tension with a knife." The drink had clearly kicked in. Luckily, he laughed.

"Well. Maybe we should go listen to these songs somewhere together." He suggested after talking about music and scrolling through each other's playlist. Another thing we seemed to have in common was our uncanny similar taste in music. This random man at Whole Foods had more in common with me than I ever would have known by first glance.

"Yeah, I like that idea." I flashed a seductive smile. Sure, I'd been out of the game, but I still remembered how to play. "Do you have roommates?" I asked, suspecting he likely lived with his parents.

"I do," he said.

"Your parents?"

He cleared his throat. "Yeah, actually. For now. Moved in after college. Saving up for a house though." College, by the way, was not that long ago. *Jesus. What am I doing?*

"I moved in with my ex and his parents after college to do the same thing, so I get it."

"You?" he asked.

I nodded. "Yeah, my roommates right now are my children and my ex-husband. I still live in the marital home. For now."

He nodded back. "Well, my parents aren't home right now and won't be for a few hours. If you wanted to come over, you could."

I smiled at him, and he smiled back.

"Sure. Let's do it." I said. On the way out, he put his arm out for me to hold. I wrapped my hands around it, hugging his strong bicep as he walked me across the street. Once in the car, he played a Justin Timberlake throwback and grabbed my hand.

"You like JT?" he asked.

I laughed. "Is this because I'm a Millennial? You think I don't listen to trendy music? That I'm stuck in the early 2000's?"

"No, not at all. I was actually listening to his music while getting ready for our date."

"That's adorable." I ran my fingers over his hand and spun the ring around on his finger.

"Does this have any cool significance?"

"This ring? Nah. I wish I had a cool story to make up for you, but I don't." He pointed at an ice-cream shoppe. "Want some ice cream?"

I could tell he was hiding any nerves he was beginning to feel. Taking a 31-year-old woman back to his parent's house for whatever might happen next. I looked at him then with an intensity and licked my lips before shaking my head.

"That's okay. I'm craving something else."

He side-smirked and squeezed his hand on my thigh.

Will pulled up to his parents' house. I'm not sure what I was expecting, but it was significantly larger and nicer than I thought it would be. It was clear he grew up very differently than I did. He guided me into the house discreetly.

"Water? Whiskey?" He laughed.

"Water is great. Thank you."

He brought me a glass of water and the sexual tension was so thick at this point, I was shocked we hadn't even kissed yet. His eyes met mine and I didn't have to say a word. He knew I was already melting. He took my jacket off for me.

"Follow me." He grabbed my hand and lead me downstairs into the family basement. He took his phone and put on a playlist. He showed it to me then. "It's my spicy playlist." I swallowed and looked at him from the white leather sofa. "Is that right?"

We listened to a few songs before I asked to play one of mine, which significantly elevated in the spice level. I climbed onto his lap and our eyes locked again.

"You are intoxicating, you know that?" he said.

"And you haven't even tasted me yet." I said, surprised that I did.

"You're right. I should change that."

He grabbed my face and pulled me in for a kiss. Sparks were flying so wildly, I didn't know what day it was, what time was, and I'd completely forgotten that I was in his parents' basement. And that he was 23 years young.

The kiss grew in intensity quickly and before I knew it, his hands were wrapped under my shirt and I was tugging on his hair, sucking on his neck, grinding the eager bulge in his pants. *This. Is. Happening.*

He slid off my shirt before I slid his over his head. Will's body was smooth yet strong. With his soft hands, he pulled my pants off next. I stood up then, and as I did, he covered his mouth and shook his head.

"Look at you. Oh my god. You're stunning, do you realize that?"

I looked down at the same body that held two babies inside of it and nursed them with swollen, leaking breasts. The same ones he was drooling over. It had been a while since I'd seen my body as sexually desirable. I can't lie, it felt incredible. I got on my knees as I unclasped the button to his pants, sliding them off slowly. I hated going down on my husband, but there was something insatiable about Will, I wanted to taste him everywhere. He pulled me away before losing control.

"This isn't how this is ending. Lay down, it's your turn."

He spread my legs apart, pulled my panties to the side and immediately sent my body into a state of bliss I hadn't felt in a while. I also hated my husband's tongue anywhere near me. But I couldn't seem to get enough of Will's mouth on night one.

I stopped him before I climax.

"This isn't how this ends." I said, looking down at his firm arousal.

"No?" he said, pressing his body onto mine. "Do you want to?" he asked, respectfully.

I nodded, his tongue sliding over mine with deep heavy breaths. He unrolled a condom, slipped it over and sat back on the sofa. I climbed back onto his lap before sliding myself down onto him. As I rode him slowly, he moaned softly into my ear. "Fuck, you feel incredible." I pulled away for a moment, observing his face. His brown eyes rolled back into his head with each stroke before they met mine. Our breath synchronized and before he climaxed, he picked me up and laid me down before stroking me again, harder, and faster. When he came, he laid there in my arms for a second. I drank in his scent. He too, was intoxicating.

"That was... insane," he said.

"Yeah. It was." I laughed a little as I realized what just happened. I'd just had sex with a 23-year-old in his parents' basement. I still needed to go home to my children tonight. I had to wake up to my ex-husband, and though in separate rooms, I would see his face. And he would see mine. And he would know that he was no longer the last man to enter my body. That ship had officially sailed. Will was the first man I'd slept with in over fourteen years since being with my husband. It was the beginning of a new era.

ON THE WAY back to my car, Will was planning future dates. It had just begun but somehow, we both already saw each other in tomorrow. A few days later, I saw him again. I had him sneak into my house when everyone left. We had blissful shower sex and he took all of me in my old master bedroom that I once shared with my husband in our old king bed. I clutched the metal headboard bars as he entered me in wild, adventurous positions. Positions my husband twelve years older than him could never imagine doing. Another couple days passed and I saw him again. Somehow, we found time to connect. The following week we had even planned a date to see the Patrick Watson concert together. I cried beforehand knowing it was going to be beautiful and romantic and perfect, and I was sad in advance because I knew I already didn't want us to end, but could feel every moment becoming more fleeting. I was sitting inside of a ticking time bomb filled with rose petals and the taste of his lips. I knew I was slowly letting go of a rope clasped tightly in my hands. Every day spent together ironically meant we were closer to the day we would no longer spend time together. He was never someone I was supposed to want to keep, but the more time I spent with him, that's all I wanted to do.

WE'D MEET AT the grocery store just to kiss. He'd sneak me into his parent's house when they would leave, and he would make my legs shake in his childhood bedroom. It was like we couldn't get enough of each other. We even walked down the stairs like we were magnetically connected to each other like Siamese twins. Our bodies were just drawn to each other in that unexplainable way.

The dates were always fun and full of chemistry, but what we craved most was a big bed for just the two of us and much needed uninterrupted time alone. Which was hard to do given our living situations. So naturally, we had the idea to book a weekend away so we could spend more time together. It was his idea to have a Top-Chef inspired cook-off since the Air-Bnb had a kitchen. And let's be honest, the main thing on the menu was sex.

"There are the men who talk the talk in the kitchen, and there are the men who roll up their sleeves, toss the towel over their shoulder and get it done."

"Which are you?"

"You're about to find out."

We showed up together hand in hand at Whole Foods, the very place we met to get our ingredients. He impressed me with the way he moved around the organic produce aisle and butcher counter. He knew exactly what to order and once we got into the Air-Bnb, he knew exactly how to cook it all. The steak was seared in butter to perfection, and as he promised, he talked the talk and walked the walk. He made me the most delicious steak dinner for us. My husband couldn't hold a candle to this man in the bedroom or in the kitchen. It was safe to say age was clearly just a number. Age doesn't make a man more mature.

"Are you going to say grace before you eat that?" I asked him, mostly joking.

He put his fork down. "I wasn't planning on it, but yeah, I think we should. We should pray."

"Alright, you say prayer, Will." I smiled at him, and he smiled back. He grabbed my hand.

He said grace and our conversations naturally picked up about real life. Religion. Family. Values. Life goals. All the serious big hitter questions you'd ask on a first date with a person you saw a future with. But because that was never the plan, we never did. We always kept things light and fun.

"Do you ever want to get married?" I asked him.

"Of course. Do you ever want to get married again?"

I thought about it for a minute.

"I used to say I'd never get married again, but I think that's because I married the wrong person. I think If it was the right person, I would."

He looked down and cuts into his steak.

"How about kids. Would you have more?" he asked and looked at me then.

"If I'm honest, I feel that I'm supposed to have one more."

He smiled. "Yeah?"

"Yeah. A daughter."

There was this strange warmth I felt when I say that. I'd never told anyone that outside of my best girlfriends. The psychic also predicted a daughter for me.

"You ever want kids?" I asked.

"Definitely. I want marriage, kids. The whole thing," he said. "Someday."

"When do you think someday will be?"

He paused and I could see us both feeling it now. The age-gap elephant in the room.

"I don't know. Like by thirty. So, seven to ten years to get married. A few after that for kids I'd say."

I'd be nearly forty and into my mid-forties if I had a child with him. Women do this, don't ask why. When we like you, we imagine our whole future with you, just to see how it fits in our mind first. But no matter how much we liked each other; I could tell this was a big problem. That no matter how good we felt together, the numbers weren't entirely adding up. I'd imagined myself re-married in the next few years, by 34 or 35. Maybe another child by 36 or 37.

"You know, we still have dessert."

"We do? I don't remember getting dessert?"

"Well, I have dessert."

I look at him with a smirk. "Is that right?"

"You."

"Mmm. That's right. Yes, you do have dessert. I brought lingerie for that kind of dessert."

"Did you? Well, I have whipped cream, too. But we don't have plates or spoons in the bedroom upstairs. We have to use our bodies and our mouths."

"I'll have to see this in action. I do have a sweet tooth now. Can you show me?"

"I can, ma'am. Right this way."

He took my hand and walked me upstairs where he immediately undressed me. Hot and heavy breaths of desire filled our mouths as we locked lips and grazed our hands all over.

"Being naked is no fun. Let me put on my sexy lingerie. Close your eyes and turn around."

While he was turned around, I slipped on a lacy hot pink

lingerie set. The sexiest thing I'd worn since my wedding night lingerie, easily.

I put on the song *"Cherry Hill"* by Russ while his back was turned. I lay on the bed with my legs spread and my back arched. I wanted him to know exactly where he was needed.

"Okay, you can look now."

"Jesus. Look at you." His eyes widened like he could swallow me whole. There were so many mysteries I was curious about that were swirling around in this man's head about me, but one thing I knew for certain was that his desire for me was apparent. And it was on fire.

He took the whip cream and put a little on his mouth before bringing his mouth to mine. Then he pulled away quickly, pulling down my bra on one side with his mouth, exposing my left nipple as he spread whipped cream all over it. He locked eyes with mine as he ran his tongue over me slowly.

"Mmm." He moaned. "That tastes delicious. I wonder where else I could eat this dessert," he said, pulling down my hot pink panties.

For a moment I thought about all the times my ex-husband wanted me to peg him or shove things up his ass to make him happy in bed. All the times I hated his fat, lazy tongue on my body. All the times I had to take my mind to other places, pretending we were both other people just to experience a shred of pleasure. How being present with him in bed was so far from reality, how detached I was from the actual act and experience with him. To now, having the best sexual experiences of my life. And yeah sure, it was with a young man. A very attractive, sexy, young man, might I add. I didn't hate it here. In fact, I fucking loved it here.

Before we fell asleep that night, he fed me blueberries and played with my hair as we confessed that we had caught feelings for each other. *This was never a part of the plan.*

We woke up the next morning with two heads of messy curls and day-old sweet cream breath.

"Mmm. Morning, sir." I said, sucking on his mouth.

"Morning," he said, sliding his hand into my underwear. "Missed you all night."

"Did you? Even being right next to me?"

"Mmmhm. Come here."

He pulled me in tighter. Before we knew it, he was inside of me again. Putting me in another wild position that surprisingly hit all the right places. Men are oddly obsessed with morning sex. After we came, we walked downstairs to get ready for checkout.

"Sit down. I'm making you breakfast before we leave."

I smiled. "Yeah?"

"Yes ma'am. How many eggs do you want?" he asked, buttering up the pan.

"Two. Sunny eggs." I said, side smiling hard into my cheek dimple.

"I got you."

He brought my plate, two sunny eggs with buttered toast and orange slices. He kissed my forehead.

"For you, miss."

"Want to get lattes after this? I don't think I slept for more than two hours last night. I lost count on how many rounds we had." I asked, kissing him back.

"I lost count, too. I practically lived inside of you over the last twenty-four hours. Coffee is definitely necessary."

We drove to my favorite coffee shop. He ordered a salted caramel latte and I ordered something seasonal and fun. Christmas was right around the corner after all. When we made it back to the car, we looked at each other, dreading the impending goodbye.

"Will, what are we doing?"

He knew where this was going. He looked into my eyes longingly, grabbed my hands.

"I don't know."

"This wasn't supposed to happen." I said, falling into this chest. Attaching to him effortlessly by magnetic forces I had no control over. My body found its way to him.

He ran his fingers over my thumb.

"I know."

"Maybe we take a week apart to think about it." I said, reluctant.

"That might be for the best. It'll be Christmas anyway."

"I'll be sad to not see you or talk, though."

"I know. I will miss you."

"I will miss you, too." I said, swallowing down the feelings that came to surface last night.

We held each other for a while until it was time to let go. This part was always the hardest.

A WEEK LATER we decided that it was time we pulled the plug on it. The feelings were deep, far deeper than we had bargained for. It was supposed to be just a fun, one night stand. It was never supposed to last this long. So, we ended it. No more checking my phone for funny memes in my inbox, no more silly texts or photos. No more songs that made him think of me during the day. No more shirtless pics to build sexual tension until we were together again. No more voice texts with his laugh throughout the day. There was nothing. Just a black hole of space and silence that was anything but quiet. It was loud and hard to ignore. A world without Will for one week already felt like torture, I was afraid to see how terrible it would feel to go any longer.

After a week passed, we decided to meet up for coffee at a small local diner. For closure, we said.

"You know I'm terrified of being in a relationship. I'm not ready and it's not what I want." Will said.

"Right. I know that."

He nodded, sipped his coffee.

"Someday you'll have to work on that, you know." I said.

"Work on what?"

"Your fear of commitment. Have you considered therapy?"

"You mean like counseling? Yeah, I mean… I did some, maybe a few years back. Didn't really like the guy. He was a little too churchy, too religious."

"What did you go to therapy for?"

"I haven't really told anyone about it. Just my parents and this counselor knows." He looked down and swallows. "It was a big deal though."

A serious look glossed over his face. I believed him and more than ever I wished I could hold him in my arms and take away whatever it was that happened to him.

"You know you can tell me, though, right? I'm a safe space." The many perks of seeing an older woman is the emotional awareness and maturity after all.

He nodded, and I could see a bit of fear take over then. Vulnerability wasn't always easy for him.

"I appreciate that. But I'm good now. I'm alright. I'll be okay."

Knowing he has scars that I can't kiss hurt my heart, too. I wanted to see the inside of his soul, I wanted him to let me in, I wanted to try my best to make it better. But he kept the walls up no matter how long I spent pounding at them from the outside in with my tired fists. He never budged. If anything, the harder I tried to climb the walls, the higher they went up. And when I reached for his heart, it slipped right out of my grasp. It didn't want to be caught, and if it was by some fluke chance, it certainly didn't want to be held onto for very long.

"Your neck is all red. You okay? Are you nervous?" he asked.

I hate that this happens when I get anxious. I considered lying, but I'm terrible at it and he knew me too well by then, anyway.

"Yeah, actually. I am nervous."

"Why?"

Sometimes I hated him. He knew why.

"Because I didn't know what to say to you. I didn't know if today was going to be goodbye forever or what we were doing."

"Well, we can't do what we've been doing. That isn't working. The lines are blurring. We caught feelings and that's not what we want right now."

I looked at him then with a longing in my eyes. I picked at a piece of fruit with my fork and swallowed the lump in my throat filled with tears. I caught feelings and I wanted to keep them. The hardest part in this moment was accepting he wanted to get rid of his. That discarding them seemed so easy for him. Even now, as he stared at me from across the table, a vacant daze and a soft smirk hung from his face. Emotionally unavailable. I nodded instead of using words that disagreed with his even though that's all I wanted to do. Because fighting for what you want comes natural to me. Giving up doesn't, and this felt a lot like giving up.

"So, that's it then? We just stop this?"

"I mean, I told you. I don't want a relationship. And we can't *just* be friends, can we?"

"You mean friends with benefits?"

He took a sip of water, looked at me and shrugged.

"Is that our last option? Our final attempt to keep seeing each other in a way that makes the most sense?" he asked.

"You think we could honestly *just* be friends?" I wagered and tilted my head in suspicion.

"I don't think we really have a choice. It's that or nothing at all, right?"

I stared at him blankly. Imagining him disappear right before my eyes forever. But with him right in front of me, a future without him in it wasn't one I wanted to live in.

I nodded because the words were stuck in my throat again. This time, my eyes fought the tears.

"What do you want then?" I inquired, my voice hollow and dull.

"I don't want nothing at all, but I don't want to keep ending up in diners and cars and having these long phone calls with each other that always end up circling in the same place."

He was right, we did keep having this same conversation. And what I wanted to say, I didn't. I didn't tell him that I thought we kept coming back to each other for a reason. That we wouldn't end up here if we had just given this a chance to see what happened. To surrender and say, "fuck it," this is fun, it feels good right now, so let's just go with this and follow our good feelings. I didn't say that. Instead, I waited for him to speak again.

The young waitress brought the check, flashed a flirty smile at him and looked at me like I was some kind of fool. The older woman riddled with a purse full of mistakes and bad choices. The obvious bad choice being falling for this charming, hauntingly beautiful man that looks like Nick fucking Jonas, with those brown bedroom eyes that melted me with a single glance.

"It's just coffee and fruit, I got it." He paid for our bill and put on his coat.

"You ready?" he asked.

No, I wasn't ready to say goodbye, Will. I never would be.

But I put on my coat, a confident smile and nodded.

"Yeah, let's go."

When we were outside, the sun made the winter chill feel more enjoyable, but it was still not my first choice to stand in it for very long. This is the part where we were supposed to hug and go our separate ways. We looked at each other, both with deep longing in our eyes. Our magnetic pull brought our bodies closer for a long, tight hug. And as always, it lasted too long.

A kiss happened. Then another one. And before we knew it, we were accidentally making out in front of the diner.

"Um. Want to sit in my car for a few minutes?" he asked.

I put my hand over my mouth to hide my smile, nodded and followed him to his car.

Once inside, he pulled my face to his and we kissed so intensely, it felt as if I'd be floating around the car like a helium balloon if I wasn't anchored down by his lips.

"How are we supposed to quit *this*? This kiss is insane." I gushed. It was true. It was the best kiss I'd ever had in my life, second to the kiss I had with my first love that passed away. His lips on mine just made sense. They fit perfectly together with his and seemed to somehow unlock a feeling inside of me that had been dormant for so long. I thought I hated kissing because I hated kissing my husband. But it turns out when you're kissing the person you crave, your soul is set on fire. And the only way to stoke the fire and stay warm is to kiss again and ignite the flame. When you kiss the right person, you simply can't kiss that person enough.

We passionately made out and felt each other up for what felt like an eternity jammed into twenty minutes. Soft moans of desire spilled out of our mouths in the parking lot.

He looked at the clock in a panic.

"I'm technically on my lunch break. I should probably get

back to work."

"Okay." I said, still sucking on his mouth.

"But I want nothing more than to spread your legs and get inside of you in that back seat."

"Is that right?" I gave him the eyes that say, *try me.*

"It is." He kissed me and his eyes rolled back into his head.

*He still wants me. I still want him.*

I pulled away and looked at him with a smile.

"So now what?" I asked.

He smiled back, licked his bottom lip, shook his head, and looked away.

I pulled at his collar, and we kissed passionately another time.

He pulled away against his will. "Okay, okay. I know we hate goodbyes. But I gotta go. For real." He laughed. And then kissed me again.

I stared into his eyes. All knowing.

"Okay, get back to work, mister."

He grabbed my hand and smiled, melting me with his direct eye contact.

"I'll see you soon." he said, leaning in for one last kiss.

I knew it. This wan't over. This isn't goodbye.

Here we go again.

◆ ◆ ◆

WE TRIED TO end it several times after this. It turns out when a genuine and fated connection like this occurs, it spreads and functions very much like an unwanted virus. And not the kind you can quarantine and hide from. The kind that comes out of nowhere, knocks you on your ass and there's nothing you can do about it. Ending it prematurely for the sake of uncertainty was like taking an antibiotic for a viral infection. It didn't work.

There was no fighting it. The only choice we had was to let something like this run its course naturally. Completely surrender to it and let it end when it ends.

Everything must eventually come to an end, right? Even though I found myself on search engines more times than I care to admit looking for "age gap" relationship success stories. Of course, for every article I found screaming at me of why it doesn't often work, I also found a lot that gave me hope that maybe it could. Julianne Moore and her husband Bart are nine years apart, her being the older one, they have two children and they've been married for over twenty years. Nick Jonas married his wife, Priya, who is ten years older than him. Yeah, the same man that has an uncanny resemblance to the young man I'm falling for, also fell for an older woman. It felt like a sign.

I was looking for evidence, a confirmation bias, that what we were feeling was real and true and that it could work. Even with the glaring "age gap issue," even if he was terrified of commitment, scared to fall in love and wasn't sure if he wanted to live in Africa for two years, move to San Francisco or stay where he was, which was a quick five-minute drive from my house. Even if our timelines weren't exactly on the same pages, but our life goals and values were. Even if I had two children and a stack of divorce papers in my office. Even if he told me several times he wasn't looking to be in a relationship, wasn't ready for something serious, didn't feel like he could give me what I needed. I was so damn hopeful. That maybe he would change his mind, that maybe forces outside of our control would bridge the gaps and keep us together. Fate brought us together in the first place, it felt like this was the very thing that would keep us connected.

Falling for a man eight years younger than me was never the plan. He made it clear he wasn't expecting nor planning to fall either. But we did. Hard and fast with the intensity of a thousand burning suns. It started off as one the healthiest relationship dynamics I'd ever experienced, feeling safe, secure, and at peace. When my head laid on his chest I melted into his presence. When I held him in my arms, I could feel his deep peace. We communicated well and often. Had a blast, enjoyed each other's company and had so much in common. And the sex, sweet Jesus, the sex. The chemistry was on fire from day one it never left. To make it all worse, he was slowly becoming my best friend. Nothing was ever wrong. Not a single conflict that wasn't handled with care, not one heated argument, not a speck of disrespect or contempt towards each other. In fact, every disagreement we had seemed to bring us even closer due to how well we handled it together. Not saying it was perfect, but there was nothing majorly wrong. No big red flags. Only an age gap and a mismatched timeline. Everything else felt right. It felt like a sick joke the universe was playing on me.

One of the most heart-breaking things the universe could do is send you the right person at the wrong time. It's one of the best-selling tropes in the romance genre for a reason. And even though it scared the hell out of us, we went with it. No regrets. Not a single one. He also made motherhood feel sexy and I hadn't once felt sexy about being a mom. He seemingly adored my role as a mother. I'm aware there's a milf porn category for a reason, a fetish amongst many men, but this didn't feel like that. It felt adoring, admiring, and like I was deeply respected. I felt seen and heard in ways I hadn't yet felt since assuming this role on the birthing table.

When he came over, he'd notice the kid's artwork hanging on the fridge and took interest in what they made. When I took them to hockey practice, he'd comment on how cute they were after posting a pic up to my Instagram stories. When he'd open the fridge and see their sippy cup still full of apple juice, he'd pick it up and say "Aww, look at this. This little cup is adorable."

And nearly every time he would come over, he would hold up their toddler shoes, smile at me and say, "Britt, these tiny shoes! Oh my God. Look at them. They are the cutest things I've ever seen. I can't get over it." He laughed while looking at me, still holding them in his hand.

There is this saying in dating, that you need to pay attention to the first date and what they say, because it really shows their truth in that single moment of time and reveals how they really feel, far more than you realize. And when you look back at the first date, the whole relationship will make sense. So far, it was proving to be true. Not only was he unphased by me as a mom, but it was also becoming evident that even more than that, he perhaps had a soft spot for it. And not only did we not expect to get so close, so fast—it just happened. Even if we tried to stop, we still saw tomorrow in each other's eyes. It was figuring out what happens after tomorrow that was always the issue.

A FEW DAYS went by and the cravings for each other were back. We met at a bar in town, and even if we didn't drink when we were together, we loved the act of going out and flirting a little in public. I wore a cute skirt, heeled boots, and a leather jacket. He wore a nice jacket, jeans, and trendy Gen Z tennis shoes, of course.

Then there are times when I remember he was twenty-three. Sometimes it was obvious, others it wasn't. Most often though, I truly forgot the age difference. Our conversations were stimulating and intellectual. And when he wore his glasses with me in public, it aged him at least a few years. We didn't look too far off visually. I often get mistaken for looking younger and he gets mistaken for looking older. I didn't feel like a cougar anymore and the relationship we had felt as normal as anyone else's. Connection is connection. It was there or it was not. And with us, it was there.

"Is your house free tonight?" he asked, sipping his water with his hand on my thigh.

"It's not, unfortunately."

I made a pouty face and he kissed me.

"How do you feel about car sex?" he whispered.

"You're serious?" I laughed.

"Let's get out of here," he winked.

He took us to a semi-secluded park after the bar. As soon as we parked, the steamy make out began. Feeling every bit of high school thrill, we began to devour each other almost immediately.

In the back seat, he slid his pants off, freeing the very part of him that I had been craving since his thigh-squeezing at the bar. The smell of his fresh skin was destroying me. His pheromones haunted me in the best way. When we were together, sexual chemistry burned us alive and it was only a matter of time before our clothes fell off and we devoured each other. Often for hours and hours. Repeatedly, as if our bodies were magnets made to stay connected through an earth-shattering bond of pleasure. I unbuttoned mine and pulled them down past my knees. Taking them all the way off would require more space than a back seat allowed and clearly, more time. We wanted each other immediately.

I sit back onto hips as I face the steering wheel and slid down slowly onto him. Drenched with desire and wet arousal, I swallowed him up without effort. I turned my head back to see his face. His eyebrows knit together as his mouth fell open, his wide moony brown eyes were so full of pleasure that he almost looked pained and pouty. I rocked down onto him, thrusting back into his lap slowly, slowly, slowly, rocking the car. The rain beat down harder and faster as if a prompt from nature. The glow of park lights illuminated little bubbles of rain falling from the windows. The scene was set for steamy late night car sex.

"You are absolutely intoxicating," he whispered. He never failed to remind me this. "Give it to me, mommy."

I stopped him there, turned my body around to face him and grabbed his jaw with my hand.

"Mommy?" I said, titling my head while making fierce eye contact. He'd never once called me that.

"Mmmhhm. Sexy mommy. Naughty mommy." He licked on my nipples. *Oof. I love that shit.*

"Yeah? And what does that make you?"

"A young, 23-year-old sexy mother fucker." *Jesus.* He wasn't lying.

He sucked on my neck, licking up to my ear. The scent of his hair sent a wave of euphoria through my chest.

"Ride me, mommy."

DAMN IT. I wasn't supposed to love this. Or everything about him. It wasn't supposed to be like this. This was not the plan. We caught feelings again and they keep catching. How could they not? This connection was intense, it was hot and it all happened fast without warning. We were both fucked. Literally and figuratively.

IT STILL BAFFLES me. Enough to be worth repeating. How on earth could he only be 23? With a face like that, a beard that full and thick, shoulders that broad. A back like that. To me, he looked like a full-grown man. And it wasn't just the way he looked. It was the way he looked at me. The way he spoke. The conversations we had. The way he lived. His values, his morals, his maturity, his lifestyle. We met in the organic produce aisle at Whole Foods, for God's sake.

A thing to know about Will was that he was a fighter, but he was gentle. His touch was tender and warm. He was strong but he is soft in all the ways I ever needed a man to be. When I talked, he listened. When I felt something, he knew before I spoke. He could read me. We could communicate by simply a lock of eyes; it was almost telepathic between us. There was a sense of safety I felt with him when we were together. A feeling of home that didn't make sense. Everything just felt right when we were together. And when we weren't? A physical ache took over and I craved him. He was becoming more than just an infatuation with some hot guy; it was more than a crush. He was becoming my drug and I was completely hooked. There was nothing else in the world that could get me as high as him. I once gushed to my best friend Audri that I even loved the shape of his teeth when he smiled.

"The shape of his teeth? Jesus, you're down bad for this guy."

She was right. I was falling in deep. And I knew I was screwed.

## Mom is Taking Stripper Classes?

First of all, it's called floor dance. Is it provocative? Yes. Is it sexy? Hell yes. Because sexy was the energy I was going for. I was newly divorced and that was the plan. That was exactly what I needed. If I was reclaiming myself as a defiant, untamed, badass woman, I needed to embody her fully. I also had a deep desire for more body movement, play, entertainment, fun and sexual expression that didn't always involve a younger man sweating on top of me. I needed to channel and harness my sexual energy in a healthy way. So, enter floor dance. It's sort of what strippers do, but it's a class for normal people who want to feel that same rush. Okay, maybe normal people don't do floor dance, but I wanted to try it. I wanted to dance on my knees and whip my hair around like someone was paying to watch. And so, when I didn't have my kids and I didn't have any plans, I did this one new thing every now and then because I wanted to. Not because I wanted to end up a famous floor dancer or end up on stage performing with Beyonce, but because I wanted to feel what it is to be deeply woman. To feel confident and comfortable strutting around, dancing in heels again. I hadn't shaken my ass in heels since the clubs in college with my friends, grinding on people under strobe lights. This was something for the new me, but also for the woman I was becoming. The new me wasn't afraid to shake a little ass in a pair of heels every now and then. The new me didn't care what anyone thought so long as it brought me joy. And sometimes joy looked like twerkin' it.

# Dating App Disasters

WHEN WILL AND I were "on", we were guns-a-blazin' ON. But when we were off, it was a ghost town. So far, this was what we did. One minute we were "on" and everything felt right and holy in the world. And the next, one of us ran away at the height of the good feeling due to fears of getting even closer. Then, like a switch, we were off again. And right now, we were off. Again.

I never saw this coming. When I walked down the aisle, I meant forever. But as it turned out, forever wasn't in the cards. So, there I was, phone in hand, uploading a witty bio selling myself to bro's on the internet. I mean, not literally, but that's what it felt like. Packaging yourself up in such a way to showcase all the goods for a swipe in the right direction.

When I was newly married at the young age of twenty-three, I envied my friends who were on dating apps. It was a new thing that I never got to try. I guess the novelty of it all piqued my interest because I was also the first person in my friend group to get married and I missed that boat. And funny enough, I am also now the first person to get divorced. It's interesting that as I write this, I realize how we always want what we don't or cannot have. My best friend who never thought she'd find a husband while I was married for nearly ten years is finally engaged to her fiancé while I am newly single and divorced. If we only knew how important it is to trust the timing of things and know that just because someone has something you want, the tables may eventually turn one way or another. Funny how that works.

As I watched Natalia try on wedding dresses the other day, I remembered how I felt when I was a bride. The whole world was my oyster. My unborn children were still just seeds to be planted, wishes, and hopes and dreams that ran through my head like lullabies on a daily basis, promising me a sense of love, safety and security that I craved my whole life. And in so many ways, I got those dreams to come true. I did get my beautiful children. I had the big house in the suburbs, and playdate brunches with the stay-at-home moms sipping mimosas questionably early on a Tuesday while complaining about our husbands. I knew what it felt like to have the American Dream and even what it felt like walking down the aisle towards it all in white lace and tulle. So, when I tell you that getting on a dating app never once crossed my mind, I can assure you that I would've never guessed I'd be here. A year and a half ago, I was slicing carrots and potatoes for a family pot roast while watching my mother-in-law slur her words and hurt someone's feelings over another glass of cheap chardonnay as my husband ignored my entire existence. And now, I'm putting myself on display in one of the most vulnerable ways yet: Online dating.

AT FIRST, IT was thrilling. It was—new. I was being courted by very attractive men (and not to toot my own horn, but I mean VERY in all caps) and it felt yet again validating. Which is why I'm sure it's also the downfall of true love and modern dating. To an insecure or wounded person, that validation can feel addicting. And hey, if it doesn't work out with one person, there's hundreds if not thousands of people just a swipe away. I wasn't particularly excited to join the dating app, but I was curious. Nothing was happening with Will, and I was ready for something more with a person willing to give it to me. However, if you have ever been on one, you know first-hand the disappointment that immediately follows.

One of my first matches, I will never forget, because it was a musician I adored. When we matched, I nearly dropped my phone. Wait a minute, this is THE guy that I saved on my Spotify playlist? I love his music. This must be a fluke. Him, matching with me?

It wasn't.

Before you knew it, he asked for my phone number. And there I was, texting this guy I admired and before that day, he didn't know who I was.

***Evan:** Hey, want to come over tonight? I'm having a little party at my house. I have a hot tub, too. It'll be chill.*

A little party with a musician I have a virtual crush on is not chill by any definition. And the possibility of being next to him soaking wet in a hot tub? I nearly collapsed. When I went to his Instagram, photos of him and his ex-girlfriend were still on his page. The girl is a freaking supermodel. What the heck does he want with a girl like me? She's a very clear ten. And I might've said yes, but I had kids after all, and I had them that night.

***Me:** I'd love to, but I can't.*

He then sends a photo of a champagne bottle.

***Evan:** Well, maybe we can get together another time.*

Further examination, the bottle says *SEX.* Is he… flirting with me?

***Me:** Let me know how it tastes.*
***Evan:** Better with you.*

Then, it happened. You guessed it. A dick pic. And I won't lie, the man was… well endowed. However, this never means good news. Obviously, the man is horny. Stiffly so. And me? Flattered, of course. But, not feeling the guy's vibe. Though, one thing about me is, I will egg some things like this on for sheer entertainment. And entertaining it was. But there was also something else coming out. His little secret.

> **Me:** *Oh really? How so?*
> **Evan:** *Well, you seem like a strong woman. Which is what I like. My ex hated that I was so submissive.*
> **Me:** *Aw*
> **Evan:** *Yeah. And she hated that I wore women's underwear.*

*Wait. What?*

> **Me:** *You do?*
> **Evan:** *Do you want a pic?*

Am I being pranked? This can't be real. Before I respond, this dude sends two photos. One of the frontal view of his bulge in a pair of pink women's underwear. And one of his ass cheeks hanging out of the thong. Still feeling pranked, I respond with gentleness. Though I am definitely freaking out.

> **Me:** *I think that's great that you're expressing yourself. I'm sorry you didn't feel accepted for who you are.*
> **Evan:** *I love wearing my thong around, it's my dirty little secret. I like wearing women's clothes too.*

He sends me a photo of him in a crop top, still in the thong. At this point, I'm running out of responses. What the hell do I say? I don't want to be mean just in case he's serious, but at the same time, I've never experienced this before in my life. Shook is an understatement.

> **Me:** Nothing wrong with being who you are.
>
> **Evan:** I'd love for you to tell me what to do. I want you to control me.
>
> **Me:** What would you want me to say or do to you?
>
> **Evan:** Something really bad. Something really subby.

He proceeded to send a video that I will not repeat in the written English language. Let's just say, it got messier from there and I never talked to him again.

What's the saying? Never meet your heroes, you're always going to be disappointed. That couldn't be more real. Dude is an incredible musician; I will give him that. But it's best I enjoy that aspect of him from afar.

My first interaction with a dating app seemed to be providing experiences and qualities that I wasn't looking for in a man. But then, of course, as an honorable mention, there were the athletes looking for a quick lay. Those were tempting for all the obvious reasons; the only cost is you must lose all self-respect. It's a steep price to pay, in my opinion. And then there were the hot young men with all their hair, smooth skin and glowing untraumatized smiles—who were also looking for a lay. There were the hot fitness men with washboard abs that you were shocked to even match with in the first place because they are clear ten out of ten. But as you guessed it, they were also just looking for a lay. Then there were the snap chat bros, looking for nude pics, and yes, also a lay. It was then that I realized dating apps cater to men and their sexual desire, needs, and fantasies and not really the needs, desires, or fantasies of women. I tried for a week, and I had seen enough. I was determined to meet someone in real life and in another way. If Will wasn't available, I wanted to find a man that was.

# Everything is Bigger in Texas
## (Objects in Mirror Appear Larger Than They Are)

**I** NEVER IN a million years saw myself flying to Texas to meet a man I met on Instagram, but there I was. Standing at the arrivals gate at the airport in Austin to do just that. My friends were stressed, my mom was having an out of body experience and I was somehow completely naïve to realize what I had actually done. I dead-ass flew across the entire country to meet a twenty-five-year-old brown eyed young man, a stranger on the internet. Excuse me, Brittany, but *what the fuck* were you thinking? With blind faith, I trusted this man I hardly knew anything about. We had mutual friends and had been chatting via Instagram DM's. From there, he got my number and we talked for hours on the phone. We had facetimed for several months, and intuitively I felt like I would be safe. This man got down on his knees during our first Facetime to say a prayer for us both as he asked God to guide our connection. He checked nearly all my boxes, too. He was spiritual, fit, seemingly health conscious, funny, driven, ambitious, and we were practically the same person. Even our zodiac signs were compatible, because honey don't worry, I checked his birth chart. Honestly, it was giving soulmate vibes and I had to know if this guy was possibly "the one" I had been looking for.

He pulled up to arrivals, stepped out of the car in a blue jacket and a big smile stretched on his face. The good news was, he was taller than he looked online and more handsome. The bad news was, I had no butterflies, no chemistry, nothing. It felt like my cousin was picking me up and we were headed to a family reunion. He hugged me then and my insides folded in half.

"Hey girl, how was the flight?" *Luke said, pushing his sunglasses over his brown hair.

"It was great, smooth sailing the whole way." I noticed that I was avoiding eye contact and staring out the passenger window.

"Did you listen to that meditation I sent you? The visualization one?"

Oh, you mean the visualization meditation that prompted me to basically daydream of Will the entire time? I nodded. "Yeah, I did."

Even when I was consciously trying to not think of Will, he was somehow imprinted in my subconscious mind. The more I tried to run away from him or turn it all off, the more he found me, in one way or another.

We arrived at Luke's apartment. In the parking garage with my luggage in his hands, he leaned in to kiss me. All of me flushed in a hot prickly sweat. I didn't like it. I think maybe he felt like he had to, or maybe he wanted to. I'm not sure. But it was very clear in that moment for me that I didn't want to. He kissed me so hard and with so much pressure my bottom lip hurt and when I looked later, it was a bit purplish. This was one of the worst kisses, if not *the* worst kiss in my life. Second to my ex-husband. I think there is something scientific and evolutionary about a kiss. I think a kiss says more than words could say about a connection. I never liked kissing my husband. His tongue never worked right in my mouth, we could never center our lips, so for years, I mostly tried to avoid it. I wrote it off as "I don't like kissing." But when I think about past connections I've had with other men, that couldn't be farther from the truth. I do love kissing. I just love kissing the right man. And at this moment, it was clear that Luke was not the right man.

A wild wave of vulnerability consumed me. I was forced to sit with my feelings in his apartment alone as he was still working. He picked me up at 11 A.M. and mentioned he had work to do for a few hours, but said I was welcome to relax at his place until he was done. Of course, I hit up the group chat and let the girlies know.

*This is a no-go. May day. May day. Alert. Alert.*

Within minutes, my friend Claire called me, and I slipped out onto the balcony, picking at my thumbs, absorbing the Austin skyline, whispering so he couldn't hear me.

"So," she says in that concerned yet amused voice. "Is he a weirdo? Have you found the drawer of toenail clippings? Anything strange? Any red flags?" I looked around, a bookshelf with a bible, other religious and spiritual books in plain view.

"No, not exactly." I tried to muffle a laugh.

"Wait, what do you mean?"

"I can't really say."

"Oh god, he's right there isn't he?"

"Mmmhm. Yep."

"Can I ask a few questions and you just say yes, or no?"

"Yep." The nervous laughs kept building, I really didn't want him to hear me.

"Do you feel safe?"

"Yes."

"Is it awkward?"

"Mhhm."

"Are you okay?"

"Yeah, I guess."

"Do you just want to go home?"

"Yep."

"What are you gonna do? Just stick it out until your flight

back home?"

"Yep."

"Well, since you can't really talk, just text me periodically so I know that you're not chopped up in his freezer."

"Jesus, when you say it like that…" I laughed a bit too loud to be inconspicuous.

"Try to have fun. You'll be fine. Text me updates. Love you. Be safe."

A FEW HOURS passed as I waited for Luke to finish up work. I sat there somber on his sofa, vacillating between staring at the wall and at my phone. Missing Will like crazy even though I knew I shouldn't while contemplating my entire life in this quiet apartment. When he finished work, he tried kissing me again. And still, it just wasn't working. My body wanted nothing to do with him. At that moment, I worried if something was wrong with me. He was cute, a good catch and had so many of the qualities I was looking for. Still yet, a hollow ache screamed at me from within. As much as I hated to admit, I was repulsed at the thought of another man other than Will touching me. The hardest part came next, communicating that outwardly.

When we talked about how I was feeling, we both cried, feeling a combination of disappointment and relief. Afterall, we both hoped this would be something, even if we didn't know exactly what.

"We're still going to have fun though, okay?" he said. "And if I'm honest, I think you should text him and tell him how you feel. Does he know you feel that way about him?'

I shook my head no. For being an author and having a knack for placing one word in front of the other, when it comes to verbally expressing my feelings, especially romantic ones, I struggle. I can be vulnerable and open and honest, but with feelings like this, I panic and freeze. Telling someone I have feelings for them has never come easy for me.

"Stop moping around, get on that skirt and let's go out. It's my friend Golden's birthday. It'll be fun!" Luke said, playfully shaking my shoulders to snap me out of the morose regret I was in. "Come on, just come! You're here in Austin. Let's go see Austin. You only live once. My friends will be there."

He was right. I flew all this way, I might as freakin' well.

I bucked up and put the damn skirt on. I puckered my lips in the mirror and ran a mauve pink over them to cover up the purple tint left by Luke. I leaned into the mirror and gave myself a last look. *Go have fun, girl. You deserve it.*

We took a taxi to a trendy bar. Luke helped me out and we walked in together. Instantly, his friend turned the corner and locked eyes with me. He was wearing a vintage tan leather jacket and black denim jeans the same shade as his hair. He also had those brown bedroom eyes that destroy me. I nudged Luke. "Um, who is that?"

"That's Noah."

I didn't say it but I was thinking it. *Noah is hot.*

Noah said his name and reached out to shake my hand. *Oof those eyes.*

"Brittany. Nice to meet you."

"Having fun with Luke here in Austin?"

We looked at each other and started laughing.

"We're having… an interesting time." Luke said. "My friends are over there." He pointed to a table with three stunning girls. Luke pulled Noah off to the side as I headed to the table to sit with his friends. It was clear they were talking about me and I was fine with it. I introduced myself to a stunningly beautiful blonde who said her older boyfriend was at home working, a cute redhead that didn't say much and then Golden, the masculine lesbian with a shaved head that was dyed blue. The other girls were so basic they were easy to forget, but not Golden.

"What do you think of Luke?" she asked.

"Luke? Oh, we're just friends."

"Really? Well, there's Noah. You know, I used to date Noah before I came out. We're still close, but now I am poly and I only date girls."

"Interesting. Love that for you. How's that going?"

"The girls? Or me and Noah?"

"Whatever you want to talk about."

"Noah is my best friend. The girls? Well, I could show you later If you want to find out." She winked. Golden had beautiful features, addictive charisma, and an unforgettable smile, but as far as I know, I am a straight woman.

"I have only been with men." I laughed nervously.

"You haven't tried me though." She licked her lips.

"Golden!" The girls laughed. "She just got here. Luke said from Michigan, is that right?"

"Flew in yesterday."

Just then the guys walked back. Noah walked up to me and pulled me aside.

"So, you and Luke. Let's talk about it."

"What's there to talk about?" I took a sip of my hard cider.

"You tell me." He said, flashing a flirty smile.

"We're just friends. Didn't he tell you?"

"He did. And he also gave me the greenlight to flirt with you. Because I don't know if you felt that when we first met, but I did."

I played dumb, but yes, I felt it. Attraction.

"And what was that?"

"Luke says you're older than him, which means you're older

than me. Which means you know what I'm talking about. You're a smart woman, I can tell."

I smirked and squinted my eyes a little.

"Who are you, Noah?"

"I'm 26, an Aquarius and I'm in acting school. Who are you, Brittany?"

"I'm 31, A Cancer, Sagittarius Moon and an Aries rising. I'm divorced, I have two kids and if I were to tell you all that I do for work it would take too long."

"A Cancer? No way. You're too fiery, but I guess that makes sense with the Sagittarius moon and all."

"I'm a pistol, what can I say?"

"I like that." He says. "Well, we have all night, you know. I can get to know you more over the course of it. I want to know all about you."

The rest of the night Noah was by my side. Funny, isn't it? How you travel to a place hoping to establish a connection with one person, but instead you end up connecting with someone entirely different. An absolute stranger. Luke's friend, nonetheless. After leaving the bar, Luke, Golden and the crew grabbed slices of pizza before walking to the next adventure. A bonfire at a house Golden was house sitting for. Apparently, she was a billionaire's personal assistant and the person was so elite and famous, she couldn't even tell us who it was. As I always do, I decided to put on my playlist while Golden passed a joint around. It made its way to me, and I took a small hit before passing it to Noah. He stopped then and looked at me.

"You like Tourist? I love this band. I bet we have a lot of bands in common if you like them."

I handed over my phone and he scrolled through my Spotify.

"Yeah, wow. You're passing the vibe check in a major way."

He didn't know this, but music was the key to my heart. A

love language. And the fact that he liked the same music as me? Swoonworthy. It started to rain just then. Luke looked at me.

"You have that flight at 5 A.M. tomorrow. It's already 2 A.M. We should go, yeah?" He says.

"I guess I'll sleep on the plane. I didn't expect to be out so late."

"I'm glad you came," Noah said.

"Me too." I said looking at him and then back at Luke. I could tell Noah wanted to kiss me, but whether Luke gave him the green light or not, it felt weird to do it in front of him.

The taxicab arrived moments later.

"Nice meeting you all!" I shouted as I stepped in. Noah smiled and waved.

"Until next time," he said.

TO BE HONEST, it was an adjustment going from living the life of a tired toddler mom to a woman that wears miniskirt and laughs until four in the morning with folks still in their twenties. I was reminded yet again how different I have been living and how much of my twenties I had missed out on due to marriage and early motherhood. I was sort of getting my second chance at my twenties all over again, and I didn't realize how fun it all was until I was toe-to-toe with girls who were twenty-five, beautiful, rested and clueless about life and the world. I didn't envy them though, not really. While they were bright-eyed, effortlessly taught and naïve, I never felt more sure of myself at 31 than ever before. And confidence, as we all know, is what is truly sexy. I didn't feel threatened in the slightest. I loved being in their energy and sharing as much wisdom as I could. I owed it to my younger self. If I could save young women from making the mistakes I made while brushing shoulders and making conversations about life in the crowded girls bathroom, I was making an impact. Even if it was slight, it wasn't small, and I knew that.

The Austin trip taught me that everything I thought I wanted was in fact not what I wanted. And everything was not what it appeared to be. And what I thought I wanted was not what I needed. Luke was seemingly everything on my list. I felt so confused and yet again, disappointed. But what I quickly realized was how badly I needed to throw that list in the trash and forget it ever existed. I found it incredibly uninteresting and boring to spend that much time with someone as similar as me. Where was the novelty? I reflected then on some of the best relationships and a lot of them were "opposites attract" where we complimented the connection by our unique differences. We invited each other into new worlds and that made it exciting. Maybe that saying is right after all, the best people you'll ever meet are unexpected. Even after all those lessons in Austin, my heart still had one burning desire. I wanted Will. And I wanted him more than ever.

WHEN WE GOT back to Luke's, I considered taking Luke's advice. *What if I texted him? What if he knew how I felt? Would it make a difference?* I wondered, in a weak moment filled with liquid courage, if I should. I missed him and I missed him terribly. My thumbs trembled around my lock screen. This was the longest we'd gone without talking, a whole month. Before I overthought it, I sent the text.

> **Me:** I'm in Texas and I came to meet Luke... if I'm being honest my body doesn't want to be touched by anyone else other than you. So, I'm currently dealing with that. I don't expect you to respond... but I'm thinking about you, haven't stopped, and wanted to tell you. I know I'm not supposed to but... I am. I don't want to overthink it or make it weird, but I do miss you.

*And physically… I'm weak for literally only you.*

In typical Will fashion, he made me wait for it. A few hours went by before he replied.

> **Will:** *Wow…this is absolutely not what I expected. It's a lot to process and naturally I have some questions. Of course, I'm going to respond, that's how I am. I won't just not respond unless there's a good reason to. You can feel however you want to feel, that's what's so amazing about it all. Thank you for being vulnerable and telling me. I'm sure it wasn't easy to decide to do. Enjoy Austin, we will talk when you're back.*
>
> **Me:** *I know… honestly wasn't what I expected either… I'm sorry … definitely not something I'm in control of. I'm just being honest and I'm glad you're at least open to listening to my thoughts.*
>
> **Me:** *Legit dead inside for anyone that isn't you… what did you do to me?*

WHEN I RETURNED home, I called Will. The result? A two-hour phone call and confession. Turns out, he missed me, too. Just as much as I missed him. From here? Who even knew what was next? I sure as hell didn't.

# Blinded by the Light
## (And Other Obvious Things)

AFTER ALL THAT time apart, the nerves began to kick in. Would he look at me the same? Would he feel the same way in person as he did over the phone? The thoughts consumed me most of the day. The plan was to meet up at night since my ex-husband had left town and the kids were asleep.

Will's text rolled in and all of me flushed.

**Will:** *I'm here.*

The door was cracked open, and he tapped on it. I waved him in with my finger. He walked in, smiling.

"Hi," he said, softly.

"Hi."

Within seconds, he grabbed my face with both hands, pushed my body against the wall and kissed me passionately. This kiss. The most electrifying kiss I had ever experienced. He picked me up then and placed me on the kitchen counter. Like the freakin' movies, ya'll. I was swooning. After melting me there, he threw his arms around me and carried me to the couch, where he pushed me down and devoured me more. With his strong arm, he pressed my legs open.

"LET ME TAKE care of you." He stared into my lustful eyes.

I knew what that meant. Me screaming a body quaking orgasm into a pillow as he massaged my g-spot and opened me up like a flower. All the while my two children slept sweetly and innocently upstairs.

Have you ever been desired by someone so much that they kiss the backs of your knees? That they grab your hand and plant a million tiny hard and fast kisses all over them in adoration? That shit will melt you faster than butter on a hot griddle. This man had learned how to turn me into a puddle in more ways than one. There were times when we fucked and there were times where we made love. When we did, the difference was clear. It was slow, intentional, passionate, and beautiful. Tonight, after all this time without each other, we made love.

"Do you want to hear a funny joke?" I asked, catching my breath post-orgasm quake while lying in his arms.

"What?" he asked.

"Us trying to stay apart." We looked at each other, raised our eyebrows and laughed. But not a "haha" funny laugh. A knowing, truth-telling, honest laugh. We were hooked. Again.

The next morning, I was up early, squinting my eyes at the light shining from my phone. *How have we become addicted to each other?* I wondered. When I don't know things and I want the answer fast, I ask the internet like a seasoned millennial. It was six in the morning and here I was searching "What does intense passion between two people mean?"

I got answers that describe what I felt when we were together. Euphoric bliss, excitement, an enamored sense of intrigue of the other person, intoxicating sensations and a feeling of craving them when you're apart. Yep. That pretty much nailed it. It was just the second part that clipped me like a bullet.

"Aside from passionate love, you also need respect, trust, intimacy, and commitment.

Without them, passionate love alone won't work. Use your passion and love to make yourselves and your relationships stronger."

This is that part where the sinking feeling in my chest hit. If it felt too good to be true, it probably was. There were the parts of our relationship that felt out of this world perfect, and then there was everything else missing from the puzzle. Thank you, Google. If being the number one search engine that has us all believing our symptoms of a small seasonal cold could equate to a terminal illness, you were now also the reason to blame for breaking my heart. The truth was staring me right in the face, so bright it felt blinding. But that was the thing about blinding light. You could still hardly see it, no matter how much it shone in your face. I was not ignorant to the facts, just blind from them.

Later that night Will sent me a riddle.

**Will:** *Teach a man to fish and he'll eat forever.*

It was my clue to our next sexual escapade and for the next several days, my obsession for finding out what exactly he had in mind.

# Becoming a Sex God

"Tell me what it is," I batted my eyes, charming my way into getting my answer.

"Guess." He adjusted his body on my couch, back in the same place where he last ruined me. Flashbacks hit like a slow-motion film. His hands, his mouth, his pleasure exploding all over me.

"I don't know. A sex toy?"

"That's a good idea. But no." He smirked.

"What else could it be?"

"Think about the riddle. Give it a minute."

"Teach a man to fish and he'll never be hungry." I repeated it out loud a few times.

"Still no clue?" he asked, leaning forward.

"Come on, just tell me." I traced his bearded jaw line with my fingertips. He reached for his backpack and pulled out a book. I read the title out loud slowly.

"*Becoming a Sex God*. This book is the surprise?"

"Yeah. I thought it would be sexy to read it together. We can try new and exotic things." He thumbed through the pages.

"It's a thick book."

"I have a lot to learn if I want to keep you satisfied. And you can never be too good at something, especially something like sex."

I shook my head and smiled at him. How the hell did I get here? It still blew my mind. The man was eager to please the senses right out of my skull.

We flipped through the book and stopped at the chapter on Tantra. My personal favorite. The mix of eye gazing, slow and rhythmic motions, intentional with soul and depth. Fully immersed, present and in sync.

He started to undress me.

"Wait, stand up again," he said. "Spin around. I want to admire you." He licked his lips and shook his head. "Look at you. Do you see yourself?"

I looked down at my body feeling like a four-course meal about to be eaten alive.

"Come here," he demanded. "Sit on my lap."

This man. *This. Young. Man.*

After, he fell asleep in my arms. An angelic chorus melody was playing softly from my speaker in the background as his skin rested against mine.

"Send me this song. It's beautiful," he whispered with his eyes closed. "I don't want to forget it."

I closed my eyes and breathed him in again. I couldn't forget any of this if I tried.

## Perfect on Paper

SOON AFTER, WILL went to Florida with his family on a vacation. When I didn't get a single text from him for an entire week, I accepted the date I was invited on with a guy who did yoga and flexed it for the 'gram. Maybe it should've struck me as cringe, but I thought it seemed mostly interesting that he had cool hobbies and shared them online. He appeared to be attractive, fit, emotionally in tune. For God sakes, he did yoga, that's always hot in my book. After telling my friends about him, we'd collectively coined him the nickname "hot yogi." After a series of voice texts in our Instagram DM's, he asked me out on a date. Again, what did I have to lose? He fit the bill and seemed to check a lot of boxes. Will was giving me zero attention and was nowhere to be found, who knows what or who he was doing, so I said yes to the date.

Arranging the date was no easy task for me. My kids were couch-bound and fever stricken. I had to coordinate two different nannies just to make it on time. Not to mention it was an absolute blizzard outside. It took me an hour to get somewhere that usually only took about fifteen minutes. As I think about it now, the universe was screaming at me, *this ain't your person, don't even waste your time*. But, I not only wasted my time. I drove in an absolute blizzard, got caught behind a train for thirty minutes, took an alternate route, all the stop lights were out of power from the snow and ice, and I arrived an hour late. When I got there, hot yogi was waiting in his car to meet me and hug me in the snow. He did get an A plus for trying to be romantic. As we walked into the bar, the power was half-out, and as we sat down, the music stopped and all the power died out. We ordered a drink anyway and sat there in the dark.

He stared into my eyes and quickly became overwhelmed with emotion.

"You're so beautiful. Wow." He wiped a tear. But across the table? I was vacant. I still only had eyes for Will and there was no hot yogi going to change my mind. But before you think he was a raging green flag, let's back up. He had many red flags. Numero one, he never gave me his phone number, even when I communicated it was the easiest method of communication. He refused and kept conversation strictly in my DM's. He also had not dated anyone in six years, and was only a year younger than me. At almost thirty, that pointed to commitment issues, did it not? He admitted to this at the date. He also didn't think he could accept the fact that I had children and was not interested in becoming a stepdad. He was wildly uncomfortable about it. So clearly, this was not my man. I found it funny to think that Will, who was only 23, never once made things awkward or felt uncomfortable about my children. Often, he expressed genuine interest, care, and concern about them. He even wanted to meet them. He loved that I was a mom and even when the kids would wake up in the middle of the night while he was over, he never once flinched. He didn't panic or freak out or snap to a strange reality of "holy shit, I'm sleeping with some kids' mom." Or "Yikes, the kids are real, and I better get out of here." No. Will would sit patiently as I rushed to tuck them back into bed when they woke from a nightmare. And when I'd return, he'd smile and say, "God, that's so attractive. Look at you. In mama-bear mode. It's so cute."

When the date ended with hot yogi, he went in for a kiss. I

just couldn't do it. I was not feeling it. Moments later, I got my SUV stuck in the snow and needed to push myself out whilst in a skirt and heeled boots. Never again will I ignore the signals from mother nature or my intuition. Hot yogi was not for me. And Will? I was still on the bread crumb trail, hungry, and stupid for more.

# Light Out, Hearts Out

ANOTHER WEEK GOES by, and Will was nowhere to be found, as usual. I wanted to hate him. Actually, make that present tense. I want to hate him. I wish so badly I could hate him. But my mind nor my heart doesn't have the capacity to entertain the thought for longer than a minute. As soon as the image of his face hits my brain, it overflows with nothing but feelings of warmth and desire for him. I couldn't hate him if you paid me, that's the worst of it.

And he certainly did enough things that should've made me hate him by then. But of course, just as I was about to start trying, he popped up.

He called me from work this time.

"I didn't want you to think I've forgotten about you. I'm in between client meetings and I wanted to say hello and check in with you."

"Oh, look at you. Sounding so important and professional. With your clients at work, doing business."

He laughed. "I do feel important. I am important." I picture him in business professional attire. The thought of seeing him dressed up in a professional setting melted me.

My eyes rolled and I smirked. *Cute, smart-ass, William John.*

"Can I see you tonight?" he asked.

"Are you asking nicely? That's new."

"I am."

He paused and waited for my response.

"You know I can't say no to you."

It was true. He was my weakness, and if he didn't know this by now, he was insane.

A few hours passed and the sun had gone down. Will usually came by once the kids were asleep. And since I was still in the marital home until the spring, I had him over while my ex-husband was traveling for work. Judge me if you want.

> **Me:** I won't lie... I'm feeling pretty slutty. Tight white tee shirt, no bra...
>
> **Will:** Idk if I can compete with that level of slutty
>
> **Will:** Maybe gray sweats
>
> **Will:** Should I leave?
>
> **Me:** Not yet... I'm just getting them ready for bed. Usually aren't down until 8:30-9pm ish. I'll text you when they're almost down and you can leave.
>
> **Will:** Ok
>
> **Will:** I'm stopping to get fuel. You have a little extra time for another bedtime story.

*Fucking melt my heart, why don't you? This makes me smile, and I hate that, too.*

> **Me:** Bad news...the power just went out at my house and the entire neighborhood
>
> **Will:** Oh no...Are the kids going to be okay?

Very cute of him to think of them. Sometimes he had a soft spot and sometimes it showed. Which made hating him twice as hard to do.

> **Me:** Yes, but it will be dark. I can light some candles, though.
>
> **Me:** It'll be romantic ;)
>
> **Will:** Sex.

And… he was definitely 23 again.

**Will:** *I'll see you soon.*

---

I LIT ABOUT a million candles to give light to my pitch-black home as I waited for him and synced up my portable speaker to set the mood. Frank Ocean *"Moon River"* was playing softly in the background when I met him at the door. I waved him inside. When he walked in, he grabbed my face and drank me in like he hadn't tasted anything all day. And when he pulled away, he looked at me and into my eyes like there was something inside of them that he craved, too. Then, he pulled me in for an even deeper kiss. Each one taking longer than the next leaving no room for breathing, just blissful gasps for air. The passion ignited an easy flame within our bodies as we peeled off our clothes. It was then he pushed me down onto the couch in the living room.

Once inside of me, something suddenly felt different. I could tell he felt it, too. Some sort of energetic shift. He stopped and looked at me. His face was washed over with a look of discernment, his lips falling apart almost in shock. We stared at each other as if we had both discovered something new at the exact same time.

"Do you feel that?" I asked, breathless. My eyes shut, weighted down by this euphoric state of bliss, as if millions of cosmic swirls were whizzing through my body. From head to toe I felt my body pulse and vibrate beneath his, along with sensations I had never once felt. An indescribable yet intoxicating feeling. When I opened them, he looked almost afraid to speak.

"Yeah… I do." he said. He held himself inside of me, still unmoving while staring into my eyes. Another wave of euphoria surged through me, making it hard for either of us to speak. "I have...*never*... felt this before," he said, his voice shaky, slightly concerned, like this was something we weren't supposed to discover together. I know it sounds crazy, but in this moment I could feel the presence of God. Like we had stumbled into some other holy angelic realm, as if something merged our souls together by mistake.

"I haven't either." I said, taking a breath. "*Ever.*" This was an entirely new feeling, a hypnotic trance seeming to alter our state of consciousness without a single substance. Like our souls were making love and had rubbed against each other for the first time. It was so beautiful and all-consuming I struggled holding back tears. He leaned his body back down into mine and when he slowly started moving deeper into me, the feeling and this cosmic energy intensified. Though he was moving, and I was too, we weren't moving fast. The rhythm was slow and tantric. His breath was synced with mine, breathing each other in. He leaned down and kissed my forehead. With our eyes still locked, we found ourselves in this new world, vulnerable and a little afraid to arrive here together. This wasn't supposed to happen, but it felt so good, it felt so right, that we kept moving through it. As the energy built between us, so did the sensations. I was moaning, making noises I'd never made, the state of pleasure I was in was a hauntingly new territory, but in his arms, I felt safe to express it all. The energetic wave built higher and higher and for the first time ever, our waters crashed into each other as we came together, staring into each other's souls. I knew I was never supposed to be in the arms of some 23-year-old guy, I was never supposed to see him again after the first date, but what we just experienced together was a moment I will never forget. His soul rubbed against mine and it was quite possibly the first time I had ever felt anything that beautiful with anyone else. There's a large part of me that doubts I will ever feel that again with another person.

He pulled out of me slowly and looked at me with wide eyes, wiping the sweat from his forehead.

"Well, I wasn't expecting that. For you to come at the same time." He paused. "And it felt so good, I usually have my timing just right, but..."

"But what?"

"I'm actually concerned that I... missed a little." He looked down at my stomach as he wiped what little there was to wipe off.

The last time I heard this was from my ex-husband and a child was born nine months later. I am not on the birth control pill. I track my cycle and know exactly when I ovulate. I had forgotten to check when my fertile window was, usually that was something I'd share with Will before we got intimate, but we clearly had gotten carried away. I reached for my phone and scrolled to my app. My eyes widened with a bit of panic to see that I was in fact in my fertile window. Smack dab in my ovulation cycle. If there was a time that I could get pregnant, it would have been right then. This was not what I had planned for my life and certainly not what he had planned for himself, either. I had two children sleeping upstairs, my divorce wasn't even finalized yet, I still lived with my soon-to-be ex-husband and if that wasn't terrifying enough, the father of this hypothetical child was practically a child himself, still living with his parents as a fresh college graduate, still figuring life and himself out. *Absolutely not. This cannot happen.*

I looked at him and covered my mouth as I showed him the fertile days boxed in the calendar on the app. I pointed to today's date highlighted in yellow and said nothing. He knew.

He collected himself calmly and pulled me into his body. We were having a very real moment where we realized what might be at stake here.

"I wouldn't have it," I said, looking away from him. I avoided the feelings of fear rising in my body. "I couldn't do that to you. And I have so much going for me right now, I couldn't do that to myself, either."

"Would you take a Plan B?" he asked. "To be safe."

I recall the last time I took a Plan B pill. It was with the other Wil when I was sixteen. I was so nauseous and dizzy after taking it that I almost vomited in the Pizza Hut parking lot. Wil held my hand and didn't let me out of his sight that whole day and night. He was just a teenager, but he was responsible, protective, mature, and kind. I knew I'd be okay if he was with me.

"Yeah, I would. But the last time I took it, I felt terribly sick for days. I hated how I felt after taking it."

He squeezed me tight. "If you need anything after taking it, snacks, or medicine, or any specific things, I got you. I'll come to the rescue and make sure you're alright."

He held me there naked in his arms against his warm chest. I closed my eyes and imagined another world, one where we were the same age, and we were together, and this was just a beautiful moment in time shared with the love of my life. But when I opened them, I saw it for what it was. A twenty-three-year-old terrified that he knocked up a thirty-one-year-old divorcee and mom of two on the couch in her marital home while her soon-to-be ex-husband was traveling for work. This was never the plan. I shook my head and let out a sigh. He kissed me on the forehead again before he got dressed and left.

I lay there on the couch, watching the candles flicker in the darkness.

I hated it here. I hated this house. I hated my ex-husband. I hated this couch. And right now, I really fucking hated God's timing.

THREE DAYS PASSED after that night and Will was a ghost. After that last forehead kiss, I wish I could say he did as he promised he would. That he brought me snacks, that he checked in on me. That he came over just to snuggle because the pill made me feel like shit. But he didn't. A beautiful soulful night turned sour fast. I wasn't sure if I could ever forget the bitterness it left in my mouth and in my heart. He wasn't who I needed him to be. He wasn't who I wanted him to be. I was waking up to it at a rapid pace. He was very much a kid. I didn't leave a painful marriage to jump in the arms of another person that also made me feel pained all the time. I needed to do better from here on out. The blinding light hurt too much.

## Valentine's Day is for the Girls

HE MAY HAVE had feelings for me, he might not have been able to stay away from me, he might have told me I was special and that he'd never felt this way about anyone else, but he couldn't, and he wouldn't commit to me, or date me. It was giving major Carrie Bradshaw and Mister Big in Sex and The City vibes. And by now, I was well aware of what was happening and how this would end. I was being strung along after all. But even with this knowledge, I was in so deep it hurt. Wild horses couldn't drag me away.

It was a few days before Valentine's Day and I'd spent all morning sobbing into a pillow waiting for him to make a plan for us. When it was clear he wouldn't, I gave up hope. That afternoon, February 13th, I headed to Whole Foods to grocery shop. As I'm in the produce aisle, I see a familiar face, one I was surprised to see. No, it wasn't him. It was my lesbian family photographer that I had a massive girl crush on. I bump shopping carts with her, and we spent the entire time shopping together, laughing our asses off and oddly... flirting. *Am I... gay?* I was pretty sure I wasn't, but she made me question things more than once. She's a masculine lesbian with amazing style. I was physically attracted to her in some capacity, but I wasn't sure what that meant or why.

"Do you have Valentine's day plans?" she asked. I shake my head no, the disappointment must be stamped on my face. "Well, have you bought yourself flowers yet?" I shake my head again.

"Come on, let's get some flowers. Because why not?"

Before I knew it, I had a date, my very first one with a woman. Of course, I called my mom and told her the details.

"Mom, I have a valentine."

"Who? Will? Is he taking you out?"

"Ummm… No." I laughed. Though it wasn't funny. It stung like hell.

"Well, who? Who is he?"

"Well. It's a she. Or a they. I'm not sure of the correct pronouns. But it's not a man."

"Is my daughter coming out right now?"

We both laughed. What a time to be alive.

"Honestly mom, I don't know. She asked me on a date and I'm going. Why not?"

"Yeah, why not? I can't wait to hear all about it," she said. "I kissed a girl once."

We laughed again.

"We all have. I think everyone is a little gay, mom."

"I think so, too. Even if only a little bit," she admitted. "Call me tomorrow morning. I need details. Love you."


PAIGE PICKED ME up in her Subaru. My nosey ex-husband peeked out the window as she arrived.

"Who's here?" he asked. "Is that…Paige? Our family photographer? Are you dating her?"

I threw my bag over my shoulder and shrugged before closing the door behind me.

She looked the same way she always had to me. Attractive, trendy. Men's jeans, baggy t-shirt, sneakers, round artsy glasses, hair pulled back in a "man bun." She smirked as I sat down in the passenger seat.

"You look nice." She looked at me, seductive eyes and all. "Actually, scratch that. You look super-hot," she said.

I laughed. "Thank you. You look great, too. Are you flirting with me right now?" A nervous giggle escaped me.

"You're literally the hottest girl I've ever taken out. I'm not kidding."

I couldn't lie. The flirting felt great. The mutual attraction was exciting. If a woman thinks you're attractive, it hits different than when a man does. It's more genuine.

"Stop. Are you serious? You're so cute. And successful. There's no way that's true." She was one of the coolest artists in Metro-Detroit and was widely known in the area. If a person were to have an alluring main character energy, it's her. She was well-known and well-loved by most and to be honest, I felt special to be seen with someone so effortlessly cool, magnetic, and charming in a way that I found endearing.

"Dating women as a woman is hard. Most women aren't fully lesbians, and the ones that are, they're hard to find. Most of the women I end up dating are straight, curious, or bisexual. They just want to experiment with me for a little while. And then I always get left for a man and end up repeating the same heartbreaking cycle."

*Ouch.* I didn't think about that and a part of me felt guilty for accepting the date, especially if I knew I wasn't one hundred percent sure of being lesbian. Maybe a small handful of times it had crossed my mind. A few of my favorite authors that I deem iconic are lesbians. They seemed to be happier and there was a part of me that was curious. What if women were the answer? Why was I attracted to masculine lesbians if I was not lesbian at all? I had so many questions for myself that needed answers.

When I was sixteen, I was hit on by a girl for the first time. She lived in town, but she was homeschooled. I worked at the only grocery store and one day she slipped me her number. I didn't think anything of it outside of friendship until when I called it, she told me she had a crush on me. I continued talking to her privately for a little while and never told a soul. Not even my mom, and I told her everything. Even when I lost my virginity, I called my mom. It turned out that I had a crush, too. And maybe that made me bi-curious. So here I was now, still curious.

A sadness filled the car. At that moment, I felt for her. I never once considered how hard dating would be if I wasn't into men at all. It significantly decreased the dating pool, that's for sure. As if dating in this generation wasn't hard enough, I had a front row seat at the LGBTQ dating scene, and it made my heart heavy.

"I have a few fun ideas for us to do, since we both don't drink."

Paige was also sober, like Will, and I found that to be refreshing.

She first took me to an old thrift shop in the hipster town I used to live in when I was in my early twenties. The energy was playful and spontaneous. You never know what might happen here and that's half the fun. We walked around holding hands and laughing hysterically at silly things that such shops have. Creepy vintage baby dolls, odd knit sweaters and vests, dad hats from the nineties, and outrageous ashtrays in every color. The scene was set for serious laughs and the two of us were serious goofballs. We were really enjoying each other's company. I tried to picture it: me with a woman. Some of it sounded like exactly what I needed. Emotional support and emotional availability. Empathy and deep understanding. A soft and gentler approach to intimacy. But when it came to sexual intimacy, I wasn't too sure. I had never gone there with a woman and never really had the urge to go there completely. I sort of think every woman goes through a lesbian porn phase. I mean, I did. But I think for me it was the only kind of erotica that depicted the kind of sexual experience I craved, which wasn't necessarily a woman as much as it was a soft, gentle, and sensual experience between two people. In heterosexual erotica, women and their bodies are often used violently. And as a woman who has a history of abuse, I was always turned off by that because it made me feel unsafe. Women always felt safe to me, which was why I had to see what this date would be like. I was curious, but I still didn't know if push came to shove, if I was sexually attracted to women.

After the fun and games, Paige had dinner plans for us. On the way to the restaurant, a song came on that made us both stop right in our tracks.

"Whoa," she said, choked up. "This song hits me in the feels."

"Wait. Me too, actually. You know this song?" I asked.

"Yeah. It's the same song I listened to with my ex. Reminds me of her. Of us."

My head fell onto her shoulder. A tear fell from my eye then.

"It reminds me of mine, too." It was the song that Will had me send him while still in my arms because he said it was beautiful. And it was beautiful. And it is. At that moment, it was clear that neither of us were over our exes. Even though, as embarrassing as it is to admit, he technically isn't my ex. He never had a label, but he was something to me. More than a friend, but not quite a relationship. A situationship.

THE SONG PLAYING was called "Wish on an Eyelash." And if I'd had a wish on an eyelash, it would have been for us both to teleport from this date and have the people we desired. Instead, we found ourselves crying in each other's arms and made out one last time for the hell of it, because sometimes that's what girls do. Afterwards, she drove me home.

For a few weeks following this, we'd hang out, go shopping, head into the city together, and enjoy the cool new artsy spots downtown. We'd bake cookies, watch Netflix, and cuddle each other when we were on our periods. Women are incredible lovers, and she made me wish I was lesbian so badly. But I couldn't deny my sexuality. I want a brown-eyed bearded man, and I want to feel him from the inside out.

# New Home, New Life

On Valentine's, my divorce was finalized and I was ordered by the court to move out of the marital home within thirty days. I couldn't find the right home to purchase, so I reluctantly browsed rentals. I found one that appeared to be perfect. It was newly updated and clean, only a mile and a half from the school, and close to everything. The location was hard to pass up, so I signed right away. I had the keys in my hands and a few empty spaces to fill. I went back to the marital home and started packing up my whole life, the only life I'd ever known. This man had been by my side since I was seventeen years old and within the next seven days, I'd no longer live with him anymore. Our chapter would finally be over. He was bitter and so was his family. They were angry with me and refused to help me pack a single box. I was leaving the marriage because of the way I was treated, and I was exiting the marriage with the same treatment. I was the mother of his children, and yet, he watched as I packed every single box alone. Not one person helped me lift a finger or helped me lift or unpack a box. With sweat dripping from my brow and my arms and back aching, I did it all by myself. I was on my new solo journey, and it was very clear that from that point forward, I was on it very much alone.

For the first time since being with my ex-husband, I was finally allowed to think for myself. Yes, I said allowed. During the marriage, I didn't have full access to our banking information, and I was rarely allowed to make purchases, no matter how small.

There was red tape around everything and being involved in any sort of decision-making was non-existent. Every piece of furniture in the house was to my husband's taste and style. He would often tell me that it was because I didn't know anything, which was why he took over. As an adult, I knew that to be untrue. At the worst of it, he convinced me I was incapable of even the smallest of things. My handwriting was mocked to the point it gave me anxiety to sign even the simplest of documents. He would hover over my shoulder and criticize the way I held the pen. I grew up near Lake Michigan, so I became a fast and early swimmer. But my ex-husband saw me plug my nose to go under the water one time and from that moment forward, teased me that I couldn't swim. And he did this for years. Not only did he convince me that I couldn't swim, but he would also tell others when we were near water that "Brittany isn't that great of a swimmer." Over time, I unconsciously started to believe that, too, and developed many slight fears. That I couldn't sign my name. I couldn't swim. I couldn't pick out furniture. I couldn't make financial decisions. I couldn't do anything that he could. When I finally had the freedom to be fully on my own and decorate my own place, it felt like a dream. One of the very first things I bought was a green velvet couch. I wanted one in our old home and of course my ex-husband didn't allow it. But now that I was making all the decisions and choosing to live a life that felt like mine? The green couch was the first order of business.

"Britt, I feel like you've escaped jail and you're finally free!" Paige laughed, sitting in the living room holding a kombucha. She had come over to see my new place, help me install my TVs, and teach me how a few things worked in the house. At the time, I didn't have a man in my life, but I appreciated Paige stepping up as one when she could.

"I won't lie, your old house with your ex was never *you*. Even the vibes are different here. You just look happy and free—like you're finally home."

Paige was right. For the first time ever, I was on my own and building a life that felt like it belonged to me. I had no one to overpower me, control or manipulate me. I was finally free.

When I graduated at seventeen, I was the only student in college that I knew of who was paying all their own bills, their own tuition, their own rent, their own car insurance, and working two jobs on campus while being a full-time student. In my family, once you leave the house, you're an adult and you're expected to make it on your own. I never intended to be hyper-independent, but I never had a choice. It was survival mode. If I wanted to survive, I had to find a way at an early age. And while my ex-husband wanted me to believe I couldn't do it without him, I'm still here. I'm not only alive, but I'm thriving without him. I am entirely independent as I write this. No man. No husband. No dual income. No corporate job. No employer healthcare and benefits. Not only did I take the solo journey, but I also took it to the next level. I am entirely solo. I am self-employed. Self-made and self-paid. The universe asked me to take a leap of faith and I said, "how high?" I not only jumped into my new life, but I jumped in with both feet. I had a dream for myself, and I was going to make it happen. There was no plan B. I was never going to work for anyone else ever again, I made that promise to myself at twenty-five years old. I was determined to figure this out on my own then and I'm determined now. Even when my ex-husband told me a million times how stupid my ideas were, how silly he thought it was for me to podcast or to write my books, I knew that's what I was meant to do. I not only trusted myself to leave my marriage, but I also trusted myself to fully provide and take care of myself alone. To be responsible for paying all my own bills with the money I made entirely on my own. I realize how crazy this sounds. Leaving a marriage with a man who provided for me, to rely solely on myself and a prayer.

I'd be lying if I said that at times I wasn't on my knees with tears in my eyes. I'd look up to the sky sometimes and say, "God, I don't even have to say it anymore. You already know." In the months following the divorce, I had been humbled to my knees more times than I can count. Sometimes I'd question if I could do this. I questioned if I was crazy to think I could survive alone. If it was just delusional thinking that I could provide a good life for me and the boys off my dreams alone. It felt worth it even if it was challenging, I never regretted leaving a man that was weighing me down. A man who was clipping my wings of new growth.

I had begun healing and to my surprise my wings were back. I was flying on my own, loving every minute. Even if sometimes the single mom journey is hard, and it's scary, and it's exhausting, and downright sad. This was never the path I imagined. But here I am, and even when I feel like I'm failing, I show myself grace. I am doing the best I can at something that often seems impossible. And when it feels impossible, my six-year-old son wraps his arms around my neck and reminds me just how good of a job I'm doing. He's right. I'm doing my best and that's all I can do.

# All Tied and Tangled Up

I DON'T KNOW how or why, but when Will and I were hooking up routinely, we ended up on the BDSM side of things. I was the proud owner of leather bondage cuffs and chokers, shibari rope, a red mood light for my room that synced up to the speakers and quite a few new toys. Together, we had a sense of comfort, ease and communication that made trying new things fun and exciting. Maybe we weren't meant to be together for a long time, but it was clear that whatever we were—we were here for a good time. Our bodies and souls just clicked. The kiss was always electric, the sex was out of this world passionate, surprisingly kinky and we fit together extremely well. We were highly compatible sexually, spiritually, physically, and mentally. But emotionally? This man was trying his very best to be dead inside.

And after a few weeks apart again, Will was back, and better than ever. Somehow, he had charmed his way back into my life and in my arms after massively disappointing me again. Usually, it would arrive in the form of a buttery smooth voice text, spontaneous phone call or making attempts to see me. And because the man made me weak, I allowed it. Besides, he was just as excited to see my new place as I was excited to show it off. I gave him my new address and waited on my green couch for him to arrive at my house for the first time. It was exciting to have the whole place to ourselves for once. No sleeping child still in the home. No shared spaces with my ex. No sneaking. We had every square inch to do whatever we wanted. This was new. And this was exciting.

I opened the door. Will was holding a bowl of fresh strawberries under the porch light with a smirk. The man loved food play. He pushed his way into the door and fed me the strawberries and sucked on them while making erotic eye contact with me. His body wasn't even halfway in the door before we started devouring each other.

"I've missed this," he said. He always said that after some time apart. Sometimes, it would slip, and he would say, "I missed you." And often he'd moan. "Oh my god. This mouth." It was like I constantly had a craving for him, and him for me. Like we would swallow each other whole if we could. We could never be close enough when we were together. When we had sex, we usually had it twice, because once was never enough.

Will pushed me against the wall then, sliding my panties down. "I want that neck," he said, kissing the back of it, slowly pushing down my bra straps, turning my body around to face him.

I sat on the bar stool; he slid his tongue into my mouth and his fingers inside of me softly. The thing about this man that made me weak was the way he handled my body tenderly and with so much care. He slid down to his knees and stroked me with his mouth so good I thought I would collapse.

We switched roles, as we do. Once in my room, he instructed me. "Grab the rope." I did. And I tied him up first. A red mood light cast over our bodies while sexy music reverberated through the walls. The energy intensified, and this time he safely used a few of his UFC fighting moves. He trained every Thursday and taught me a few good, safe, chokes. I cuffed his throat with my palm, as he showed me.

"This cuts off the blood supply, not the air supply. You never want to block off the windpipe." He smiled slightly, he was loving the power and control dynamic of the BDSM world, and together we were playing along perfectly. Will was just as naughty and adventurous as I was.

Like usual, we had post orgasmic dopamine high sillies and stayed up until 3 A.M. laughing until we cried, feeding each other fresh orange slices, and dancing naked in the kitchen. All I'd ever wanted was this. Someone like him. And I was so close I could taste it. Then, before the sun would rise, he rolled out of bed to go home and refused to stay the night.

"Before you know it, I'll have a toothbrush here and you know what that means."

"What?"

"That we're dating and I'm your boyfriend."

"So?"

"So, I don't want that. You know that."

"It can be whatever it is. Why are we stressing about labels again? None of that really matters, we agree on that. If you want to stay, then stay…"

"I do… and I will. I just shouldn't. Not tonight." He looked at me with a twinge of sadness in his eyes. "Oh, come on," he said, "don't look at me like that. Don't do the puppy dog eyes."

I definitely did do the puppy dog eyes. I couldn't help it. I wanted all of him. And deep down, I knew he wanted me, too. It was never clear if he was fighting it, if he was afraid, or if he just didn't feel the same way. Regardless, he was not ready for what I was ready for. I wanted a boyfriend. He couldn't do that.

"I'll cuddle a little longer, okay? I'll set an alarm for 4 A.M."

"Will. That's basically staying the night. You're being stubborn for the sake of proving a point now."

"No, I'm not. Please. Come on."

I looked at him blankly again. His whole body softened as he stares into my soul the way that only he does.

"Roll over. Come here. Come here. Come here. I'll hold you."

I melted into his chest and he fell fast asleep. I watched him as he breathed peacefully, his skin on my skin. He felt like home.

The alarm rangs at 4 A.M. He startled awake. He kissed my forehead and rolled out of bed.

"Don't be sad, I have to go. I have a lot to do tomorrow."

We both knew it was a lie.

"Please, don't look at me like that," he whispered.

I was looking at him like this was the dumbest thing in the world. A couple more hours in bed, a peaceful night sleeping next to each other, having organic coffee and pasture-raised eggs with caracara oranges from Whole Foods sliced the way we like it in the morning. Why couldn't we have that? Why was he running away from this? It was clear to me that he didn't want to leave but felt he should. The alarm clock was more than a reminder to wake up, it felt like a signal towards his feelings. Conflicted.

There's the saying in dating, "If he wanted to, he would." Well, with us, it had always been complicated. Age gaps and mismatched timelines weren't the easiest to navigate. Friends and family talking him out of it. Because it didn't sound great, and any mother would have their doubts about this for their son. Trust me, it's not ideal and neither one of us intended to stick around each other this long. I had no intentions of us ever getting past date one. I never thought I'd ever get along with a man so much younger than me, let alone feel this deep of a connection with one. Whatever was happening between us, it was not in our control. It was clear. This was not just a matter of the heart, it was a matter of the soul. His soul was intertwined with mine. We never planned this, it just happened by accident. A happy accident. Serendipity.

I walked him to the door to let him out. Standing in the

doorway, he kissed me, holding onto my waist. Our messy curls were tousled wildly from another passionate night together. We always had crazy sex hair and it's one of the little random cute things that I loved about us. If we weren't already similar enough, his curly hair was just as wild as mine. I didn't consciously mean to, but sometimes my mind wandered. If we did have that baby, how curly its hair would've been? The thought would make me laugh. A cute baby with some serious curls. We stood there holding each other for twenty minutes, kissing a million little kisses as if we'd dissolve if our lips weren't locked together. We were terrible at goodbyes. We always had been.

Have you ever pulled two magnets apart? Because that's what it felt like when we left each other's side. This was not an easy situation, but when we were together, nothing felt easier.

# Lessons from a Fiddle Fig

WHEN MY EX-HUSBAND and I first bought our house, his mother gifted me with the most beautiful fiddle fig tree I had ever seen. Over the years, that plant had become like a baby to me. I nestled it in a warm, sunny, cozy corner of the house, watered it routinely, dusted its leaves, and even talked to it like I'd been told to so I could really see the plant thrive. Thrive she did. I named it Jesse. At one point, Jesse had grown so lush and so tall, she had reached the ceiling. I had never seen a fiddle fig so big and so healthy in my life. I was so proud of this beautiful plant; she was a showstopper. Anytime people came over, they noticed her right away. Her presence and her growth demanded attention. You couldn't miss her if you tried. I loved this plant as much as a person loved a household cat. But one day, out of nowhere, I came home from running errands and saw that my ex-husband had cut her leaves down to the studs a year before I filed. No longer was she towering with her greatness, she was chopped down to mere bits and pieces. Branches were broken and scattered on the floor, the body of her was so short, it was unrecognizable. It didn't even look like Jesse anymore. My jaw hung to the floor. I couldn't believe my eyes. He knew how much I loved this tree and how proud I was to get her to such heights, and still, he chopped her down to almost nothing. I was so devastated about it that I cried for weeks. Every time I saw her like that, unrecognizable and sad, it stirred something inside of me. It became a daily reminder that the tree was an example of me.

I was that tall, towering tree full of growth and charisma, and my husband hated me for it. So, like he did with the tree, he cut me down as often as he could. Nothing I did was ever good enough. Every hair cut I got came with a horrifying remark to stab at my confidence, to which he would say, "I'm just joking, can't you take a joke?" I never folded the laundry right, the house was never clean enough, even my body at its most fit was still not enough. I was too fit, and he didn't like it. He once showed me pictures of girl's bodies that he did like and that he wanted my body to look like instead. When I wrote my first book, he held it in his hands, and said "Do you think the cover looks crooked? I think it does." Not "Congratulations, you wrote a book!" Instead, he could only speak of its flaws. When my cookbooks hit the best sellers list on Amazon, he teased me and told me it wasn't that big of a deal and that I could hardly call it a bestseller. That winter, the sales from the cookbook had paid for our family's Christmas while his job was uncertain. When I started my podcast, he laughed at me and told me I was the one millionth podcast ever started, so it wasn't worth trying. The next year I was a global podcast streaming in multiple countries and topping charts, ranking in the top 50 podcasts worldwide. Nothing I ever did was ever enough, in fact, it was despised by him. For every step I took forward, he would try to shove me two steps back. He hated everything I did and constantly tried to cut me down. Jesse and I had that in common.

When the divorce was finalized, he still had Jesse in his possession. Though she wasn't where she used to be, I managed to get her growth near close to what was it was before. She was on the up and up and so was I. I saw myself in my fiddle fig. She was more than a tree; she was a reminder of who I was and where I was going. And where I was going was a place that I could grow in peace without anyone cutting me down anymore.

After a few months of my ex-husband having Jesse, her leaves were dry and her structure was brittle, lifeless and dull. She didn't have the same shine as she did when I took care of her. I was determined to get her into my new home without the man who could so easily cut us down. I couldn't wait for her to breathe in this new air of hope, safety, and possibility. To get her into a new space, one with a higher ceiling and a sky light window shining like a spotlight over her. A place where she and I could both grow and thrive. Now that she's here, she is healthier and more beautiful than ever. The people who see her now, really appreciate her, and notice her right away. She's in a much better place and so am I.

What Jesse taught me is that an insecure man will try his very best to cut you down and tear off all your leaves, but no matter how much they try, a strong woman is resilient. She grows like a lotus through the mud. My fiddle fig and I both did just that. Jesse was my daily reminder that your environment matters. That you can always rise and grow above the bullshit in life. That even if someone tears you down repeatedly, you can always grow through what you go through.

## This Isn't Good Night, It's Goodbye

"Y**OU KNOW YOU'RE** single, right? You can see other people." Will said this to me while I was lying on his chest. We'd been seeing each other more frequently again. "I know, but I only want you." I said, looking into his eyes, tugging at the button on his jeans. "Isn't that sexy to you? This is the only one I want." I pointed at it. He smiled a little.

"Just wanted to remind you," he said, and my chest tightened. I didn't want to dig deeper than the surface. So, I kept quiet while inside I was screaming. *I just want to be yours.*

It was as if Will purposely wanted to maintain the empty void between us, because if he were to fill it, then it would be something. He made it very clear that he wanted everything to mean nothing. More than anything, I wanted it to be *something*. I wanted everything to mean *everything*. I was disillusioned, too afraid to accept the truth. He didn't want me, and I'd been losing parts of myself trying to prove to him that he should.

"This isn't going to end well. Besides, what would your kids call me? What if they don't like me? What happens if in eight years you change your mind about me, like you did with your husband?"

"That's not fair. He was awful to me. That's why I left."

"Please don't tell me that," he said. "I can't hear it."

He got this way when I opened up about my past. He didn't want to know about it, as if knowing made me become a real person with real feelings. Real feelings meant he'd have to have real respect and accountability, things he lacked, either because of his age, or maybe a character flaw. It was hard to know which was which. And I was starting to see it, the age difference, his youth and immaturity. Even though I was in denial from the beginning, the immaturity hurt a whole hell of a lot.

He'd go around and around in circles with me aiming to push me away yet keep me reeled in enough to hang on by a thread. Until this night, he said something he hadn't before.

"I just think I should be with someone my age."

As much as I wanted to agree with him, because I wanted what was best for him, it was hard for me to swallow. Especially when he's what my heart wants. Maybe on paper it all made sense, that he'd find someone his age and all his dreams would come true. But this wasn't a thesis, this wasn't a resume, this wasn't a job application. This was two hearts on the line. Something that defied any logic. I know it didn't make sense, the fact that we didn't choose this, maybe that's what made it real. Isn't that how fate works? You don't choose fate, it chooses you.

"You want someone your age? Fine. Go find some brunette that works in HR for some corporation she hates. And listen to her gush about the Beibers and what Netflix show she's watching. And when you're bored, because so far you have been with women your age, and because she can't think for herself, don't come back to me. Go find your young wife and leave me alone."

He said nothing. He didn't interrupt. He just listened. Sometimes I hated his patience. I hated his stillness. I hated when he heard me and tried his best to understand me. Because even after he did, the outcome was never different. Sometimes I wished he would be arrogant or rude. I wished he'd raise his voice or threaten my personal space like my ex-husband did. I wished he'd be abrasive and volatile and angry and violent. I wish he'd scream in my face and send shivers down my spine. Because that was the only kind of man I'd ever known. His gentleness and softness only made me want him more. And I was constantly looking for every reason not to.

"You want to know how this ends if you run away from it? You're young and a little clueless, so let me tell you. You're going to run away from something extremely rare, but you have no idea at this very moment just how rare it is. You will search for me in every person you meet from this point forward. And someday, you might even get pretty damn close to finding her. It still won't be me, but at this point—you'll settle for close enough. And years from now, when the night gets lonely, and you're staring off at the moon, you'll think of me. You'll remember the nights we had and how amazing everything really was. And you'll wonder what would've happened. Around that time, you'll search for me online, when you miss me most. You'll stare at my photos with those big brown beautiful longing eyes, still curious and full of wonder. You'll be tempted to call me, but by then it'll be too late, you're years in with someone else and you can't. So, you'll swallow a lump in your throat, walk back to your wife, shutting the door and everything else you ever felt behind you. Never really knowing, and never really forgetting. That's how it'll end if you walk away."

I looked at him with tired resentful eyes. I said nothing else, but the silence meant more than that. He looked at me, still quiet. I could almost see the wheels spinning inside his brain, calculating a response. Processing what it would mean to lose me.

"You think the worst thing that could happen is that I'll fall in love with you. Or that you'll fall in love with me." I shook my head. "I'm fucking amazing to be in love with by the way."

Pain filled his eyes then. He said nothing. Still. He didn't have to.

"But I think the worst that could happen is me hating you."

He shifted his gaze towards me then. "You couldn't. You don't. Do you?" His voice shook.

What I wanted to say, I didn't. I didn't tell him that I'd already tried and that I couldn't. That I prayed more times than I care to admit for my feelings to leave. They didn't. Instead, I looked at him blankly. Words weren't enough at this moment. I closed my eyes and shook my head again.

"Look. You deserve someone that has their life together, someone that has the same values, same goals, good head on his shoulders. Someone that lives the way you live. Someone who doesn't really drink, because you don't. Someone fit and healthy like you. Who likes the same music you like. And bonus points if he shops at Whole Foods." He smiled, trying to add his charm and warmth to gloss over the pain.

"You just described yourself, Will."

"I know. Someone *like* me... because it can't be me."

"Why not?"

"You know why." He put his head on my chest. "Your heart is racing."

"Why do you always have to be my heart monitor?"

"Because I know you. What's wrong? What's making it beat like that?"

I didn't say it, but I was dying to.

*It's You.*

The entire time he pretended not to care, started to feel like maybe he didn't. When he ignored his feelings and mine, it started to feel more like neglect over self-preservation or protection. When denial of what was happening between us started feeling like abandonment, I knew I had to walk away. For real this time. If the seven stages of grief were in full effect, I was on stage five—anger. Truth is, I was slowly grieving it the entire time. My heart just seemed to take a while to catch up.

# If the Devil Can't Reach You, He'll Send You an Aquarius

IT WASN'T SOMETHING I was meant to understand when it happened. Instead of grasping at straws, I allowed myself to become available and open for new moments and new connections with new people, to help me move forward on my own. Waiting for Will was getting boring. I was ready for some fun.

A couple weeks after Will and I broke it off again, I heard from Noah. Yes, the Noah that I locked eyes with at the bar in Texas, when I was visiting Luke.

**Noah:** *I'm coming for you.*
**Me:** *Is that right?*
**Noah:** *I'm booking a flight and I'm taking you out. Watch.*
**Me:** *I'll believe it when I see it.*

And that he did, to come see me the following week. I can't lie, I was excited. It was an adorable meet-cute. Someone I wasn't expecting to run into while I was traveling. And since things with Luke or Will were a no-go, this felt kind of promising. Noah was interesting. He was attractive and he too had brown bedroom eyes that ruined me. Noah was also an aspiring actor and creative. I felt seen and understood by him. As an artist and creative, finding people who get you makes all the difference.

I picked Noah up from the airport on Easter Sunday. I didn't have my kids that day, and it made me sad, so I made us both

Easter baskets. Noah thought it was adorable and hilarious, which was the goal. I filled them with funny things like candy cigarettes and a friendship bracelet making kit for us to make together. Things with Noah were going so well, that when my mom called, he asked me to put it on speaker so he could talk to her. He seemed so curious about me, my work, and my life. This was such a change of pace from Will. This was also the first time another guy had spoken to my mom since my husband. To me, it felt like a big deal. Will hadn't ever talked to my mom on the phone. Once we hung up, things took an interesting turn. Noah looked antsy.

"Want to go for a walk? I want to see this cute little city."

One thing about my new place is that it's walking distance to downtown, which has been extra fun for me as a single lady. It's a different life than the cozy suburb tucked away from the city I used to live in.

We walked into town and stopped at the only fancy bar open on the holiday. I ordered a prosecco and he ordered a Manhattan.

"That's an old man's drink for such a young man," I teased.

"Oh, please," he says, "You're not that much older than me."

I sipped my drink. "Five years."

"Honestly, what's five or even ten years older when you're in your forties, fifties, sixties? No one cares how old anyone is anymore. Some of the best marriages I've ever seen included an older woman and a younger man."

"Hmm. Is that right?" This perspective was something I needed to hear. It felt that ending up with a younger man was likely my destiny. I found Noah's take to be refreshing but also painful. Why couldn't Will see it that way?

WE WALKED BACK to my place and Noah's demeanor shifted a bit more. He still hadn't kissed me, which I found to be odd. *Maybe I'm reading into this too much*, I thought. When we were at my place, it was clear that one of us was going to make a move. There was attraction and tension after all. Finally, he kissed me. And when I was down to my underwear and bra, he started to body-worship me in one of the most intense ways I have ever experienced, almost to an unsettling amount.

"You are a literal queen. Wow." He kissed me all over. When it came to the next part, he froze.

"Is everything okay?" I asked.

"Yeah, yeah. I'm just nervous."

"We don't have to do anything. It's okay." To be honest, it was all feeling off anyway.

And so, we decided to opt out of it. Instead, we found ourselves finishing the night by making pasta together and watching my favorite movie, which happened to also be one of his favorites. *LaLa Land*. It felt also a blaring metaphor for what this was between him and I. Two creative dreamers that saw the world differently but weren't meant to see it together. The next morning, he woke up next to me and things got naturally physically intimate, until suddenly he stopped, again.

"I can't do this," he said. "You're right. Something is wrong. I need to come clean."

"What is it?" I say, panicked.

"I actually have a girlfriend. It's the redhead girl that was out with all of us that night when you were in Austin. And she's been blowing up my phone since I've been here. She found out I'm here and it's a whole big mess. I feel terrible for doing this to you both."

"No. No fucking way. This is a joke, right?"

"It's not. I'm serious." He covered his face shamefully and rolled off me.

"Noah. I met her. She is so pretty and she's so nice and so cool. What is happening right now? I don't want to do this to her. Oh my God. I had no idea. I hate this so much." Tears fell from my face instantly. My father cheated on my mother for seven years. I have a brother out there in this world that I've never met because he had a lovechild with another woman while still married to my mom. I'm a lot of things, but I am not a liar or a cheater. I could never hurt someone the same way that my dad hurt our family. Being the other woman in that moment, even unknowingly, turned my stomach.

"Please leave." I said sternly. "Get out. I'm dead serious. Delete my number and forget this ever happened. I never want to see you or talk to you ever again. This was disgusting. I'm beside myself."

And he did. He spent the rest of his time in my guest room without me even breathing in his direction, took an Uber to the airport and left. I spent the entire day crying in bed feeling physically ill and wildly betrayed. I blocked him on everything, and I never spoke to him ever again. This was a lesson for me in trust. I learned that just because I have pure and genuine intentions, not everyone else does. This was the moment I began guarding my heart and my body more intensely. Monsters are real and no one is coming to save me. I'm my own hero in this story.

It was clear that this was yet another life raft teaching me a few things: That "if he wanted to, he would." He would put in the effort and book the flight just to see you. And that age gaps don't really matter. My level of self-concept and self-worth was working, slowly but surely. I was noticing that I was beginning to attract a man that put in the effort, but clearly, I had some work to do, because it also showed me where I was emotionally—unavailable. Just like he was. My heart still belonged to someone else. It was at that moment I realized I would be removing myself from the dating world until I was ready, which meant being over Will and fully moved on. I couldn't find my soulmate if I was still deeply attached to someone else.

So I did what any heartbroken girl should do. Cry about it, a lot. Then shift the focus back onto me. I spent three months celibate and "man sober." I shifted the love I was searching for back on to loving myself. I got massages, booked reiki energy healing appointments, had my first facial, and started getting bi-weekly mani-pedi's. I actually kept my hair appointments without canceling, started meditating daily, journaled several days a week, made exercise and fitness a priority again, indulged in a new wardrobe, bought myself a fancy Prada wallet, new shoes, new makeup and invested in a new skin care routine. I couldn't get to where I wanted to be by remaining who and where I was. If I wanted to feel like a million bucks, I needed to act like I was worth a million bucks. I needed to embody being a millionaire, investing in myself like I was one, too. You attract what you are. I needed to do better.

# Meeting Your Life Partner

I DROVE TO a sketchy art district neighborhood in Detroit for an ecstatic dance party. Just me, myself, and I. I told no one I was going, not even my friends. When I did, they thought I was a little insane. Was it safe? Eh. Debatable. But I knew I had to go dance my little heart out. I wanted to feel free. At ecstatic dance parties, everyone is sober. There are no substances allowed as it would alter your state of consciousness. The point is to gain consciousness by connecting deeper within and to let whatever is inside of you come out in its full authentic expression. Instructors are usually very skilled at creating a safe dialogue and safe space to foster genuine authenticity. Anything goes at these kinds of things. Hippies and freedom seekers of all ages and from all walks of life usually show up. The room was decorated with silk tapestry from the walls and ceilings, bongo drums, streamers to dance with and tambourines were scattered about. When the session began, music played, lights were flashing, and the people started to let loose. Letting loose for some might include gentle swaying to the music, and for others it might include chanting wildly while convulsing on the floor. There was no judgment, and your inner child was safe, which is why I spent an entire hour pounding away at a set of bongo drums with a Rastafarian man and a smile plastered on my face so big, you couldn't tell me that I wasn't a child at that moment. I felt free. I felt alive. I felt like me. It was working.

Then, as the music began to slow down, the instructor said

something that changed my life forever.

"Look at your life partner in the eyes," she said. My eyes watered as I looked around the room, alone, heartbroken, empty, and divorced. Other couples look at each other in adoration.

"Not at another person," she said stoically. "Look in the mirror. There's your life partner." Several times I had looked over at the couple feeling sorry for myself and the others, I realized, she's right. I am my life partner. I hugged myself, caressed myself. Made myself feel beautiful, worthy and loved. I danced with myself and her beautiful shadow, embracing my curves and edges. I was realizing just then how I was falling in love with me. My reflection, my shadow, my energy, my own wholeness, my own life. I never needed anyone. I am enough on my own. I am my own life partner. When you choose the love of your life, you must choose yourself. That is the ultimate life partner.

# Falling Over Facetime

NOTHING WAS EVER the same after April 27th 2019. It was the day my first love passed away. He went to sleep one night and didn't wake up the next. And again, I don't find it to be "just a coincidence" that April 27th is the same day my divorce was finalized, four years later, in the state of Michigan. I cried so hard to God on my knees that morning—"Please God, no more endings. No more hard lessons. I'm ready for my new beginnings. I'm ready for a change. I'm ready for some love." Sure enough, just hours later, I met Mason, a man that would forever change my life.

"I'm willing to give you my number if you want it," he said. He had found me on social media and had just begun following me as he anticipated my book's new release about losing my first love. He mentioned he'd lost his wife and his first love, too. He seemed kind enough, but I needed to do my due diligence and thoroughly creep through his social media accounts just to be sure. Since his Instagram was set to private, I went to Facebook and searched his name.

*Holy shit.* This man was gorgeous. Brown flowing hair, kind brown eyes and a smokin' hot beard. I wasn't expecting the poor widower to be so attractive. I just wanted to make sure he wasn't weird. Not only was he easy on the eyes, but it was also very clear from a handful of photos how much this man loved and missed his wife.

"I'll take your number. That sounds nice, thank you," I wrote back.

What did I have to lose? It was Wil's death anniversary, it was the day my divorce was finalized, I was grieving him, the divorce, and the other Will if I was being honest. I could have used someone to talk to. And the bonus was that he was that he was stunning to look at. Before he called, he sent a voice message.

"I was born very early and had a brain hemorrhage as a baby, so I have a pretty bad stutter," he said. The stutter was apparent and hard to understand at first.

"That's okay," I reassured. "My oldest son has a speech disfluency, and he stutters. He's been in speech therapy for years. This is normal in my world." I responded.

That must have eased his nerves, because that night, we talked well past midnight when he called me. He struggled to get the words out, but as a parent of a child who stutters, I know that meeting new people and emotional topics are triggers that often make it worse. When I talked to Mason, I made sure to slow my pace and use a few speaking techniques taught to parents to help their stuttering loved one. I never thought I'd use it with anyone else, but quickly realized how well it worked with him. I seemed to understand Mason on every level and that made the connection easy. From knowing how to communicate with him, to deeply understanding his grief. And Mason knew how to hold space for my emotions and support me in my endeavors.

Butterflies rested in my stomach as I waited for his Facetime. When I answered and saw his face for the first time, he lit up. A wide, perfect dimpled smile took over the screen. Mason was radiant and beautiful. He harbored a natural, calming presence that made me feel safe instantly.

"Hi." he said, still smiling.

"Hi." I giggled and my cheeks flushed like a schoolgirl. This was definitely turning into a crush rather quickly.

"It's late, but I'm glad we could talk," he said, his words breaking on the way out. I found the stutter endearing and vulnerable. "I know what it's like to lose a person you love." These words broke the most on the way out. "I'm sorry about my stutter by the way. I wish it was easier for me to talk. If you find it easier to complete my sentences for me, I won't be offended. Everyone does it and it helps me out. So feel free," he joked. I could tell this bothered him and I imagined how hard it must have been to struggle getting words out.

"It's fine, I hardly notice." The last thing I wanted to do is make him feel worse about a condition he couldn't control. Besides, a part of me found it adorable and I couldn't explain why. "I'm sorry for your loss, by the way. I can't imagine how hard that must be to lose your wife."

"Thank you, I'm sorry about your loss, too. Do you want to tell me about him? I can tell you about Lyss, too. Sometimes it's nice to talk about your person, isn't it? It helps."

WITH MASON, IT was easy. From our first call, we began to Facetime every day, often for hours and hours. And as he grew more comfortable, he stuttered less and less. He was even comfortable enough speaking with me that he bought my book and read it out loud to me on Facetime. It was never supposed to be romantic with us, until we realized it was. A slow burn.

MASON STARTED BUYING me cute little gifts "just because" he was thinking of me. And to my surprise, he even texted me all the while he was on a Bachelor weekend with his friends. *If he wanted to, he would.* And Mason did. He was so excited about me, I even met his mama on Facetime, talked to his dad, his brother, and his best friends on the phone. Mason texted me daily just to check in and wanted to know little things, like how my day was. We would talk on the phone for hours and hours, unable to hang up. Finally, he booked a flight to come see me within one week of meeting me. He said he "just knew."

This was seeming to be a classic "friends to lovers" trope, but there was one thing stopping us. Seven hours, a six year age gap and two state lines. Though Mason made it very clear that he loved that I was a mom, would be honored to be a stepdad and thought the age gap was wildly attractive. "Lyss was an old soul and I've come to realize that they don't make girls like that anymore. I like older women because they seem to understand me more. We just work better. And it's pretty damn hot, I won't lie. I prefer it."

I agreed with Mason. This dynamic was becoming my favorite. Age was nothing but a number here. The hard part was the location. He was in Maryland and I was in Michigan. I couldn't legally leave the state due to the divorce and my kids. And he didn't think he could leave his family, his friends, his career, or his life in Maryland. Mason was torn. To move to a new city, quit his job, leave his town, his family and everything he ever knew behind in small town Maryland? Could he leave it all to shoot for the moon with his dream girl? Mason often told me I was his "to the moon" girl. Because with me, he could see all of his wildest dreams coming true. After meeting me, he started to dream bigger and began to imagine his greatest dreams for the future were possible. It would just require living almost five hundred miles away from home and starting completely over.

Regardless of our obstacles and the uncertainty of it, Mason was showing me how a man treats you when he sees you as a potential wife. Because when that's the case, that man will move mountains. It looked like good morning texts and "just because

I'm thinking of you" notes. He would call just to hear my voice. He didn't ghost, leave my text on delivered and he didn't ignore me. He didn't make excuses and he was never too busy for the woman he adored. He complimented me often and made sure I felt special.

A man who sees you as a wife invests in you from day one. He isn't afraid to talk about the future, he isn't afraid to plan dates and trips months in advance, because he sees you in his future. He isn't afraid to be vulnerable, talk about feelings, your hopes, and dreams. He sees your scars and wants to love you anyway. He sees your baggage as something that he's strong enough and willing to carry. Two kids and a divorce to boot? He's ready and he wants to show you. His actions align with his words. He follows through. He is patient. He is kind. He doesn't just love bomb you with grand plans and empty promises. He isn't future-faking you to manipulate you. He genuinely sees you. He hears you and understands your precious value. He supports your dreams; he is your biggest fan and cheerleader. This kind of man does exist.

Meeting this man showed me this is real. Rare? Yes. But very real.

THE WEEKEND OF Mason's planned trip to Michigan to meet me, he was also supposed to meet everyone important in my life—my closest friends, my family and possibly even my boys at my book launch party. We weren't dating, but he was important to me, and I was important to him, and the way we met was not just coincidence. We both felt that our angels on the other side brought us together. It wasn't clear what was happening with us, but it was clear that whatever it was, it was meant to be. Divinely so.

However, as a plot twist would allow it, we both didn't feel ready two days leading up to his flight. Mason and I felt the distance was too scary, too heavy. We both just didn't want to risk the heartbreak.

"Should I just cancel my flight? I wonder if it's all just too much to consider. It hasn't been that long since Lyss passed. A part of me feels guilty for even trying to move on."

"I understand, Mase. It's okay. We don't need to over complicate anything. What's meant to be, will be. And if it's not, it won't be."

A week went by of us trying to let this go. He didn't make the flight and I went to my book launch party alone. I was trying to move on from the connection when of course, he reached back out. Through Facetime. I reluctantly answered it.

"So, I finished your entire book. Can you talk?" And just couple weeks later, he booked another flight to come see me. "I need to see you. I need to meet you." he said. "I'd regret it if I didn't."

There had been so many serendipitous moments and points that had connected us which seem nearly unbelievable. It felt hard to say no even though I wanted to. There were so many fated signs that had been too obvious to miss. The last place Wil lived before he passed away? Maryland. The way my book ends? (Spoiler alert) The main character ends up with a brown-eyed bearded man that "heaven and angels" brought together. I don't believe in coincidence, not when heaven and angels are involved. We found each other in pieces and were healing together, finding peace. This connection, especially with the distance, brought up many uncertainties, but one thing we knew for certain was that we are meant to be in each other's lives at this very moment. Mason was one of the most beautiful tender souls I had ever known and I was forever grateful that our angels on the other side were guiding our next chapter.

Even though higher realms were guiding the connection, I must admit, Mason and I weren't always on our best behavior.

"I WANT TO see you shake," he said from our nightly video call. "Stop. Did I say you could touch yourself?" he looked at me with a devious grin. Our clothes were off at this point and we were up to no good.

"Feel up and down your body, grab your tits for me, open your legs. Good girl, now shift to the left." I angled my body to the camera as he instructed. He bit his lip and nodded at me.

"Mmm. That's a good girl. Now spread your legs wide for daddy. You have permission to play with your toy. Grab it and put it inside of you."

He propped the phone on the floor next to the mirror. He was on his knees, but sitting back a little, enough to make his abs pop. A shoulder vein was bulging and suddenly I wanted to sink my teeth into his thick neck. I stared at his naked body, admiring all of him, with his thick flesh erect in his hand.

MINE. I thought to myself. *That's all mine.*

EVERY DAY WITHOUT fail, Mason Facetimed me from the shower. I watched him as he massaged shampoo into his gorgeous long brown hair. Suds dripped down his body, flat lining down his abs. He turned around to rinse his hair, water streaming down his strong back and broad shoulders. When he faced the phone, he was firm and aroused. He stroked himself for me, moaning a little as he made eye contact into the screen.

"Mmm. Wish you were here," he said. "I'd love to bend you over right now and fill you up."

And when he was out, we were back to what we did best.

"Grab the lube and rub it all over your tits for daddy. Can you do that for me, baby girl?"

I nodded. *What has this man done to me?*

"I want you to ride it like you're riding me. I want to fill you up. Can I fill you up? You're such a good slut. You look so good riding me."

*This man. This young man.*

"Breathe for me. Relax. Breathe. That's it baby girl. That's it. Yes. I want you to come for me, okay? Can you come for daddy?"

He was on his knees with his phone propped up and me watching as he pleasured himself. As I start to climax, his head fell back, his eyes closed tightly, his mouth fell open and he exploded everywhere. He grabbed a towel then. "Look at the mess you made me make. You're such a naughty girl. Such a good slut."

Some girls like a praise kink. And sure, sometimes it's nice. But sometimes, a girl loves being a man's good slut. It's me. I'm *that* girl.

"I want to rail you, but handle you with so much care. I want to wreck you, but I want you to feel safe," he'd tell me. *This* was the masculine energy I desired and craved. Trust me, I was here for it. The man was built to provide and protect. To keep me safe. What woman wouldn't swoon over that?

EVERYTHING WITH MASON was good and fine, but I just had to know. So, I prayed the prayer that never lets me down.

*God, please do not give me another lesson. Please, bring me my soulmate to keep. I'm ready for my person.* I wasn't sure if God was listening. It was starting to feel like he wasn't. I journaled and I asked him out loud: *"God, if this isn't my person, please send a sign. To Mason and I both. A sign so obvious, we can't possibly ignore it."*

Later that afternoon, I got a text from Mason.

"Britt, I'm at my buddies house. Helping him with a project outside. You'll never guess what I found."

"What?

He sends a pic. It's a giant piece of driftwood. Mason knows I'm writing this book and I told him the title and what it means. He knows that seeing a piece of driftwood is a sign that means I'm close to my desire and destination. Not exactly that I've arrived.

"This isn't a good sign," he said.

I asked and God delivered. Is Mason is the driftwood? The sign that I'm almost there? Or was it the sign that he was not my person to keep? Even though we had this very clear sign, we sort of wanted to ignore it and definitely didn't want to decode it. Ignorance was bliss, right? Mason was still planning to come visit me, until he panicked.

"Britt. What if that sign meant that we shouldn't do this? Should I still come? I don't think I should."

Two. Freaking. Days. Before his trip to Michigan. I couldn't make this up. He got cold feet. Overnight, he pulled the plug on our connection. I was devastated, mostly because I was growing tired of these games these men were playing with me. I'm not a drinker, but I took a bottle from a case of champagne I had in my office for my book launch party, the one in which he was supposed to attend. I proceeded to recklessly drink half of it. Rock bottom was waiting at my feet like a hungry snake ready to swallow me whole. I was so done with men loving the idea of me, but never choosing me. I was at the end of my rope, sobbing into the carpet. *Not again, lord. Haven't I been on this floor long enough?* I had been on my knees for years praying for my person, and when Mason revealed that he could never move to Michigan, and that it had to be over for that reason only, I crumbled.

Another potential person had slipped through my fingers. I had encountered yet another man I couldn't keep. I physically and emotionally felt as though I could not endure another lesson of the heart. My heart by now was tattered, worn down, broken, bruised, and shattered. I didn't think it had another lesson in it. I truly didn't think I would be able to survive another lesson if it came my way. But, my mama always told me, "God never gives you more than you can handle." And if that were true, I really felt like I couldn't handle another failed "almost" relationship.

MY FRIEND CLAIRE'S new boyfriend, who I might add is one of the most emotionally intelligent men I've ever met, called me the next morning.

"Wanna talk about it?" he asked. Though he didn't know me at all, I just started sobbing to him. But more than the emotional release, two major things were revealed in the phone call. One: a limiting belief that it was always my fault somehow that things didn't work out and that I was never enough. He said, "I'm hearing the belief that you don't think you're enough. That you're too much. That these men had said you were too far away, too successful, too far ahead in life, too old, too much in one way or the other. But you need to flip the script and understand that this is not about you. It's about them not being able to meet you where you're at. It's them falling short, not being able to rise up and not being enough for you."

*Holy fucking shit.* I owed this man money for the free therapy because wow, that was legit advice. As we cycled through all my mental and emotional garbage, I also realized something else. That really, Mason could have been yet another mental distraction for me and it was very possible that I was yet again trying to move on from a person I still longed for and craved. I wasn't ready to be with him or anyone else because I still had all my texts and photos saved from Will. And while that might sound like a silly point, it was clear that I had not let go and if I was honest, I still didn't want to. I wasn't ready. He still had saved memory to my phone and was taking up space there and in my heart.

Eight months had gone by at this point, and many dating blunders and failures, but the one thing always remained the same up until this point. All roads led back to Will in my heart. My only choices now were to stay alone and heal from the heartbreak and pain of not having the one man I desired most or continue to hold onto that last strand of hope that maybe it could still be us in the end. Nothing was certain and by now I was tired of dating and tired of waiting. No one else fit like he did. I fully surrendered to the universe at this point. Knowing that I'd arrived at the messy middle where anything could happen, and the possibilities were endless. The ending of the story was not yet written. We were still working on the ending in real time. Everything after this just had to be smoother sailing now. It just had to be.

# The Messy Middle

IN THIS MOMENT, I was the loneliest I've ever been. I lay in bed on an overcast day. My home was quiet. And my refrigerator hummed me its lonely lullaby. When I was in the thick of motherhood, marriage, and life, I prayed for days like this. Where I was cozied in bed under a knit blanket with the window open, listening to "Fade Into You" just to set the scene as I lay in my own crumbs of whatever I was too lazy to eat at the kitchen table. And some days, I loved it here. The melancholy pang of heartbreak and suffering reminded me that I was alive, still feeling something. And other days, it was as sad as it sounds.

My family lives three hours away on the other side of the state. All my best friends had moved away. I lived in a new neighborhood and city. I moved to metro Detroit to live with my ex-husband and his family, none of which were actively in my life anymore. I was starting from scratch with a blank canvas. I was alone. I had always enjoyed being alone. As an extroverted introvert, I'd always required a disgusting amount of alone time to recharge and feel my best, but being lonely and being alone are two separate things. I was feeling equal parts of both right now. This is the messy middle, after all. The uncomfortable place you end up before where you get to where you want to be. It's not the place you imagined you'd ever be. Often, the messy middle is a place you end up against your will. You're a part of the club you never wanted to be invited to. There's a vacancy and longing that lives in our bellies in this place. And it bubbles up, stings, burns, and oozes from time to time. Just to remind us not to stay here.

# It's Not Always What's There, Sometimes It's in What's Not

A FEW YEARS ago, I listened to a podcast episode that flipped my world upside down. It was from Rachel Hollis, and it was the episode where she talked about her divorce. I was upstairs very much married to my husband, folding our family's laundry with my earbuds in as the kids napped. She talked about her journaling practice, and I nodded along because I also journal faithfully. And then she mentioned a bit about what she was manifesting her fortieth birthday. She said she had journaled every little detail down to what she was wearing and who was there. But what she didn't realize in hindsight, was how when she went back and read that journal entry, she didn't mention her husband Dave. She saw everything else, but he was missing. She swears that she felt like her intuition and her subconscious knew before she did. I covered my mouth and dropped the pair of socks in my hands as it hit me then. When I thought back to my visualization meditations of my dream life, whenever I journaled about my dream life in the future, I never saw him there. Not even once. And I didn't realize it until listening to that podcast episode right at that moment. When I thought about it, I never once saw my life growing old with my husband. I could see myself in old age, and I could easily see him in his. But I could never imagine his old wrinkly hand in mine sitting in a rocking chair or walking in the neighborhood together. When I saw my future, I saw me and my boys, but I couldn't for the life of me see my husband. This episode changed my life, because after I was done folding laundry, I did a quick visualization meditation just to see if anything changed.

As crazy as it sounds, I wanted so badly to see my husband, even if things were shaky. Even if I was feeling uncertain and like my heart had checked out already, I was still hopeful for the sake of keeping my family together. Still hopeful for the sake of avoiding a divorce and the uncertainty that came along with it. I pushed the laundry to the side and laid down on our king bed. I put on my favorite manifestation visualization, and to my surprise, there was still nothing. He wasn't there. Not a trace of him. In a panic, I searched for a random soulmate meditation on YouTube hoping his face would be the one to pop up. I prayed to God to show me my soulmate. I told God I was ready to see who it was, whether it was my husband or not. I closed my eyes and let the guided meditation do it's thing. And when I saw him, my eyes leaked tears. God showed me an image of my soulmate and I hiking together—we were laughing while he was playfully giving me a piggyback ride up the mountain. And I knew then that man I saw in this visualization from the future was not my current husband, because this man had brown eyes, brown hair, a beard, and an incredible smile. I could feel him so intensely, that I knew my person was still out there. And I knew then that the only way I'd ever have him in my arms was to get a divorce.

Sometimes it's not about what's there. Sometimes it's about what's not. And in the words of Tina, my therapist, she was right. Something was missing. Someone. And I was still trying to find him.

## That French Guy

HONESTLY, IT WAS a peak moment for me. The night I went to a concert with my best friend to watch a band that I absolutely adored. I had cried to their music for an entire year during my divorce, so this was the cathartic release I had been waiting for. The outfit I had on was fun, fresh and youthful. Black vans, a crop top, flared faded black denim because flares are back in, and I even tried my hand at winged eyeliner. Was I meaning to meet anyone at the show? Not in the slightest. But, as my best friend and I know, we always meet concert buddies. We're two blonde extroverted chatty gals with bold personalities, we make friends without even trying. And I love that about us. So, tonight was no different. We shimmied our way to the front of the crowd, she grabbed my hand and led me like a big sister bestie would. We made it to a great spot and the vibes were high. To my left? None other than a tall, dark, handsome French man. Of course, we were vibing, dancing together, laughing and joking with each other. Full on flirting. I mean, I did say he's a tall dark handsome French man, right? Right, okay. So of course, I'm wide eyed and crushing hard. I was dancing with him behind me and I was leaning into his chest. At one point, he leaned down to kiss my neck and all of me melted. Was this really happening? It felt like a dream. He grabbed my hand and said, "Let me get you a drink." So, we head to the bar and that's when I saw it. His wedding ring.

"Oh. You're married," I said. I couldn't see it in the darkness in the crowd. But at the bar with lights all around us, it was clear. A band around that left finger. He looked down, disappointed.

"Yeah…" he said.

"Well, thanks for the drink," I said, and headed back, trying to avoid him the rest of the concert. I ain't no home wrecker. I wish I could say that was the last time I ever heard from him again, but it wasn't. He remembered my name and found me on Instagram. Sent me messages for an entire month after the concert. Asked me out to coffee. Asked to come hang out. Asked to be my friend. And while it was hard to say no because he is a hot French man, I had to.

A COUPLE OF months later, I was hanging out on my hammock when I looked down to see that I had a phone call from none-other than him. It wasn't entirely a surprise however, because he was flirting hard at times. He even asked me out to coffee twice. I declined both times since he was married with an infant son. I could never do that to someone's wife. Even if he was unhappy and wanted to leave, he still belonged to someone else. That was drama I was unwilling to participate in. Even if he was tall, dark, handsome, sexy with a French accent to boot, it was territory I couldn't go down. And he knew it too.

The universe had sent another lesson. Another shiny trap to see if I would fall in. Did I want to? Yes, I'm sorry. I'm only human and have fleshly desires. And, because he called to tell me that he was in his car and was holding himself back from trying to meet up with me because he felt that he had experienced love at first sight.

"I know I only met you once, and it's crazy because I don't really know you, but I couldn't keep my hands off you. I have never felt that before. I've worked in Hollywood with extremely attractive actresses and celebrities, and it's not that you're not attractive, because you are, and I have a painful crush on you, but I felt something. Like, I could see that you were the girl of my dreams and so clearly see a future with you in it. There's just something about you. And it kind of breaks my heart right now."

Okay so, pause for a moment and re-read that in the sexiest French accent. It makes it ten times more adorable and dreamier. But then read it once more with frustration because the man is married. With a baby. We talked for about an hour. I laid on my hammock and listened as he told me about his marriage falling apart and his dreams that he had that were rotting along with it. He also told me incredibly nice things about myself, which if I'm honest, were all things I needed to hear. That being 31 and a mom of two didn't make me lose my value, if anything, it made me more interesting and added to my value. He also said he had never once cheated and was not a cheater, so he wouldn't be asking for my address to lay together in my hammock, even if that's what he wanted to do. I respected him, and I was proud of us both for having the strength and willpower to not to do something we'd regret. But I also felt sad for him. For letting his dreams slip away, settling in his relationship and in his marriage, staying in situations that made him unhappy and having this feeling for a girl he couldn't have. Because man, had I been there. It felt like I was talking to a much hotter French male version of myself from a few years back. Another guy where there's a spark, who's close but just far enough away to be out of touch. On to the next one.

"Come see this movie with me," he asked a couple days later. "It's a romantic story about two people who probably were lovers in a past life."

It was a terribly romantic gesture. More than anything I wanted to. I was lonely as lonely could be. A romantic date with a nice attractive French guy sounded amazing.

He sent a screenshot.

"I bought two tickets. I'll be waiting at this theater for you."

I didn't show.

I couldn't. Even if he was painfully gorgeous, a married man is not an available man and I was ready for a man to keep.

"I'm sorry, I can't. I hope you enjoy it, though."

Some time passed. He wrote another message.

"You know, I think you were French in a past life. It's crazy to me how similar we are."

It made sense. I dreamt of writing in Paris off scenic balconies often. My boys also have French names, Julien and Jean Philippe. My guilty pleasure was slow living and I adored sexy French music.

"I probably was, Andre. I probably was."

"I hate how much I am into you," he wrote again. I read it in his beautiful accent.

"It really is a tragedy, I will admit."

# Yin Yoga Lesson on the Art of Stillness

WHEN YOU FEEL like an orphan in your 30's, it can make you do silly things. Like google local meets up and to seek connection outside of your norm. I was also working on healing my attachment style and actively trying to become more emotionally available to myself. One of the ways I was doing that was by making commitments to myself and following through on those commitments. How could I expect commitment from someone else if I found it challenging to give it to myself?

So, I found a yin yoga and massage drop-in class, booked it, and went. It sounded easy and relaxing enough. I thought, maybe I'd bump into a cute man in class, but once I arrived, I discovered otherwise. I was shocked to see that only three other people had shown up, including an old Asian woman wearing a straw hat that went by the name Taki and answered her phone in the middle of class several times. I was expecting a full class. Besides, it was Sunday early afternoon. But as the instructor shared, it's one of the hardest practices, as it focuses on the art of stillness. Sitting in discomfort in your body and in your mind. Committing to that stillness, knowing there will ultimately be rest and reprieve. Giving yourself compassion through your breath.

"The peace is in the breath, in the present moment. Surrender to this stillness. Surrender to the discomfort. Long uncomfortable poses without distraction. What has been your distraction? Where are you avoiding discomfort?"

Again, I felt divinely led to this muggy humid hot yoga studio. I felt sweat roll down my chest and tears from my eyes. Her gentle voice echoed through the studio.

"Where have you been judging yourself in your journey? The real work is in the stillness. And it begins after this class."

We held a pose for what felt like forever, embracing the discomfort.

"Change is around the corner. There is movement in stillness."

I needed to hear those words. *Change is around the corner.*

Trying my best not to move, not to cry, I remained still. Unmoving, though stretched to the point of aching all over and the only thing that would bring me comfort is movement. To unpretzel myself from the very position that felt as though it was ripping my limbs apart.

"Humbly surrender to the empty spaces of time and stillness. Sit with it. And breathe into those spaces. There's a lesson there."

She was right. The discomfort of Yin Yoga, the difficulty of surrendering into stillness was my lesson. I was in my season of stillness. My slow down back to my homeostasis. And I needed to learn how to be okay by just sitting in it. Peaceful violin music filled the warm space. I laid on my mat and stared at the ceiling before closing my eyes. *I release to receive*, I thought. *I am safe to be. I am whole and complete on my own.* A blur of key moments over the last 365 days from when I filed for divorce raced through my head all at once like a fast-forwarded film. Key moments, concerts I'd gone to, dates I'd had, kisses I'd tasted, laughs I shared, classes I'd taken, my home, my friends, nights out, nights in, all of it—I was finally accepting this was where I was. And more than that, I was feeling grateful and loving it all. I surrendered with a smile. And a little sweat.

Even though I felt lonely at times, doing this work was a gift. I was thriving. I was glowing. I was having the best time. We are often not alone in our singleness for very long, even if it feels lonely and that it will last forever. It's not. We have our whole lives ahead of us to be partnered and with someone. But how many years do we truly spend alone? I was reflecting. From zero to seventeen I lived with my parents. And from fifteen to seventeen I was involved in committed relationships, never really spending time alone and single. I was also married for nearly ten years and together nearly fifteen. I hadn't really spent time truly single. It hadn't been very long either. One year. One whole year of being alone. Was it that bad?

The more I thought about it, I realized that I think I might love it here. I think I might be okay. There is beauty in these empty spaces of time. Breathe into them.

## Navigation with Your Inner Compass

I MAKE SNAP decisions all the time. My friends know this about me. It's not to be cool or edgy, it's because I trust myself. So yeah, I've been known to take a spur of the moment trip to Texas on a whim to meet a man I met on the internet, known to get a spontaneous tattoo on a random Tuesday at four P.M. because they had walk-in hours and I was feeling brave that day. Known to sign myself for a bikini competition, purchase a $7,000 business course from my car because I felt like I needed to, chop my hair off to my ears and dye it blonde, go gluten-free and dairy-free and stay that way for 15 years, go full on vegan for three years and one day decide it wasn't right and stop just like that. Known to write a book or ten across every genre there is because I felt like it. Known to take a big risk and start a new business or three. But also known too deeply to commit to something and see it through. My word is everything, and people know that when I say something, I mean it. I say what I mean, and I mean what I say. And when I trust myself, others seem to trust me. It's a beautiful conscious loop of love. It sounds silly, but I trust myself and what I need, even if that is a tattoo out of nowhere. Or jumping in the pool with all my clothes on because I wanted to feel alive and rebellious. Our inner child craves that freedom, that spontaneity, that sheer element of surprise. I make sure to gift myself that all the time. I also make big and fast decisions for myself all the time. The book *Think and Grow Rich* says that high performers and achievers have one principle in common—they have the ability of quick decision making. What's beautiful about people who can make a choice and stick with it demonstrates their ability to trust themselves. They harness their intuitive sixth sense and like Nike, they *just do it*. Most things in my life have appeared to be a snap decision. I just decided to do a bodybuilding show. I just "decided" to get a divorce and start a new life. I just decided one day to quit my 9-5. I just decided one day out of the blue to start a podcast, to write a cookbook, to write fiction, to share on social media, to start a new business, to go talk to that guy at Whole Foods, and just now, I decided that in twenty-four hours, I will be doing a 12 hour hike in the middle of nowhere.

I wonder where your inner compass is guiding you?

## Sail, Don't Row

MY POOR MOTHER has been put through the ringer with me. Not in a bad way, just in a Brittany sort of way. I'm a bit of a loose cannon in the sense that it's not unlike me to Facetime her with a headlamp on at nine P.M. and break the news of some brilliant idea I had.

"Mom, I'm waking up tomorrow at four in the morning to leave for a 12-hour hike alone in the woods."

"Brittany. Are you serious?" she laughed. "Why are you like this? Why can't my daughter do normal things and not dangerous things?"

"I wish I had the answer to why I am like this, ma. But I don't. And I'm goin'."

"Of course, you are. That's what you do. You set your mind on something and you follow through. I expect nothing less. But can you at least let me know where you'll be so I can make sure you're safe?"

"My phone won't be on. You can't use your phone. You can't go with anyone else. You can't listen to a podcast. No technology, nothing. It's just going to be me, my thoughts and nature. For twelve hours."

"Keep the phone on for emergencies. Please? Other than that, call me before you leave and call me when you're done so I know that you've made it alive. I'll be tracking your location, too."

"Deal."

It doesn't matter how old you are, a good mother will always mother and guide you. And at that moment, I was grateful for mine. I'd always been my mother's warrior because she'd always been mine. I was headed out for a 12-hour solo hike with no man to know my whereabouts, no man to come and rescue me if I needed help. Just a protective mama bear that still looks after me in my thirties, and me, myself, and I.

THE WEATHER WAS chilly for early June, so I was grateful to have packed for the different elements and to be dressed in layers. Something deep inside of me craved this experience. My heart was broken and, in the past, retreating alone in the woods always seemed to help. However, this was different. I couldn't escape my reality and zone out to music or a podcast. I had to stay out there in nature for 12 hours. The rules were simple; it didn't matter how far or how fast I went; it wasn't an endurance challenge or race. It didn't matter if I trekked one hundred miles or one mile, it was all the same in that way. I'd never done anything like this before, but I was searching for peace. I was ready to let it all go and I knew that the only person to let it go was me.

There are no shortcuts or cheat codes or life hacks when you're feeling the call to do the work. It's a journey you've got to go on alone. So, with my meals in my pack and my hiking boots tied tight, I was headed to get lost again in hopes of finding myself.

I won't lie. The first six hours were a challenge. It was partially due to the nature of the hike, but also due to the route I chose. I walked ten miles though the sandy dunes along the coast of Lake Michigan, in a small beach town called South Haven, the place where I grew up. My soul called me back home to heal and feel and process, and when I picked it, I knew this was just the place to do it. I walked the first half of the hike through tall grassy dunes, emptying the sand that filled my shoes every few miles and journeyed through the dark canopy of the forest. Just me, my pack and a new walking stick I acquired on the hike that I still have in my car to this day. You never know when you'll need a good walking stick.

To be honest, I wasn't sure what to expect, but I had a hunch it would be emotional. I was right. Within the first few hours, tears poured out of me. Feelings I'd ignored and shoved deep down bubbled close enough to the surface to finally feel them. And in those woods alone, I surrendered and allowed them to come out. It was time. Everything was catching up to me, to the point where every mile there was a new memory—a repressed point in my life I didn't want to face. Seeing the childhood face of my estranged sister flash before on Christmas morning flash before my eyes when we hadn't talked in years, or the oddly adorable way my ex-husband looked on our wedding day when he had toilet paper stuck to his upper lip because he cut himself from the nerves. How my little cousins would pretend to have big wedding ceremonies in my grandma's backyard and pick flowers from her garden for me to walk down the imaginary aisle with. How badly I had always wanted to be a man's bride and how devastating it was that I wasn't one anymore. When these memories surfaced, they took my breath away. It all choked on the way out, but when it did, I felt something I'd been longing for. Permission to finally be free.

IT'S WORTH NOTING that I am not much of a navigator. I still GPS my way around the city I've lived in for the last ten years, so of course I didn't carry a compass on this hike. And I was so off-grid, I didn't even have cell service to GPS if I wanted to. To say that I got lost during the twelve hours would be understatement.

Often, I found myself looping around the same areas over and over. Instead of accepting my surface-level frustration, I went deeper. *What is this teaching me? How can I apply this lesson in real life when I leave this day behind?* What I found was simple. Getting lost wasn't all that bad. Getting lost could be enjoyable when you trust you'll eventually find the path.

Sometimes the lesson is winding around the same spot over and over again to learn your lesson.

Why not trust and enjoy the journey?

We have plenty of time and we always end up where we need to be, don't we?

When I turned off the outside world and my own internal noise, I could hear myself. And when I heard myself, I heard God. When we let ourselves be quiet, we can allow the magic to pour in.

GOING BACK HOME was a blaring metaphor for everything in my life. Before all else, I first needed to come home to myself. To become aware of the lighthouse shining and guiding me from within. When I opened my eyes, I could see the signs all around me. Even the rip current warning on the beach was a reminder of just how much I needed to stay in balance with the rest of my life, that I couldn't expect to swim against such a universal force. To survive, I needed to learn how to swim across it and alongside it, with respect for its power. Life works best when we are in balance with the water, earth, wind, fire, rain and all the elements and its beings. It gets easier when you allow the river to unfold as it should, when you sail and don't row. If you find yourself trying to navigate the choppy waters, you have to trust in your own lighthouse to show the path toward the shore.

HALFWAY THROUGH THE hike, even though I was getting powerful messages and downloads from above, I still wanted to quit. Around the ten-mile mark, I stopped to take a quick nap in my car since I didn't get any sleep the night before and felt like calling the whole thing off. I was tired. Tired of dumping sand out of my shoes. Tired of sand whipping in my eyes from the wind. Tired of my aching shoulders and joints from carrying my pack. I just wanted to go home. But again, I also noticed another lesson. It was to learn to rest, not to quit. So, I got back out there, walked to a coffee shop because I didn't want to pee in the woods again, grabbed an iced latte for a little reward and kept on going for the second half. I was careful not to slow down and rest too long. And before I knew it, I walked twenty miles in twelve hours. I walked until my body ached, but my soul and heart didn't as much. Maybe that's the price you pay for when you're searching for freedom.

# Fourteen Lives in a Day

I WOKE UP to texts from Mason wishing me good morning, and asking if we could talk. He told me was at Assateague beach alone, that he was heartbroken and needed to clear his head. He was hurting from the depth of our connection, still grieving his wife and now me, too. Grieving what happened and what didn't happen.

I ignored his first two texts. I was trying to move on. He also unfriended me on Instagram because he said it was unbearable to see me and not have me, so I went another step further and I blocked him. To me? We were over and I was ready to move on. I detached fully. The result? He was blowing up my phone. Finally, when he called me twice in a row, I answered.

"Britt. I have to tell you something. It's important."

"What is it this time?" I huffed.

"This morning, I'm sitting around a small fire that I made on the beach drinking coffee alone. Everything made me think of you. I imagined you here and then I put on your favorite playlist. The one I showed my brother and he laughed at, but the one I've been listening to all summer because it reminds me of you."

"Mase..." I said. It was terribly hard to stay angry, annoyed or frustrated at him. Even if that was how I felt.

"Britt, that's not even all of it." he said. "I'm tearing up right now. There was this little girl on her bike that was heading into the beach house next to mine. She had gotten lost and was afraid until she finally made it home. It made me think of you. I want to be your home."

He then cried to me on the phone as he told me that he appeared to have a third realization that I was "the one." That after reading my book, it made him feel even more connected to me. He had the qualities I desired in a safe masculine man. He showed me what to start requiring in relationships. It was either going to be a man that could give me what Mason could, or better. I still thought, maybe it could have been Mason, even though my heart was attached to someone else.

He FaceTimed me and I answered reluctantly. Seeing his face was nearly impossible to turn down. Those dimples got me every time. But old habits die hard, ya know? He was in the shower, his phone propped so I could watch all of it. He was naked, he was hot—It was—hard—to resist. One thing leads to another, and he guided me into another phone sex induced orgasm.

"Mmm. I missed you." He said, panting.

"I know you did." I said.

"Do you miss me?" he asked.

"I don't know. Do I?" I winked and left the mystery.

*Do I?* I wasn't sure. Was this fun? Of course, it was. The silly little things, the little joys, the frivolous freedoms of being single I know I will miss. I'm no stranger to a good nude or phone play, and Mason always delivered both.

I pulled my skirt back over my hips when we finished, blew a kiss goodbye to Mason, and headed to my best friend's going-away brunch at a new upscale place in the city with a post-orgasmic glow plastered all over my face. If there was anything about my dear sweet Pisces bestie Audri, she always knew when I'd been up to no good with a boy. It'd be written like Sharpie on my forehead. I was feeling boujee that day, wearing a floral mini skirt, white plunge neck bodysuit tank and white chunky heels. The hair was straight for a change and the makeup was done for sex. Sometimes, I can't help myself.

I was running too late to worry about parking, so I valeted, which made everything feel sassy and classy. Fancy and fun set the tone and I was back to the energy of living my best life. The sun was shining, I was out and about, I was unbothered and unphased with boys or anything else. Whatever happened, happened. No stressing about Mason or the situation, just remaining present and living life. The very attractive, tall, dark and handsome valet driver boldly made a sexual innuendo with me at the door. Never did I ever think attention from young men would happen so often after motherhood or after turning 30, but here we are. And it doesn't feel bad for the ego if I'm honest.

"Sir, you look awfully young." I've been here before. Here we go, again.

"I'm nineteen. You look like you're in your twenties, yeah?"

I smiled, throwing my bag on my shoulder. "Cute."

As I wait at the valet stand, I run into none other than the hot French guy, *with his wife,* who are on their way out. We locked eyes, and our jaws dropped in slo-mo like a movie scene.

"My friends bet me $200 I couldn't get your number," said the valet driver.

"Well, I guess you owe them $200. You're barely legal, young man."

"What's your Instagram then?"

That felt harmless. He handed me his phone and I put it in.

"I'll be in touch," he said on my way out. *Oh, boy.* Young men had been fun, but this felt a bit too young for me. I smiled, waved, and he drove off. I called my best friends immediately with another "You're never going to believe this!" story. By now, no one was phased with the stories and situations I encountered anymore. It was just a part of this big bold life and I was the main character.

Later that night, we headed to a BDSM sex dungeon party at a private warehouse. Yes, you read that right. Why were we going? Well, for the plot, of course. And to study the scene and environment for the new book I was writing. We *had* to. It was decided. The entire theme for the night was: do it for the plot. What I saw in that dungeon I can never unsee. I'd tell you all about it here, but then it might spoil the next book. A little mystery is seductive, is it not? But I will say, it's not what you think. Not even close.

THINGS GOT MORE interesting when I get home to a message from none other than Will.

"Say it," he wrote to me in my Instagram stories. Breaking a three-month long silence between us, the longest we'd ever gone without communication or seeing each other.

"Say what?" I asked, knowing exactly what he wanted me to say.

"You know. Just say it."

"I don't know what you're talking about, mister."

"I think you do. And you just might get it."

He wanted me to say I missed him. That I wanted to have sex with him. When I wouldn't, he said, "Don't make me come over there to force it out of you."

"I dare you," I said. What was I doing? It was almost two in the morning. I just got home from a sex party with my friends and here I am, talking to Will again after months of not hearing a word from him. My hands were shaking. This could not be real life. More than anything I wanted to see him, but more than anything I worried about starting the same damn cycle all over again. There was no way he would come over.

Just then, a text lit up my phone.

**Will:** *Open the door*

*No fucking way.*

I opened the door and immediately shut it in disbelief. He showed up at my door at two in the morning, standing there smirking under the front porch light.

"What are you doing here?" I said, covering my mouth.

"I want to hear you say it."

All of me melted. He looked good. Better than ever. I still wanted him, and he knew it.

"Say what?"

"You know. Just say it."

He walked into the doorway and brushed up close to my body.

"Say it," he breathed onto my neck.

"I want you...."

He pushed me into the wall and kissed me passionately. He pulled away from my lips and looked around.

"Where are you writing these days?" he asked.

"My office, why?"

"Good. I want to fuck you there."

And that is exactly what we did. He pleased me to an intensity that sent me screaming so loudly I covered my face with a pillow to try to muffle the noise. The things he could with his hands and his mouth baffled me. It wasn't fair for any man who tried to compete. Once he finished me off, we headed back to my bed, and he ruined me again until we both climaxed. *God, I missed this.* After three months celibate, this was beyond glorious. Worth the wait.

"Do you know your neighbors?" he asked, wiping his pleasure off my stomach.

"Yeah, why?"

"What are they like?"

"They are a bunch of old ladies, why?"

"Because I'm pretty sure you woke them up. Unless they're up playing late-night bingo."

I shoved him a little and he fell into my arms. "I'm not going under the covers with you, or I'll never get out.

"Good idea. They have magnetic powers, so there's no chance of you getting out once you get in. You know this."

"I do. Which is why I'm not getting in." He got up, put his clothes on quickly and asked me if I wanted some water.

"You know this was the first time I've had sex in three months. You broke my celibacy streak."

"I hope this doesn't give the wrong idea. I don't want to give you the wrong impression. This doesn't mean anything," he said.

"Okay, got it. You're still an asshole. Nothing has changed."

He looked away. He told me he'd been stepping into his masculine energy, preparing for the day when he finally becomes a husband and a father and how he'd had a new shift towards desiring a wife and a family. He talked about fatherhood with passion, and I sat there listening, melting, daydreaming. It wasn't hard to picture. He was gentle in all the right ways and tough in the ways that mattered. The thing about Gemini's is they like to talk and often have these big ideas they've been thinking about. The thing about Cancer women is that we're usually great listeners with a deeply understanding energy that welcomes and nurtures such ideas.

Will and I always had the best conversations. Deep down, I knew he would be back. I had written in my journals, I saw visions often popping into my head out of nowhere, saw signs everywhere and I just knew it wasn't over yet. It'd been nearly nine months since we met, and we still had something together. What was it? I can't really put my finger on it.

A kiss with Will was otherworldly. My body shook in the arms of his, and I could feel our hearts sync up every time he drew his lips to mine, slowly finding safety and comfort with our breaths. I couldn't say that I knew how or that I knew when, but I did know he would be back again after this, slowly but surely. We would be back to where we end up. In each other's arms. Drawn together like a moth to a flame. Neither one of us was ready to fully let go, but it was clear he wasn't ready to dive all the way back in again. So I let him out the door, not really knowing what was next for us. Just his mouth saying, "I'll see you around eventually, right?"

I smiled. I knew it was his way of keeping me on the hook without any promise of tomorrow. Because a promise of tomorrow feels like commitment. And Will didn't do commitment. Not yet at least.

"Yeah, maybe. Maybe not." I shrugged. "Who knows. Good night, Will."

He looked back and smiled that knowing smile. He would be back. Sooner than we both planned. The cycle began again. This time, it was different. It had to be. He seemed more mature and had grown up a bit since. And me? I was stronger than before. Less clingy and needy. I was more secure on my own. We needed the space. From here, only time would tell. Though right now, I couldn't get the image of a cute, brown-eyed, curly-haired baby girl out of my head. And a bearded man. A daddy.

A WEEK HAD passed since that night and Will was per usual nowhere to be found. Not a text, not a call, not a single message. He disappeared, as he always did. In a moment of weakness, I wanted to get his attention. So I sent him quite possibly the best nude photo I'd ever taken. I was tanned from the sun that day, my abs were showing, and I had just gotten out of the shower and oiled my skin. I was glowing and shining. I looked good and I knew it. And for having two babies, I was pretty damn proud of it. His response to the award winning nude? Literally nothing. Crickets. He even stopped watching my stories on Instagram. He didn't reply to my message. Though the rejection hurt, and it felt confusing, it also felt like closure. Hurt me one last time, so I could really let go. The next night, I deleted his number and all the photos, videos, voice messages that were ever sent. I released him and all the attachments to him. I wrote a long paragraph in the notes section on my phone, a message I never would send. I was hurt and I wanted him to know what he did to me, but I also knew that he didn't care enough, and I knew it was time to let go. I wondered if I'd arrived at one of the final stages of grief—acceptance. The last stage is hope. That was a feeling I was looking forward to.

I FELT ASHAMED of the nude I sent, but I tried to also find some grace for myself. Regression is a part of growth, I'm almost certain. Sometimes we take backward steps in our process of moving forward. Sometimes we need to revisit old lessons and stories just to make sure we learned enough to keep moving forward in the right direction. I could beat myself up for caving after walking 20 miles and for 12 hours trying to move on, only for him to show up on my doorstep three days later with the temptation to get looped in the same toxic cycle, or I could begin my healing process all over again. I could forgive myself and accept this as a necessary part of the process. A week later, when he finally texted me back, I ignored it. I grew stronger in my "no."

My sacred no was becoming powerful, fueling up for my

sacred yes to arrive. The more we allow ourselves to use the power of "no," the stronger our "yes" becomes.

THAT NIGHT I got a FaceTime call from Mason.

"I have to tell you something," he said, his voice hurried and frantic.

"Yes?"

"I have been doing a lot of thinking."

"About?"

"About dating you. I think we should see what happens. I have feelings for you, Britt. How could I not? We are both rare and real. We make sense. I want to see you soon. I think it would stupid not to. Why wouldn't we just try it?"

I could not fall for this again. Instead, I laughed.

"Oh really? We're doing this again. Alright, well. I will believe it when I see it."

I didn't know what to think anymore. all I knew was that at this point, I could always count on one hell of a plot twist.

## Let Yourself Eat Cake

THIS ISN'T THE part where I talk about calories and body positivity. This is the part where we talk about self-love. Not bubble baths and face masks, but in loving yourself enough not to settle and accept crumbs any longer. After leaving a toxic and emotionally abusive marriage, I was so starved for love that my first helping of crumbs from other men were tantalizing. My mouth was salivating, and I couldn't get enough, even if that was them meeting the very bare minimum and not treating me to my full value. It was still so much more than what I had experienced with my ex-husband. Did I ever feel full? Of course not.

You could lick a plate full of crumbs entirely clean, but it would never be enough to satisfy. I was getting a sweet taste of something I hadn't enjoyed in years, but after a while and some minor heartbreak along the way, I realized something. I didn't leave a whole marriage behind for just a little taste here and there. I left because I was starving—for *love*. After several finger-licking good times with a handful of crumby men, I was ready for the whole damn cake. When the whole cake arrived, I panicked. After being starving for so long, I almost didn't know what to do. I found myself afraid of it, unsure if it was too good to be true. No one warns you about that.

What it feels like to open yourself up to a healthy love from a safe, emotionally available man, after not ever having that in your life, is to love *yourself* enough to feed yourself cake. To walk away from anything that appears to be a plate full of crumbs. Know your worth, know your value, and respect yourself enough to say no to anything that is not in alignment with your best self.

Being ignored as a child taught me at a young age that I wasn't worthy to be seen, heard, or validated. It wasn't until I did the work to unlearn that, that I realized I have been subconsciously searching for men who would trigger my old wounds from childhood. Men who really were no good for me, who weren't ever going to meet my needs or fulfill me.

No one tells you that healthy love, when it shows up, is gentle. It's not a tidal wave of intensity. No one tells you that you might feel like leaning out at first, versus sitting still.

# On His Way Back to Me

WHEN I WAS in my sad bitch era, I posted a sad TikTok as one might do. I missed Wil, my dead ex. I missed the feeling of love. And his love was the only love I'd ever known that was honest, pure, and real. The post immediately went viral. My fiction novel inspired by my experience with Wil, *On His Way Back To Me,* became such a massive success, I could hardly believe that I had somehow with one click completely launched the writing career I'd been dreaming of all my life, basically overnight. The book went viral, sales were so insane I would cry happy tears for days. People loved the book and became instant fans. The launch surpassed my expectations, becoming an instant three times best-seller on Amazon. The readers adored it just as I had hoped. I was even interviewed by the *Seattle Times* and other media outlets. I was in shock with what God had done for me. In His timing, certainly not mine.

A month after I published the book, Wil's grandma sent me a message on Facebook.

> Hi, Brittany,
> I just finished reading your book. It was amazing! Do you have any of Wil's ashes? If not, I can give you some.
> Wil's Grandma, Georgette.

At first, my cheeks reddened. I had spicy scenes in there and now she knew about it. She knew the things I did to her grandson in explicit detail. But that embarrassment quickly left as I realized this was a full-circle moment I didn't expect I would ever receive—that he would literally be on his way back to me. I dropped to my knees and began to sob. Of course, I wanted his ashes. I was unable to make it to his funeral. I went into labor two days after he passed away from the shock of grief. I never really got my last goodbye. We never had any sort of closure when he was alive, and even worse to not attend the funeral once he left. Such a huge part of me died when he did. I just wanted to touch him one last time. And the fact that I didn't get to, made it harder for me to move forward.

The first year he left this earth, I did everything I could to numb the pain. One glass of wine turned into a half bottle. And once a week quickly turned into every night. I hated myself for not choosing him while he was alive. I drank myself into a deeper sea of regret, and it made me ever sicker. I was the sickest I had ever been in those three years following his death. I hated my life as it was. But one day, I woke up and decided I needed to start feeling my pain because what I was doing wasn't working. It was only making it worse. It was literally killing me. I had to learn to sit in my grief. And I learned to heal it by feeling it.

There wasn't an ounce of me that didn't still crave even the slightest molecule of him. Even though he had been gone for four years, he was still the person I wanted more than anything. The most painful part of this divorce was knowing that I had my chance with him when he was alive, and I didn't take it. It still haunts me if I'm honest. It likely always will. The bill of regret lasts forever. I often wonder what it would've been like if I would've been with him. Maybe he would still be alive? At my worst, I blame myself that he's not, because he loved me—he truly, madly, deeply loved me and I didn't let him in. He struggled without me, and I wish I had known. I tell myself that maybe I could've saved him. I will never know if that's real or imagined, but if I could go back in time, run into his arms, never let go and never look back, I would.

**Me:**

*Hi Georgette,*
*I would be honored to receive some of his ashes. That would mean the world to me.*

**G:**

*I thought it might. You know, I know more of your story than most people think. You were very special to him. Where do you live? I'll send the ashes out in the next few days.*

He was finally going to be close to me again. It had been so long without holding him that I couldn't wait to have him back in my hands again. I never imagined that when we would make our way back to each other, that it would look like this. For days, I anxiously checked the mailbox and my doorstep. When he arrived, I fell to my knees again. After all these years, we were together again.

Upon my divorce in 2022, I told myself that I wanted to wake up next to my soulmate in the following year. Though it arrived differently than I expected, I wear his ashes on my chest in a necklace with his initials engraved on it. I wake up next to him every day. True love never dies.

# A Ride in the Jaguar

I HADN'T RIDDEN in many luxury cars, especially one as nice as a Jaguar, but since moving to an upscale part of town after my divorce, seeing them had become my norm. When my Uber driver showed up, it was almost natural for me to expect a luxury car. In the back of the Jag I felt it—the deserving feeling of abundance. I was sitting pretty with my summer tanned legs crossed feeling every bit like the queen that I was. My self-concept was improving, so much so that I had landed a date that night with a model. The outfit was summery and sexy. Tangerine bodysuit with cute white cut off shorts and white platform wedges that made my legs look a mile long. My blonde wavy hair was short and sassy. I looked and felt like a vixen, that happened to also be a milf. The model was younger, of course, and he was a real estate agent, which is how we connected in the first place. I had just begun investing in real estate. At first, I wasn't sure if it was a networking meetup or a date.

"We'll have a reservation at eight P.M. at Market North End," Anthony said.

"Who's we?" I inquired.

"Just me and you."

"Let's do it." Damn it. Why couldn't I say that without it sounding sexual?

When I got there, we sat down next to each other and there was definitely some tension, a little chemistry, and a nice sense of comfort. The man was attractive, fit, and had that flirty suggestive smile. We talked about wealth, Lamborghinis, closing million-dollar deals, fitness, mindset, relationships, all of it. The date was going well. My classic move was to suggest listening to music at my house in private. We played a few songs before he put on his spicy playlist. The one with all of the songs a person would practice making babies to? Yeah, that kind of playlist. One thing leads to another thing and before you know it, the 6'5 tall, dark and handsome bearded model had me up on the counter. The passion was there, and the spice kicked up quickly. So much so that I had accidentally turned the water faucet on with my shoulders and it was flooding the sink and counter, drenching my clothes.

"Mmm, you're all wet," he said. He slipped his fingers inside of me then and my head fell back. "You should probably take off your clothes."

"You think so?" I said. He sucks on my neck, massaging my nipples through my shirt with his thumb. I hadn't worn a bra tonight and now I was glad that I didn't.

"Yeah, I want to make you feel good. Can I do that?"

Another young man in his twenties focused on female pleasure. How could I say no?

After everything else I had been through, I deserved a few more inches, a Jaguar ride, and a tall, dark and handsome bearded model. This was definitely all for the plot. I wasn't mad about it.

# Whole Foods Man and the Plot

A TEXT LIT up my phone late in bed. It was Will. At this point, we were off again and I hadn't been reaching out at all. If he wanted to, he would. This time, he made an attempt.

**Will:** *I think you should let me read some of your memoir. You know, being such a pivotal part.*

His confidence was exactly what I loved and hated about him. This asshole was fully aware of the chokehold he had on me.

**Me:** *Eh, you might have to wait until it's published like everyone else. I might send you a teaser scene…Maybe. I do have a personal favorite scene.*

I liked to hit him with a little mystery and intrigue. A good cliffhanger is something no Gemini man can resist. He was so curious.

**Will:** *That might not be good enough, I was thinking more of a chapter preview.*
**Me:** *I like surprises, don't you?*
**Will:** *Not very much, honestly.*
**Me:** *Says the guy who shows up on my doorstep at two A.M.*
**Will:** *Don't confuse that with spontaneity.*
**Me:** *It was hot…*

I admitted it.

**Will:** I know, that's why I did it.

**Me:** What's that like by the way? Knowing you accidentally stumbled into a sex goddess at the grocery store, but she's also a writer… and now you're stuck in some plot of her next book… "The Whole Foods Man."

**Will:** It'll be a chapter in my book. That I won't ever publish so you'll never know.

**Me:** You'll let me read it right? If I'm in it, I gotta see my parts to fact check.

**Will:** No

**Me:** Rude

**Will:** Oops. I can't have it leaked.

**Me:** I don't share company secrets.

**Me:** Though I will say, a 2 A.M. performance wasn't the best it could be. I'm not against a do-over…

TWO DAYS WENT by. Classic avoidant Will.

**Will:** Wow, very forward of you, ma'am.

**Me:** When have I ever been anything but forward, sir?

**Will:** That was a valiant effort.

**Me:** Hardly. Just sayin'… we could do better than that.

A WEEK LATER, another text from Will.

**Will:** Question

**Me:** Yes?

**Will:** Do you like Post Malone?

**Me:** Who doesn't? lol

**Will:** Word

Gosh, he was still so young. That was my reminder yet again.

*Will:* *Wanna go see him tonight?*
*Me:* *Who's all going?*
*Will:* *Would just be us*
*Me:* *What time?*
*Will:* *Starts at 8*
*Will:* *Should I buy tickets?*

Mason would be here in three days. We were still talking everyday. He'd kept his flight this time. I didn't expect Will to be back in the picture right at this moment. But now that he was, I was having a hard time saying no. *Am I going to attend this concert with him?* It didn't feel right not mentioning it, so I did. I asked Mason and he said he didn't care, though I knew of course he did. To be honest, it was a blind-side. Everything felt off balance, aimless and unpredictable. I had no idea what was happening anymore, and it showed.

*Me:* *Do it*

He sent a screenshot. It was a $500 date. We love a young man with his money right.

*Will:* *I'll pick you up at 7*

I was always passenger princess with him. That clearly hadn't changed.

WHEN HE GOT here, the nervoussness was inside my stomach and everywhere. Just a few weeks ago he was on my front porch at two A.M. wearing nothing under his zip-up, pushing me against the wall to eat me alive in a ravenous passion. And now, he was acting calm, cool, and collected. Almost like it never happened, treating me like I was his cousin he was picking up to see a PG-rated movie. I got into the car, and it hit me then. The intoxicating smell of his essential oil-based fragrance and the subtle hint of coconut always lingering on his skin and hair. I did meet this man at Whole Foods, after all. I expected nothing less. Like a clean-cut hippie man. I absolutely adored the hell out of it. He was basically the male version of me and his scent is a constant reminder.

We kept our hands to ourselves for the first time in forever while he drove. Usually, he rested his hand on my thigh the whole way we drove anywhere. Physical touch is our love language, but tonight, he was trying his best to play it cool with me. So I followed his lead and kept my hands in my lap.

He broke the silence.

"Can you believe it's been 10 months. Us. Knowing each other."

For him to bring that up felt significant. That he'd been counting the months and recalled how long I'd been in his life. Also, that he felt the need to share it with me. A way to build connection, emotional connection. It felt like a small shift towards vulnerability, which I knew didn't come easy for him.

"Honestly, no. It feels like a lifetime I've known you, yet also feels like I just met you yesterday."

He smiled then, eyes still on the road in his trendy shades. The young man had style.

"You're that guy, aren't you? The one that wears sunglasses even when the sun's not shining anymore."

He laughed. "There are two kinds of people who do that."

"Who?"

"Blind people and assholes."

I couldn't help but laugh. "Ah. So, you're the asshole."

He smirked. "Guess so."

I looked out the passenger window and we both attempted to make a little small talk. But small talk never lasted very long with us. It quickly turned into big talk. Hopes, dreams, random inner dialogue, something new we just learned, what our friends were up to. When he mentioned his friends, he mentioned that most of them had girlfriends and he'd been the third wheel lately. This was new. If his friends were in relationships I wondered if maybe he had been thinking of starting to be in one, too. I'd be foolish to think maybe he'd consider us finally being together, but I'd be lying if the thought didn't still swirl around in my mind.

I pictured it then. A few months from now, he'd be my boyfriend and we'd finally be a couple going on dates, he'd be buying me flowers and random gifts, maybe we would even hang out with other couples together. A delusional girl can dream, right?

Just the week before I saw him tagged in a photo with a baby and I immediately cried. The way he looked holding this tiny toddler hand made me melt from the inside out. The smile on his face, lit up with the wholesome purity that being in a child's presence can bring. I thought back to the Air-Bnb weekend we had together and the way he smiled at me when he asked if I'd have another child someday and I said yes, I think I'd have a daughter. I knew at that moment, he likely imagined it all with me. Even if only for a second. And the last time we talked, I knew that becoming a father someday was very much becoming a new purpose in his life. He made it very clear he hoped for a wife and kids someday. And the thought melted me every time.

WE ARRIVED TO the concert venue and the subtle touching began; it truly was impossible to keep our hands off each other. This was us trying our best. First came the subtle shoulder touches, then the arms squeezes, light back caressing, an accidental hand gliding against mine a few times. If he was trying to keep the fine line at "just friends," romantically showing up at two A.M. on my front porch unannounced and then railing me into my headboard until four in the morning probably blurred a few, I'm afraid. But we'd been here before. Desperate to be in each other's lives, afraid to be more than friends, yet absolutely terrible at remaining only that. It was the same closed-loop cycle we always find ourselves in. Not just friends but also not fully dating, either. I tell myself that if it were anyone else, I'd never settle for this madness. But something kept reeling us both in. It always did.

It took a minute for us both to loosen up at the Post Malone concert, but when we did, we were an absolute vibe together. We always had a blast at concerts together, since the beginning. Going to concerts was our thing, and for him to rekindle this again with a concert date felt significant. It felt special and telling—like this was maybe far from over. It was as if it were signaling a new beginning together, taking something from our past we used to do and creating new memories.

We were dancing, being playful and being silly together as we always were. It was easy with him. No matter how long we went without seeing each other or talking, we picked right up where we left off. The chemistry was still burning red hot. When Post Malone grabbed the mic and started talking about heartbreak before playing his next song, I could feel it and see it on Will's face. As if he was talking directly to us. It was clear in that moment in our energy alone, we'd both felt heartbroken by this connection and this relationship. Post Malone sang "I Fall Apart" and Will pulled me into his chest and held me as we swayed to the chorus. Fall apart we did, right in each other's arms. At that moment I knew he was hurting, and I was, too. If there were ever moments where I didn't think he cared about me, about our connection or the time we spent together, the truth all came out now. At one point his heart also beat for mine, and when I walked away, his heart broke, too. If I got anything out of this concert and never saw him again after that night, I could walk away knowing that the feelings I had were not unrequited. He felt them, too. I needed that more than I knew. To know I wasn't crazy. That this was real. To us both.

The concert ended and we were stuck in traffic. He decided to sing to me.

"You're the only one I do this around. I only sing in front of you, you know."

"Really? Wow, I feel so special. I get my own personal William concert. I'm the luckiest girl in the world."

Will had a beautiful voice and I could listen to him sing for hours, and lucky for me, I'd had the opportunity many times. I watched him with wide adoring eyes. A smile spread across my face as he belted out the most beautifully romantic lyrics. How could I not? He was so dreamy and perfect to me sometimes that it physically hurt.

We got to my house. Our eyes met and we stared at each other, unsure how to move forward, but the tension was pulling us together like magnets.

"Well, this was fun. Thank you." There was a shyness in my voice, a vulnerable suggestive tone that was quietly screaming for him to kiss me.

"You want me to walk you to your door?"

"Well, I don't want the boogie monsters to get me, so yeah." I bit my lip a little and gave him that look.

We walked to my door. He left the car on.

"You're not coming in?" I asked once half-inside, glancing at the car still running.

He looked at his car and back at me.

"You're being shy, Will. Are you a shy boy now?"

He looked at me deviously, tilted his head and smirked.

"Give me two minutes." He walked back to turn his car off and headed inside. He sat on my couch and grabbed my book from the bookshelf. Started reading a line out loud.

"Geez, verbal punching? Tell them how you really felt."

It was his way of acknowledging the book I wrote and the work that I'm doing. That he saw me and wanted me to know. Though he hid in the shadows, he was well aware of my success. And for the first time, wanted to show me in person. Of course, through our love language of roasting the absolute fuck out of each other. A good teasing always did us well. First with our words, then with our bodies.

I looked at him then and he locked eyes with me.

"So." I said, nodding, as I sat on his lap.

"So," he said with his soft warm voice, gazing into me, setting me on fire.

"So, you are shy?"

"No, I just didn't want you to think that all I wanted was to have sex. That wasn't even my intention. Which is why I purposely left my car running. I just wanted to hang out with you."

"Because no one else wanted to? Because the other girls said no?"

He laughed. "No, I didn't ask any other girls. Just you."

I tried to hide a smile, but I couldn't. I could feel myself opening up from the inside out. Arousal flowed out of me. I was so wet sitting on him with my tiny white cut off shorts, it wasn't even funny.

I inched towards his face, and he took off his glasses and leaned in to kiss me. The passion ignited quickly from there and we began to devour each other. This time, he was vulnerable. I could feel his emotions pouring out with every touch. And the eye contact, my god, his eyes hadn't left mine since he walked in. The way he looked at me, like I belonged to him and always would. Like I was the only one.

"Here, put on a song," he said, handing me his phone to scroll through his playlist. Like we did on the first date nearly ten months ago. Never in a million years did I think ten months would pass and I'd still be next to him. Doing this all over again. But here we were.

"What's the mood?"

He looked at me and grinned.

"You pick."

As I was scrolling his playlist, one thing that stood out right away. It was our playlist, pinned to the very top, titled: *Will & Brittany*. When I broke things off, I left the playlist and unsaved it. Not only did he still have it saved, even after being out of contact for three months, he had it pinned to the top. It said nothing while saying everything all at once. He missed me, was still attached, and had not let go. I didn't say anything out loud, but inside I was screaming: *"I knew I wasn't crazy! I knew you felt the same way as I did!"*

WHEN HE WAS inside me is when he expressed it all. "I'm in love with your body. I love the way you feel. I love how good you taste. This is all yours. You're all mine. I missed this. I missed you. Just like that, baby. Fuck, baby. Yes, baby."

God, I missed him. Now I knew for certain, he missed me, too.

"I guess this means we're addicted again, aren't we?" he joked, but we both knew it was true. Sex was better when we were having it together. I knew in my soul that this man could travel all around the world, but anyone he met wouldn't hold a candle to us and our connection, passion, and energy towards each other. It was him for me, and me for him. He knew my body at this point better than anyone, as did I for him. He knew all my spots; I knew all his.

"It also means we're toxic, doesn't it?" I asked, somewhat joking, somewhat serious. I licked the sweat from his neck before burying my head into it.

He shook his head. "No, it's not. We aren't toxic. It's just complicated. It's a complicated relationship."

He was wrong, yet he was not wrong. It had been a complicated relationship, but it didn't have to be like this.

We kissed goodbye and just like old times, it took us three times as long to say it.

He left and ten minutes later he texted me.

**Will:** *I definitely left my glasses at your house*

I looked around. There they were on the green couch that just witnessed it all.

*Shit. He definitely did.*

**Me:** *Wanna come back and grab them now?*
**Will:** *Nah, I'll get them another time*

He lived five minutes away. He could easily grab his glasses on his way to work or on his way to the gym, while he's running errands. But no. He was plotting. I knew him. He liked a little distance to make the heart grow fonder. The chase. He liked to build a little tension before the big release. He knew now there are other men who had my attention and wanted to date me. If he was coming back this time, he knew he must come correct. He needed to act right. I wondered when and how this would all shake down. But for now? I was preparing for Mason's Maryland departure and Detroit arrival. I wasn't waiting around playing miss nice girl for anyone.

The plot was plotting.

# Summer Fling before the Ring

WHEN MASON DIDN'T come after the last flight he booked and after the countless phone calls we had trying to end the whole thing, I must be honest when I say that I did not see this coming. He had done some thinking, was beginning to face his trauma, and "called his own bluff." He was scared to fall in love with me, but even more afraid to have never taken the risk with me at all.

"I'm seeing you this summer," he said over Facetime.

"Sure. I bet you are." The sarcasm was thick. I couldn't trust his words as far as I could throw him.

"Summer fling?" he said.

"Summer fling before the ring," I said smugly. I would only entertain this situation on the way to meeting my husband. To pass the time. Besides, the last time I had a summer fling was in high school. I was fifteen years overdue.

"I'm smiling so big right now," he said.

"I hate you, I really do."

"You don't. You love me, actually."

Oh, love. What was love, anyway? Don't ask me. I was still figuring it out. All I knew was that this 26-year-old small town country boy with long flowing brown hair and muscles would soon be touching down in my neck of the woods, and soon be devoured by me.

THE DAY BEFORE his flight, we argued. It felt every bit like we were already an old married couple. When I went on the concert date with Will and told Mason about it, he wasn't happy. Would he be coming? Or canceling again?

"What do you want me to do, Mason? I'm single and looking. I'm shopping around right now until I find a boyfriend."

"You're not shopping around. You go back to the same shopping cart every time, knowing it has a bad wheel. Then last night you didn't see the bad wheel because it's filled with free groceries." He meant Will and our date.

My friends would constantly tell me he's not this dreamy "Whole Foods man" I made him out to be. He was just some "half foods guy" they said. Maybe my friends and Mason were be right. I did keep going back to the same grocery cart, even if it had a broken wheel. It was the cart I knew best. I had an emotional attachment to it. I thought it was special, and even though no one else saw what I saw, maybe they were right. They didn't see the good in this wobbly thing, it was still broken, imperfect, off balance, yet oddly reliable. But so was I. Maybe that's what I liked about it.

"Am I still coming or not?" Mason asked.

"I don't know. Maybe you shouldn't."

"You know what?" he argued, "No. I'm still coming. I'm meeting you, goddammit. We're not doing this again. I'll sleep on the floor or on your hammock outback. I'm seeing you tomorrow. And that's that."

"Great," I said angrily.

"Great."

We were both angry with each other and now he'd be here tomorrow night. The whole argument, I kind of hoped he would cancel. Last time he canceled when all was going well. Now, nothing was going right, and he wanted to show up? It didn't make sense. He was driving me crazy, and I had royally pissed him off. We were off to a great start, weren't we?

I WASN'T EXCITED to pick him up. I was annoyed. I had been here already with two men from the internet that required air travel and an overnight stay and it never went well. I didn't even go out of my way to put on makeup or wear my cute lounge clothes. I was in my frumpy pajamas, had messy hair and wore sandals with socks. I was not trying to impress a man that I wasn't looking forward to seeing. I just didn't care anymore, and my expectations were on the floor. I was honestly just looking forward to getting it over with so he could meet me and just go home. I was prepared for a terribly tense and awkward weekend together, so we could finally both move on from this connection knowing we tried, but that it wasn't a good fit. "Best of luck."

**Mason:** *Hi.*

He texted me from arrivals. And called me a second later.
"I don't see you. Where are you?"
"Sorry, there's traffic. Which is odd for one in the morning. But I'm parked a bit down on the right side. It's a short walk."
"White SUV?"
"Yeah, that's me."
"I see you." He walked closer to the car, his brown hair flowing with each step forward. He flashed a dimpled smile and waved as he approaches me. *Fuck, he's hot.* And while I knew that before, seeing him in person made it real. He was *really* hot. And he was *really* here.

Whether we liked it or not, we had a bond. It was a bond that was formed through grief and love. Through heaven and angels. How could we stay angry at each other?

The drive to my place with him felt natural, as if we were old friends passing time again. When we walked into my house, he placed his bags in the guest room.

"Guess I'm sleeping in here," he laughed.

"Where else would you sleep?" I asked. I could feel it then. The sexual tension. We had seen each other naked and had phone sex on FaceTime more times than I could count.

"I don't know. You tell me." He walked into my room and looked around. "It does look extra comfy in here."

"It is." I tried to hide a flirty smile. My plan to ignore and avoid him was being derailed by his dimples.

"Well, good night, then," he said, laughing a little.

"I mean... you can hang out in my room for a few if you want before you sleep."

He looked at me then and we both felt it. Chemistry heating up.

"Okay," he said, sitting on my bed. "This is really comfy."

"Hate to brag, but the sheets are like silk. They're so soft." I pulled the comforter down and ran my hand across the soft fabric. He did too and his hand touched mine. Our eyes met then.

"Hi," he said.

"Hi."

"I can't believe I'm really here. Doesn't feel real."

"I know. It really doesn't. It's crazy."

I pictured his naked fit body with soap running down his stomach and I swallowed hard.

"It's almost two in the morning. Aren't you tired?" he asked.

"Yeah, but suddenly I'm feeling... alert. You woke me up."

"Did I? How so?" he asked, his voice lower then. Flirty and seductive.

"That. Right there."

"What?" he said, smirking into his dimples again.

"You know."

"Do I? Hmm."

He leaned in to kiss me then. To my surprise it wasn't awkward at all. It was warm and inviting. I pulled away and gave him the "what are we doing" look.

Before you know it, all bets were off. All clothes were off, too. He was on top of me, making me feel so good I could hardly believe it. When it came to sex, I can say with sheer confidence that not one man has ever made me come the first time that we had sex. I had low expectations and low hopes for the first time with anyone. But Mason? Magic must have been in the air because he sent my body into orgasmic bliss rather quickly and on the first try. If this was any indication of how our weekend was going to be, I was pleasantly surprised and looking forward to how the rest would unfold. He was a giver, and I was happily receiving it all. Every last inch.

We woke up the next morning and went straight into morning sex. I had two orgasms by nine A.M, before coffee and breakfast. When we finally got our clothes on, he came outside with me and sat shirtless on my front porch. We are doing two of my favorite things, listening to music and drinking coffee together. There was a light summer rain pattering when I had a brilliant idea.

"What are you doing?" Mason said, looking at me puzzled.

"I'm lying on the ground in the rain." My indie romantic playlist hummed from my speaker.

"You're a little crazy. You know that?" he shouted out at me playfully.

"Yep," I said, catching raindrops on my face, letting them fall down my cheeks.

"That looks refreshing, actually," he said.

"It is. You should try it."

"Done," he said, running out into the rain. He dropped his body down to the lawn and lay next to me. He grabbed my hand.

"You're a good crazy."

I smiled. "You are, too. You're crazy good."

We both felt it then. From chemistry to romance. In real life. *Is this real life?*

We dried off and brought the speaker into the house. Mason poured us both another cup of coffee. He put his hands around my waist and pulled me in.

"You are literally so perfect." He smiled and started to sway with me.

"Are we dancing in the kitchen right now?" I asked.

"I think we are."

Michael Bublé's 'Home' comes on then. There we were, stuck in the most romantic scene. This did feel a little too good to be true.

"I think we should go to Vegas tomorrow and get married," he says.

"You're hilarious, sir."

"I'm not joking, check the flights."

I looked at him like he'd lost his mind.

"You're my wife. I'm so sure of it. And I'm your husband."

My stomach sank a little. Thoughts of Will crashed into my brain without warning. Getting married meant I'd never have Will ever again. The thoughts were starting to haunt me and steal my joy. How could I even consider marriage if I still had my heart with someone else? How long would I feel this way? I started to worry about my future, one where I married someone else and longed for Will for the rest of my life.

"You're adorable." I said with a giggle. "But we are not going to Vegas."

"But you are my wife. I'm 99.9 percent sure of it."

"What about that one percent?" I asked. "Why not a hundred percent?"

"Because you don't live in Maryland. And the distance is a big barrier to the relationship. It would be a hundred percent if we lived in the same place. Without a question," he said. "By the way, I have something for you." He walked into the guest room and pulled out a letter from his bag.

"What is this?" I asked.

"It's a letter to you," he said. "From my mom."

"Your mom wrote me a letter? That's so sweet. But why?" I asked.

He shrugged and smiled into his dimples again.

"Mom thinks you're the one, too."

LATER THAT MORNING, when we were intimate, he whispered in my ear.

"I love you."

I pretended I didn't hear it. I wasn't ready to hear it. Then he whispered a different version, one that was easier to digest. "I really want to love you." What is love? It's reciprocal, isn't it? And the Will-sized hole in my heart wasn't allowing anyone else to climb through it. I liked Mason, a whole lot more than I did before this weekend together. But it wasn't love for me. Not yet at least.

We were out on a date that afternoon when I noticed an incoming call from Will. I didn't answer, but seeing it ring in my palm and going unanswered burned a hole through my flesh the longer I left it there. His voice was on the other line and this was the first I'd ever ignored his call or had been too busy to answer. I'd always been right there when he needed or wanted me.

A text flashed in seconds after.

**Will:** *Are you home?*

**Will:** *I'd like to grab my glasses.*

My stomach dropped. *Oh, fuck.* My fear was coming true. He needed his glasses while Mason was here. *Shit. Shit. Shit.*

I looked at Mason and he knew by the panicked look on my face. He knew about Will, I'd told him everything. And like everyone else, he wasn't a fan.

"He texted you didn't he? He wants his glasses?"

"Yeah… What should I say?"

"Just tell him to come get them. I'll hand deliver them to him," he smiled.

I shoved his arm playfully. "Um, that is a horrible idea." We both laughed, but inside I had this awful sinking feeling. The time had come where I needed to face the facts. Will had put himself in the position to lose me repeatedly and now there is the very real possibility that he might lose me for good. He'd have to accept that whatever we'd had, was maybe coming to an end, and that maybe, just maybe, I was about to have the love and the relationship I was always looking for. The clarity I had prayed for was arriving, the fog was lifting, and I was realizing that it was likely it might not be Will in the end. The fantasies I'd brilliantly constructed in my head were crashing down and I was hand-in-hand with a man who was ready to offer me his whole heart and soul. Even if it terrified me.

It felt like a fork in the road. To choose to prioritize Will once again and continue to bend and sculpt myself to fit into his life on his terms or choose a new path for myself. One that didn't have him on it at all. One with a new person. A pang of grief hit me then. It was time to do what once felt impossible. Peel Will off the pedestal I had unknowingly put him on and choose myself. And in choosing myself, choose someone else that had the capacity to show up in the ways that were fulfilling, in the ways that I deserved. This was my second chance at love, and if I was going to get it right this time, I couldn't make any decision lightly.

THE PROBLEM AND the solution always started with a man's eyes.

It's the way a man looks at me that tells me everything I need to know. With Will, I could stare into his eyes for miles and miles, as if I could see an entire wide-open galaxy inside of them. They were seeking and vastly mysterious, full of wonder and possibility. When I'd investigate them long enough, I would get lost in his gaze for what felt like all of eternity. Time would stop and there I was, free-falling into the great beyond with every blink. There was a comfort, a feeling of home and a sense of fullness in that. When I investigated anyone else's eyes, I didn't get lost in their depth. I didn't get the "diving into the abyss" sensation that I had grown used to. In fact, they didn't pull me in or take me to some far away place at all. When my eyes met theirs, they were usually grounded in this realm, in this dimension, and there was nothing to seek, nothing to search for—it was all right in front of me.

With everyone else, theirs said, "Here's everything I've got, and it's all for you. You don't have to look for it, chase it or deep-dive for it. You won't have to fly around the star-studded universe to find it, because it's all right here. Effortless and available. And if you want it, don't look away."

I always looked away.

I craved the kind of eyes that set me on fire deep and send my soul into the cosmos. I wanted depth and dimension. A surface level connection would never be enough after having the soul connection I had with Will. I wanted something cosmic or nothing at all.

    The day after Mason left, Will stopped by on his way to the gym to grab his glasses. He appeared to be in a rush, but deep down I could feel that he knew. There was someone else. And he wasn't sure how to feel about it.

## Every Moment is a Movie

T HE DAY BEFORE I turned 32, I was out on my front porch journaling and sipping coffee when I got a phone call from the French guy.

"I saw it's your birthday tomorrow."

"It is," I smiled and shook my head a little.

"I got you a present. Is it okay if I drop it off? I promise that's all I want. Nothing more. I know I'm married and everything. I don't want to make any mistakes, but I do think you're a special girl. And so, I got you something special. I picked it up this morning."

"You really didn't have to. That's very sweet of you. Thank you. Yeah, I don't mind. I'm just out on my porch." I gave him my address and a half hour later, he showed up in his brand new Mercedes Benz. As if him being tall, dark, handsome, and French wasn't bad enough, he dressed and drove in style, too.

"I don't have to come in or anything. Just to see you is enough." His accent destroyed me. It was painfully attractive.

"Do you want a cup of coffee?" I asked. "It's still on."

"Yeah, that would be nice." He ran his hand though his soft black hair. "I can't stay long. I'm supposed to be grocery shopping."

I brought him a cup of coffee and we caught up a little. He told me about his time in Hollywood and all about his dreams within film and cinema. The dreams were as gorgeous as he was.

"You know, we think a lot alike, you and me. I think that's

why I feel like I can't stay away from you. I see everything as a movie and you do, too. I live my life as though it is art, as though it's cinematic. Every night I walk my dog and I smoke a cigar listening to sexy French music. Every moment is a movie to me."

"You're right. Life is art. Every moment is a movie. Life is cinematic. We're all the actors on the big screen of this life."

"Open your gift."

"Now? You sure?"

He nodded and smiled.

I unwrapped his gift. It was the *La La Land* soundtrack on vinyl. My eyes widened and I covered my mouth.

"Do you like it?" he asked.

"I absolutely love it. Andre, this is my favorite movie and story of all time. How did you know?"

"I didn't. You just remind me of Mia from *La La Land*. And funny enough, that's what I saved you as in my phone." He pulled out his phone to show me it read "Mia Dolan," who Emma Stone played. A chill shook over me and my eyes filled with tears. This movie and its theme seemed to be following me everywhere in this chapter of my life.

"If I'm Mia, does that make you Sebastian?" The character Ryan Gosling played. If you don't know the moral of the story, I hate to spoil it for you, but they don't end up together. Regardless how well they connected, they went their separate ways to pursue their dreams, which they couldn't do if they stayed together.

"I think so."

I smiled at him and leaned over for a hug. I drank in the smell of his expensive cologne. I closed my eyes and imagined another world where this could've worked. A pang of sadness hit then. Some people are life rafts and others are ports made for just passing through.

"Thank you, Seb."

"You're welcome, Mia. Happy Birthday."

THE NEXT DAY I decided maybe it was time for me to stop the self-sabotage and allow a healthy love in. I called Mason and shared that I also was beginning to develop feelings for him. I was ready for a love that was in the here and now, ready for the taking, and that meant the possibility of embarking a long-distance relationship with Mason, who lived almost 500 miles away.

On my way from one side of the state that used to be my home to the other side, metro Detroit, I liked to stop halfway in between, in the town I used to go to college, and grab a latte for good old nostalgia's sake. It was raining and I'd cried the entire drive into town feeling sorry for myself for having a lonely birthday. One without a man and feeling down about love and life and the cards I was being dealt in my relationships. As I was leaving the coffee shop, a homeless man sitting outside in the rain asked me for food. I gave him my breakfast and the cash I had left in my wallet, which was a $50 my mom had given me for my birthday.

His eyes welled up.

"Today is my birthday," he said to me. The rain began to come down a little heavier.

"Can you sing to me? Can you sing me happy birthday?" he asked, a tear falling from his face. "I just had my birthday, too." I said. And as I did, he clapped for joy.

"I will sing you happy birthday." I said to him gently.

And there in the rain, I sang this man happy birthday and we both cried. He told me he hadn't seen so much money in such a long time and he was happy that he could buy his medication and a blanket to sleep on someone's porch for the night. If everything is a lesson, this one was teaching me a few things. That the best gifts in life aren't the ones we receive, they're the ones we give. Life could always be worse, our feelings are valid, but try to appreciate the smallest of things. Like having a bed to sleep in, money to buy medication if you need it and food in your belly. I grew up rather Christian and my southern Baptist father would always tell me, "Be kind to everyone you meet, you never know if that is Jesus in disguise." I'll never know if that homeless man was Jesus in disguise, a test from the universe to see if I was harnessing an abundance mindset, another lesson in gratitude or a gift in giving itself. But I will say that after that moment, things looked a little brighter for me. The rain cleared up half-way through my drive and the sun began to shine. I suddenly didn't feel like crying anymore. I suddenly felt content, happy with being exactly where I was. I felt less lonely, more hopeful. And financially had an abundantly blessed week that I didn't see coming. I was being blessed for blessing others. And while I didn't do it for those reasons, that's just the way the law of karma works. The good you do comes back to you.

## Take Two? Take Three?

"Mase, maybe you're right. About Will not being good for me. About us being good for each other." I expressed this on our daily FaceTime. It took a lot for me to be honest. To open myself to someone new and to be vulnerable in sharing my new perspective with him. Even though I told Mason everything, this didn't feel easy.

He looked at me and looked away.

"Britt, don't hate me for what I'm about to say."

"Which is what?"

"I just don't think I can ever leave Maryland. Which means, it seems pointless to continue. Don't you think? If we never end up in the same location, why bother?"

Once I expressed I was open to exploring deeper feelings with Mason, he panicked and we found ourselves back to where we had once started. He was certain he never would, no matter how many times I tried to share a new perspective, one with him possibility in my state which is only a one-hour flight and a seven-hour drive, it was never convincing enough. He couldn't leave and that was that. But did he tell me he thought he was my husband, that he loved me and wanted to marry me on the way out, making it twice as traumatic? Yeah. Yeah, he did.

Again, I found myself wrecked. I was so close to having exactly what I was looking for and I was finally looking forward to opening my heart for once. But I knew he couldn't be my person, because my person would choose me. My person wouldn't give up on me and choosing me would be the easiest "yes." For those reasons, I told him goodbye, for real. When he texted me the next day asking if we could be something casual, I laid the boundary down and said absolutely not. I knew I had learned my lesson, those situations never served me. There would be no more settling and accepting halfhearted, luke-warm and inconsistent men. If he was in, he was in and so was I. I was ready to give him what I was certain he couldn't find within ten miles of his home from almost 500 miles away. But the rejections came one after the other, and the only reason I was being rejected this time was because of distance.

"Britt, I would try if you were closer. But it isn't practical if I'm never leaving here. I do think you're the one, you're just not where I need you to be. If you were here, it would be us. I'd build us a house, you'd bring the boys and we would live a dream life here."

But I couldn't. I was bound and tied to Michigan. So, another one bit the dust. I walked away in a new direction, swimming through the water again without a life raft this time. But from here, knowing the light was shining down on me from the lighthouse. Mason maybe wasn't the final destination, but I knew with the light he shed on me, I was headed in the right direction. Maybe he was the driftwood. Reminding me where I was headed and what was possible. That I'm closer to the shoreline than I thought. If anything was getting me through the soul crushing heartbreak of having something and losing it again, it was that. That he was a glimmer of hope that a love like his existed and was possible.

LATER THAT NIGHT, I prayed on my knees again. *God, please keep anyone not meant to be in my life out of it.* The next day, I got a text from Will.

I swear, it was like every time I ask for a sign, he popped up. But why?

**Will:** *Can you do me a solid?*
**Me:** *Maybe… it depends.*
**Me:** *What?*

He sent me a screenshot of this giant container of aloe vera juice.

**Will:** *Can you run to Whole Foods and grab this for me before they close, and I'll pick it up later?*

That was cute, Will. He wanted to see me and was thinking of any excuse to.

**Me:** *I have so many questions lol. Why can't you get it? I was planning on going to get coconut water anyway, but if I go then you owe me big time.*
**Will:** *Nevermind, I should be able to get it if I go now.*
**Me:** *Okay, bring me a coconut water then*
**Will:** *Ask nicely*
**Me:** *Please bring me a coconut water, William*
**Will:** *I'll leave now*
**Me:** *Text me when you're close, I'm thirsty*
**Will:** *Be there in a few minutes*

We both knew this had nothing to do with aloe vera or coconut water and everything to do with us being addicted to each other. It was August now, almost a full year of us doing this. If we couldn't quit each other for over a year, then what were we going to do? How long could we really keep this up? As long as I tolerated it? Until we found someone else? There was one part of me that was ready to throw in the towel, yet another side that said, "Why not just have fun with him while I can?" Well, maybe because it hadn't always been fun and games. It'd been painful and challenging, too. Every time I tried to let go, he showed up again. A part of me wondered if it was just a big lesson I still hadn't learned yet or if maybe this was something that wasn't supposed to end yet.

He knocked on the door, and I yelled from the corner of the living room on the sofa, "Come in!"

"Where are you hiding?" he asked.

"Over here. I'm in my writer's cave and I can't get out."

The lights were dimmed in the house, and I had romantic indie music playing softly.

"How's everything going?" he asked. "Here's your coconut water." He handed it to me. His Will smell hit me then and I began to crave the taste of him.

"Thank you." I looked at him and his eyes met mine. And instantly, there was that feeling I always had when I investigated them. They pulled me in, and I couldn't get out. We held eye contact and smiled a little too long for "just friends."

"So, you did all of this just for me? Just because?"

"Yeah. But you do owe me."

"Mmm. Really?" I bit my lip, not breaking his gaze. "What's that?"

"I think you know what that is."

"Do I?"

He nodded. "Yeah, you do."

He crossed his arms and leaned against the wall.

"So, you're shy again? Is that right?" I asked him.

"You keep saying that."

"Look at you. Arms crossed, like I'm a stranger." I laughed. "Do I make you nervous, Will?"

He uncrossed them.

"No. You don't."

I said nothing, I didn't have to. I could feel it then. He had that look in his eye and he walked closer to me. The one that was ready to make me shake underneath him. He took my hand.

"Come on. Let's go." He smirked and walked me into my room, pressed me down onto my bed. And for the next two hours, he dominated me with relentless pleasure. It'd been a while since we dabbled in BDSM, but that night, I was submissive, and he took complete control over my body.

"To me, you're so fragile and sensitive. I don't want to hurt you."

No wonder he touched me so gently, so tenderly. He was afraid to break me. He was afraid to hurt me. He said so much without saying much at all.

## Maryland, Motorcycles, Man Buns and Mountains, Oh My!

O F COURSE, THE next day, Mason reached out. Why do men *always* come back?

"Long distance?" the text read.

Not again. Was he serious? How could a person be so wishy-washy? He was giving me major whiplash and to be honest, it was making me dizzy.

"I know this sounds crazy, but… come see me this weekend? Meet my family and friends. I think we should at least try to do this."

Feeling heartbroken over how things went with Will. Feeling lonely and wanderlust, I decided I had nothing else to lose. With Mason, I knew I was safe. I knew he cared about me. I knew we would have a great time. So I booked a flight. I guess this made me crazy after all.

When I landed, Mason was there at arrivals in his big pick-up truck and two thermoses of coffee he made for us. He knew how I liked it from the last time we were together. Almond milk and a little honey to sweeten. He took my bags and threw his arms around me.

"I missed you," he said with a big smile that hung from his dimples. Gosh, he really was adorable. I smiled back.

"Did you?" I was reluctant to say the same. It felt too vulnerable, and I was still unsure of my feelings. There was this big part of me that would regret not seeing where this could go one last time. Whether I cared to admit it, I knew that I would always have a special connection with him. We held each other through grief, and he was someone that I knew wanted the best for me and my life.

"I want to take you on your first motorcycle ride today. I'll take you through the mountains, to see the property I bought to build my house and then stop at the car show in town to see Dad. And you can meet everyone there."

We pulled into the driveway, and I was amazed when it looks like we'd arrived at a literal castle.

"Mason, this is your house?" I asked, the shock coating my voice.

"It's my parents. I live in the guest house for now. I sold my old house once Lyss passed."

Someone pinch me. I was literally in some sort of Disney movie. Small town hottie locked away in a castle, waiting for his princess charming. Okay, okay. I'll stop with the dramatic romantics. But the scene was set for romance with this castle, his long hair and dimples. Add a motorcycle ride through the mountains and I had myself a dreamy situation. Somehow, I found myself in these often.

It had been a while since I'd been single, so meeting someone's family and friends was a big deal to me. I hadn't done that in over fourteen years. I was definitely feeling overwhelmed.

It's cheesy, but we planned matching outfits for the motorcycle ride in advance. Black shirt, black denim jeans and black Vans. With his Vans next to mine, and me straddled on the back of his Harley with my hands around his waist, he put on my favorite playlist, and we were off.

WE CROSSED BABBLING rivers and dreamy little bridges. We wound around the mountains, farmland and took the long back roads, because the main roads made me nervous at first. Being in Maryland reminded me of being back in my small hometown, except his was a little smaller, less developed. Here I was, chest pressed into a strong bearded country boy on the back of his bike. This felt like a dream. *Is this real life?* Was I really divorced with two kids in Maryland with a 26-year-old hunk who was pretty sure he was in love with me? Someone who saw my baggage and wanted to stay anyway? Someone who couldn't wait to show me off to his friends and family? When Will never once mentioned me to either. It was clear, Will didn't want anyone to know about us. Like I was a piece of forbidden fruit that he kept to himself. That stings. Even now.

Mason showed me that I was worth it to someone. That I had value. That I was worth loving. Flashbacks jumped to my mind the first time we met. The way he looked at me then and the way he looked at me now. *You're literally perfect.*

We made it to the small-town car show, and everyone already knew me as "that city girl writer from Detroit."

"I'm actually a country girl at heart," I told them. "I grew up in the country, my dad has a blueberry farm. I grew up four wheelin', baitin' my own line, you name it. I ain't afraid to get my hands dirty." I said with a smirk. My faint southern accent popped out when I was comfortable enough.

"We like her, Mase," his dad's friend said from the sack chair with his hands on his belly.

"Mason has good taste. If he likes you, you're a good one. You wouldn't be here if you weren't," his dad said. His dad was stern yet gentle. Common for an old blue collar country man.

"We're headed to Rube's Crab Shack after this for dinner, Mase. You guys comin'?" he asked.

"We'll be there," Mason said, looking at me with a smile. Even though I know Wil, my first love, is dead, I found myself looking around for him. He lived in Maryland before he passed away. It felt serendipitous to be in the last place he was before he left. Somehow, he is everywhere always. Guiding me on my path.

Only one big problem. I'm allergic to seafood, especially shellfish. The last time I ate I had a near death experience. *Shit.* I pulled Mason to the side and tell him.

"Umm, I'm allergic to seafood."

"That's okay, no one minds. Maybe get a salad or something?"

That was the plan until I broke out in hives and my throat started closing a few minutes after sitting down at the table in the crab shack. In my marriage with my ex-husband, he had zero patience with me. But with Mason, he took me outside immediately and didn't leave my side. He didn't act embarrassed like my ex did when this happened to me. He didn't try to force me to eat something anyway, like my ex did. Instead, he took me to get fresh air and helped me relax.

"Breathe through your nose, drop your shoulders, remove your tongue from the roof of your mouth, okay?" he said, holding my hand.

He knew how to handle me and my anxiety.

"How are you so good at dealing with me, with this?"

"I was married, remember? I had a wife and she had anxiety. And it got really bad before… you know," he said. It was then that I remembered, because sometimes I forgot. She sadly ended her life due to mental health. He knew what to do with me due to the most horrific circumstances.

When we got back to his house, I couldn't help but cry.

"I love that I'm here with you and that I get to know you. But I also hate it. I wish your wife was still here. The only reason

I'm here is because she's not. And that breaks my heart for you. It shouldn't be me here. And I'm sorry," I said sobbing into his chest.

"Hey, it's okay. I know what you're saying. And it is hard, and I hate it, too. But I'm glad you're here. Okay? This is my new life and I'm learning how to be without her. It's not easy, but I'm trying." Just then, a few tears fell from his eyes. We squeezed each other tight. His pain was palpable, and I wished I could take it away. I wished I could give him his wife and his old life back, even if that meant I was never in the picture.

The rest of the day he took me through photo albums, shadow boxes full of all her things, dried casket roses, her jewelry, and cards she wrote him. I watched videos of them together and sat with him in his grief once more. He showed me the perfume she wore, and where her ashes were. It was then that I remembered the way he kissed his cremation bracelet every night before bed. No one loved his wife more than he did. That was clear. It will forever break my heart to know he's without her.

Eventually, we collected ourselves and Mason had plans for his mom, cousin Chloe and me to go to a small cozy winery up the street. Mason had been sober for a year, but he knew it would be something fun to do for the rest of us. The evening was coated with guilt and grief. As much as his family welcomed me, I knew I wasn't who they wanted across the table. I wasn't the girl they wanted. They missed his wife. I knew they liked me and were grateful I was in Mason's life, after all, his mom pulled me aside and thanked me for getting him into therapy. But I also knew I was never going to be her. And I sensed that she was all Mason wanted. I could tell that he was feeling overwhelmed with his decision to begin again with someone else. And to be honest, I was too. I wasn't sure if I was ready for this, either.

Still yet, we had two days left together so we planned on

making the most of it. We had nights out with his friends, dinner dates and spent so much time cuddling, I thought our bodies would fuse together. And when we weren't cuddling, we were doing other things. The attraction between the two of us was wildly alive. We showered together and we had so much sex each day that I was sure we'd get sick of it. Spoiler alert: we never did. Because he was once married, he knew his way around a woman's body. He knew how to please, and please a woman's body he did, let me tell ya. I will never forget what it felt like to have his body pouring sweat over me with his hair pulled back in a man bun giving me back-to-back orgasms. How could I ever? When I signed on the line for my divorce, I knew it would give me life. But times like these, I realized I got way more than I bargained for. I'm living my very best one.

THE NEXT MORNING, I woke up to a text from Will.

**Will:** *I didn't know you were Amish now.*

He had watched my Instagram stories and saw that I was in Maryland. I shared a quick video of me on the back of Mason's Harley and set the location to that small town. I felt protective over Mason, and I knew Will was being arrogant because he was jealous.

**Me:** *Good one.*
**Will:** *You're breaking the rules, by the way.*
**Me:** *What rules?*

He sends a screenshot of Amish rules and highlighted in yellow the part where using technology was prohibited. He felt threatened by this Maryland man and was having no problems throwing shade at him.

**Me:** *Good thing I'm not with the Amish.*
**Will:** *Yeah, who is she?*

He asked, trying to get me to say I was with another guy.

**Me:** *Who said it was a girl?*
**Will:** *I don't know, figured maybe you switched teams. The Amish are probably crazy like that, anyway. All there is to do is have sex I bet.*
**Me:** *Maybe you're right. Maybe that's all I'm doing here.*
**Will:** *Having sex?*
**Me:** *Maybe I am.*

I wanted him to feel the jealousy I have felt every time I knew he was with someone else.

**Will:** *Good for you. Who is she? Is she any good?*
**Me:** *What part of your dick in my mouth ever gave you the impression that I'm a lesbian? I'm painfully straight, Will. You know this.*
**Will:** *Good point.*
**Will:** *When are you home?*
**Me:** *Couple days, why?*
**Will:** *Just curious. Would love to see how straight you are again.*

This was all code for: *I know you're in bed with some guy from Maryland, I absolutely hate it. I'm jealous, but I did it to myself. I miss you. Can I see you? I don't want anyone else to have you.*

IT'S BETTER TO have no one than half of someone. I hopped on the flight home knowing that Mason would never be mine. And I was headed back home still unsure if the man I wanted to be mine was sending bat signals to be caught or what he was trying to do this time. But what harm did I have in finding out?

# What Goes up, Must Come... Back Again?

A FEW DAYS later when I got back home from Maryland, I saw Will. As he said, he wanted to see me when I got back and he followed through. I was hesitant, but still slightly powerless to him. Something, I can't tell you what, kept me hooked. My kids were home this time, but they were in their beds sleeping. He snuck in from the side door and followed me downstairs, like old times. Instantly, he gave me a passionate shove onto the wall and kissed me so intensely, I could hardly come back up for air. He kissed my stomach and down my thigh and then back up again.

"We should probably wear protection. You were with someone else," he said with a cold undertone.

I looked at him blankly. "You were, too."

"Well, I only went unprotected with you."

This was his way of trying to see just how close I got to Mason. Unprotected sex is an obvious level of closeness, and it was clear he wanted that to himself. What man wouldn't?

I didn't say anything. He could tell. Mason and I got extremely close.

"I'll just be safe and wear it."

Sex this time felt cold, off and disconnected. There was tension between us in a painful and obvious way. Our bodies were clearly holding onto jealousy and they weren't in sync like they once were. When we finished, I couldn't help it, the tears just started to fall.

Will looked at me then as he pulled his pants back on.

"Brittany. You're crying…" he said.

"It's just…" The words choked on the way out.

"What? Tell me."

"What if I end up with someone else? What if you end up with someone else? I'm afraid to date a person and be in a committed relationship with them because then I'd never see you again. And maybe I'm afraid to keep doing this to other guys. Like the guy in Maryland, who is amazing, and kind, and loves me. And I could never hurt someone like him. I would never be unfaithful to him or to anyone. Being with someone else means losing you."

"Why are you saying that right now? Are you in a relationship with this guy?"

"No. He just really made me think about things. He's the type that would be a great boyfriend and great step-dad. And he sees my value and wants to love me."

He nodded and swallowed. Time seemed to be slipping away like sand through an hourglass.

"It's inevitable, though. We will eventually meet other people." A sadness coated his tongue.

"That makes me sad, Will."

"I know. It is sad to consider. I'd like to always be in your life. You know, if I dated anyone and they were upset that we were still friends, I'd choose you. You would always come first. I'd rather lose her than lose you. A person that doesn't understand what your friendship means to me isn't a person I want anyway."

More tears fell. *If I mean so much, why not be with me?* I didn't say it, but I wanted to.

"I had the craziest thought today, it popped in my head out of nowhere," he said.

"What was it?"

"I had the strangest feeling come over me and the word 'stepdad' popped in my mind. And I couldn't shake it. But now I think maybe it's this guy and the fact that he wants to be a stepdad to your kids. I knew it couldn't be me. I'm not ready to be a step-dad."

"He does want that, you're right."

He looked into me with depth and all the life left his face at once.

"I just don't know."

"Well, you need to be sure. Your kids deserve that." He adjusted a hair tie on his wrist. Likely another girl's. I noticed and look back at him.

I nodded.

"You know, I met someone, too," he mumbled.

Everything in my lungs escaped all at once, but on the outside you wouldn't notice. I tried to hide the broken by sweeping it under a blank stare.

"You did?"

"At a wedding. In West Michigan. She's young, a dancer." He raised his brows like I was supposed to be impressed after he grinded himself on top and inside of me for the last thirty minutes. "She was the waitress. My mom was rooting for it the whole wedding. And I don't know what happened, but she just disappeared after a week. I tried texting her, and she stopped responding."

Karma is funny, isn't it?

"What did you send her last?"

He pulled out his phone and faced the screen towards me. A photo of a sunset.

"I was up north at my family's lake house, and I sent it to her, I thought of her and I thought she'd like it." He made a frustrated face. "And she just ignored it."

The sunset photo I would've done anything for. The simple

photo I wanted so badly when he was in Florida, the one he had so easily sent to someone else. A girl he didn't know. A girl he hadn't rubbed his soul against. A waitress. Another girl that wasn't me. The brokenness was hard to hide now. The tears bubbled back up, but I swallowed them down. Bitterly, I replied.

"That's your answer then. She doesn't like you."

"Maybe I'm not being patient enough. I know she's super busy, it's summer and she's slammed with work. Maybe I should text her back and see why she didn't like me. It's driving me crazy."

"Will, no girl who likes you is ever too busy. I'm an exceptionally busy single mom running multiple businesses, writing two books and if I like a guy, I will answer his message from the bathtub. We make time for the people we want to prioritize." My own words stung on the way out. I wasn't the girl that got the sunset photo. And I wasn't the one he wanted to ever prioritize.

"Maybe you're getting your karma." I blurted. It came out like hot lava.

He sat there for a second and let that sink it.

"Yeah." He opened his mouth and exhaled. "You're probably right."

As much as I wanted to be shitty and say, "you deserve it," I met him with empathy and kindness. I hugged him and said I was sorry he was feeling that way.

IT WASN'T THE bad sex that crushed me nearly as much as the photo of the sunset he sent the girl that didn't want him. I wanted him to think of me when he saw the sunset. I hoped that when he stared out into the horizon and watched the waves crash, that memories of me and of us laughing on the floor together at three in the morning and thoughts of me would flood his brain. I waited for that photo, and I never got it. I waited for the texts he never sent. I waited for the smallest crumb of affection and attention from him that I craved with an ache that pressed into my ribs. I was always waiting for him. To realize how great we were, how great we could be. How great I am. I waited for him to see me. To really fucking see me. I ripped myself open and waited for him to pour himself inside. And when he didn't, and when I had finally been emptied out entirely, I finally stopped waiting.

I gave him everything. And I never got anything in return. The hardest pill to swallow was that he had been holding the entire cake in his hands the whole time, but he was just hiding it behind his back. Even when I was around, even though he knew I was starving. It wasn't that all he had to offer was crumbs, it was that I wasn't the person he wanted to give the whole cake to.

# Like a Kid with a Kite

MOM FLYING HER first kite at 54 is one of the most beautiful things I've ever seen, because not all of us had the childhood we deserved. My boys raced down the beach, sand kicking up behind their heels, trailing the big red ladybug kite behind them. Until my youngest accidentally let it go and it slipped away from the grip of his tiny little fingers. Immediately, there were waterworks from them both. They were having so much fun and they didn't want the fun to end. I know grief when I see it. I know how hard it is to let something go, especially when you weren't ready to. I knelt next to the boys and summed up this experience as best as I could, in a way that a four- and a six-year-old could understand. At 32 now, I oddly feel wise beyond my years. Trauma, heavy life experiences and motherhood will do that, won't it?

"Look, I know the kite was so much fun, but it still served a beautiful purpose, even if it was short-lived. Didn't it?"

They looked at me blankly and I knew then I had to explain it simpler.

"Letting go is hard, especially when you had other expectations for how things were supposed to go or how you wanted it to go. This kite was supposed to fly forever, wasn't it?"

They nodded tearfully.

"And when time was up, it was hard, wasn't it? But just because it's over, let's not forget how it was still a magical time. Wasn't it so much fun?"

"Yes, we just want the kite back. And look, mom! It's so far away now, we'll never catch it."

"I know, baby. But maybe that kite wasn't meant to be yours forever. Maybe that kite was ready to bless someone else's life with its magic. Can we picture that for a minute? Maybe the kite had a different journey in store and it's on the way to more kids to play with. Can we still be grateful for the time we shared with the kite?"

The boys nodded again and wiped away their tears. They also knew ice cream was around the corner and all hope was not lost.

And then it hit me. That message was for me, too. I had reached one of the final stages of grief for all the people who have entered my life but didn't stay.

Hope.

# The Counterfeit Always Comes before the Blessing

GOD IS NOT the author of confusion. You'll know it's God when there's no confusion, no miscommunication, no anxiety. That will all be replaced with peace, security, and love.

However, my rose-colored glasses had turned shit brown. I have had enough of these dusties. And we were done with dusties. You know what settles? Dust. I am done with settling and done with dust.

Feeling sad after leaving Maryland because Mason freaked out again, and after Will somehow found a way to shatter me another time, I did something that felt against my value system and logged back into my dating app. Not without any hesitation or reluctance. I went back on that app kicking and screaming. The night I signed back into my account, I had a painfully depressing evening. However, the day started out on a high note. It was the day I had my *Seattle Times* interview about my viral TikTok video and my book, *On His Way Back To Me*. It was also the same day I had my rebrand photo shoot. I had a $100 worth of professional make-up and lashes still intact. I looked like a million bucks, and felt it, too. Naturally, I wanted to celebrate. I wanted to go out and enjoy the good news. So, I texted Will. He lives just aroud the corner and I always enjoyed his company. But of course, he ignored it. When I realized I had no one else to go out with, I said, "Fuck it. I will celebrate myself." I took myself out to the nicest newest cocktail bar in town, sat at the bar and ordered myself a prosecco. Just me, myself and I. I had decided then that I was worthy of celebrating, even if I was the only one celebrating me. I didn't need anyone else to validate my existence. If the lesson was finally accepting that I was enough, I was sitting in the front row seat in class. However, at the bar, I was reminded of my blaring singleness as I sat next to the cutest couple I had seen in a while. After a little small talk, I asked how they met. I was curious afterall. Where do people find love? They looked at each other and then at me before answering.

"Wouldn't you know it, a dating app of all places," the woman said. "I was just about to give up and delete the app. And then I heard my gut instinct say, give it three more days. And on the third day, he messaged me. And here we are. And that was two years ago."

I smiled and nodded. "Oh, I'm so glad that worked for you. I don't think my person is on those apps, though."

"How can you be so sure? Maybe this is your sign to give it another try."

In some weird way, it did feel like a sign. A sign I was apprehensive about, but like most cases, what did I have to lose?

I drove home in the pouring rain thinking about how angry I was at Will for flaking out and ghosting me. How disappointed I was at Mason over his back and forth antics. How sad I was about celebrating big news all alone. I opened the door to my tiny home, collapsed onto the floor, let out a good cry into the carpet, and re-downloaded the dating app I was trying to avoud. While still on the floor, I adjusted my profile a bit and started the swiping. *Here goes nothing.*

SHORTLY AFTER LOGGING on, I had a match with a guy who sent me a playlist. The playlist read: You Are So Beautiful Can I Ask You on a Date? He was funny, cute from his profile pic, romantic and seemingly sweet. His idea for a date was to have a taco Tuesday dance party and cook for me. It sounded like a blast, what's the harm in that? Could he murder me? Possibly. But at this point, I was already dead inside.

I looked out of the window when he arrived. To my surprise, the man drove a brand-new Mercedes. He was also in real estate, and I liked that he seemed ambitious. He seemed to have so many qualities I was looking for in a man. Except, I felt kinda catfished. His profile said he was six feet tall, and when he showed up not being as tall as his profile said he was, I felt shocked. Why lie? What was the point? I instantly felt sick. Not because he wasn't a 10/10, but because he lied. And no matter what kind of guy he was, I feared that I couldn't build a relationship off that foundation. But he was very kind and at the very least, showed me what I deserved. A man that went to Whole Foods and got me "one of everything just because I wasn't sure what you liked" kind of guy. A man that let me whine about my emotions and my period. Patiently listened to me vent about my broken heart. Did my dishes. Heard about my baggage and didn't run for the hills. There were so many things the universe was showing me. I was a vibrational match for a man to come in and give me everything, but I had my doubts. Maybe this was possibly another piece of driftwood? The one thing I thought I was looking for, but when it showed up, I questioned if it was the real deal. I worried if it was merely a mirage of 'the list' I had made before I met Luke from Texas, if I was just scared because he was emotionally available and ready for a real relationship with me, or if we just weren't right for each other. He was totally a nice guy and quickly became a wonderful friend that I enjoyed spending time with. But I feared that deep down this wasn't my guy, though after meeting him I felt like I was finally getting closer to attracting a real relationship with the man of my dreams. Even if it's unclear who that man is.

# Facing My Own Emotional Unavailability

"I'VE KNOWN YOU a long time now. You're a fearful avoidant attacher," my therapist said to me. "Every man you've been attracted to or have attracted into your life has been emotionally unavailable to a high degree. Think back to when you met your husband, was he emotionally available? Was he ever emotionally available?"

I shook my head.

"Then we have the age gap relationships. The men from other states. Long distance. Even the married men or men in relationships that pursued you. The widow who is also long distance, had an age gap and is grieving his deceased wife. All of them are very much emotionally unavailable and unable to enter a real relationship with you. You find them the most attractive because deep down you're not ready for serious commitment. You're choosing the ones who aren't ready because you're not."

She was right. So, why did that happen? My therapist explained it like this. It's because if we're honest, everyone in our energetic field is a mirror to where we are and where we've been in the past. I had subconscious blocks due to my need for space and my fears of intimacy. Letting people love me was a journey I craved, but at some level I wasn't actually ready for it. In fact, I was subconsciously terrified of it.

My journey with unrequited love from men started young for me. Heck, probably even from the playground in primary school to the boys who weren't allowed to date me back in my teens.

One of the first boys I had a crush on was the class bully in kindergarten. He often teased me and threw sand in my hair on the playground. But to my childhood self? That's what boys who love you do. That's their way to show love. That's how my dad showed it to my mom. "If he's mean to you, he likes you." I was drawn to them like moth to a flame. And the ones that did have any sort of longer relationship with me were relatively aloof, unavailable, immature, hot and cold, inconsistent, often mistreated me, ignored me, never prioritized me, and never fully chose me.

Now, in my 30's, single, healing, and ready for real love, what better time to break the pattern and the cycle. To stop chasing and attracting unavailable men. There was work to do to fix this and it began with not just choosing myself, but also learning what love was and what it felt like. To also recognize that I was worthy of real love. Unconditional love. I had been on the journey of loving myself and felt myself mastering that lesson and felt confused why I wasn't getting what I was asking for. I upgraded my wardrobe, got my nails done every month, until I realized I still unconsciously didn't think I was worthy of it. I had been successful and often felt worthy of recognition and admiration. But love? I wasn't so sure. If my own father and household couldn't show me love in a healthy way, how could anyone else? To get to the root meant several things, there was still more work to do on my self-worth when it came to accepting and receiving it.

I am worthy to be loved just as I am. To accept love fully, to feel it entirely, to appreciate it, to let it wash over me without fear. To sit in its glory and its discomfort.

Choosing healthy love after only being served toxic love is an experience to me akin to what Edward experiences with Bella in *Twilight*. Edward is a vampire built and wired to kill her by drinking her blood. But, no matter how much he craves her in that way, he chooses not to, even if it takes everything in him not to eat her alive. He values love enough to do the safe, right thing, even if it doesn't feel natural to him. What felt natural to me was unhealthy love from unhealthy men. What I needed to do is be more like Edward. Lean into what isn't as natural for me, in the name and desire for pure authentic and real love. Sometimes love is a sacrifice, not for them, but for me.

I BELIEVED THE love I wanted to receive would come when I did more work on not accepting unhealthy love. During my childhood, I lived in a chaotic home where love was scarce, uncertain, and poisoned by alcohol. To forge a new path for real love meant looking under the rug at my past, riddled with the trauma of abuse, neglect, betrayal, and abandonment. To get to the other side meant I had to face myself. Weather my own storm. To heal forward and into wholeness. Because everything I desired was on the other side of myself and the obstacles I'd held there for so long. Almost like I had swam up to a glass wall once I made it to the middle. I could see the horizon, but there was still a block. I knew I had to remove it somehow. The only way out is through. It might hurt to knock the wall down. I might bruise my knuckles trying to tear it down and I may have to swim with painful bits of glass on my way there. It'd sting and remind me of all the hell I'd been through. But the waters were calm, they were healing. With each glide forward, the glass bits fell away, and my skin began to heal. In fact, everything started to feel more pleasant. As if I was beginning to enjoy the swim so much that I started taking my time, float on my back a little and take in the view. The present moment finally felt like a gift. Even if I didn't have all that I desired in my hands currently, I could see it, and now that I'd removed the block, I knew I was on my way. The how and the why when I got there was less important. The journey was becoming one that was worthwhile.

# A Fated Lesson in Surrender

OF COURSE, I was so done with that damn dating app by now. It appeared to be one epic fail after the next. But the voice of my therapist was buzzing through my head still.

"The real work comes through relationships, not avoiding them and calling it art." She meant isolating myself and writing, which is exactly what I did best. Isolate and call it art. I'm doing it now if I'm honest. And by relationships, she meant friendships, too. At this point, I had zero romantic expectations on the dating app. I was just looking to heal through making connections with all kinds of new people and was actually having fun meeting new friends. And I can't lie, I was starting to enjoy the flowers, chocolates, doorstep deliveries, cute dates, rooftop drinks, fancy dinners and activities planned and paid for by men. I was finally allowing men to treat me like a queen and that was its own magic healing energy after spending 32 years of my life shit on by nearly all the men in my life. This was a beautiful lesson in allowing myself to receive gentleness, adoration, kindness, romance, and positive attention from men.

When this new guy on the dating app asked me to an expensive concert that would be a blast to attend for free, I had a hard time turning that new, fun, exciting and spontaneous kind of adventure down. Worst case scenario? I see an epic concert with a guy I'm not interested in. But hey, it's an epic concert I wasn't otherwise going to attend, especially alone. Per usual, I didn't have much to lose.

**Thomas:** *I have good news and bad news, Brittany. Good news is, I'm looking for an excuse to spend a stupid amount of money to see the Hozier concert tonight and would love for you to join me. Bad news is I'm here on a work trip and I leave tomorrow.*

**Me:** *I can meet you for a drink to make sure the vibes are good. And if so, we can go together.*

**Thomas:** *Sounds good. Let me know when and where to meet you.*

Usually, I'd prefer the guy to set the date and the time, but he did say he wasn't from around here. I gave him the benefit of the doubt. We made plans to meet at a popular local spot for happy hour drinks for six P.M. The concert didn't start until eight P.M, which gave us plenty of time to see if we vibed or not.

I showed up and he was standing outside of the bar, looking the other direction. When he turned and saw me, his eyebrows raised as he gave me the, "*oh my god, look at this girl,*" look. It was clear within the first few seconds of seeing me, he was attracted to me. Sometimes you meet someone on a dating app, and they are nothing like you'd expect. They might be shorter, have a little less hair than their photos, smell weird or just simply not vibe with you. I've experienced them all, I'm afraid. But lucky for us, we both looked like our profile pictures. And to be honest, he looked and he smelled better than I thought. I was attracted to him, too. What was not to love? He was 6'4", wickedly handsome, still had hair (this is a thing when you're dating in your 30's), had a sexy beard. I don't know what it was about him, but I loved the way he smelled. His pheromones drove me crazy in the best way.

We walked in together and headed to the bar while we waited for a table to open.

"You look amazing, by the way," he said.

I looked down at my shoes and scanned my outfit. I'm wearing what I wear to most concerts—black Vans, jeans, a cute little crop top, and a black denim jacket. Nothing that screamed overly cute, in my opinion. Besides, I didn't really plan on making it to the concert with Thomas. My plan was to get one drink and likely head home after being wildly disappointed again. But to my surprise, within the first ten minutes, Thomas and I really hit it off.

"Order whatever you want, I got it," he said.

"Champagne. I'm in my champagne era," I said.

"Then let's get this girl some champagne."

A woman turned around. "I'm sorry, but you two are so cute together."

We looked at each other and smile a little too hard.

"Yeah," I said. "We really are. So," I said, sipping my champagne, leaning into the bar. "You're here for work?"

"Yeah, though my boss asked me a couple weeks ago if I'd consider relocating to Grand Rapids. Should I?"

"Of course you should." I said, thinking about how things with Mason didn't work out due to distance. Looking back, I now see that redirection is divine protection. It was never going to be him regardless.

"Yeah? You'd move with me?" he asked. Of course, he was being funny, but there's always a hint of truth to people's jokes.

"Totally. My best friend just moved there. It's super cute. I think you'd love it."

Just then, our table opened. I wasn't sure if it was because we never thought we'd see each other ever again, but the conversation only grew deeper, into vulnerable territories. We talked about his spiritual awakening he had two weeks ago after attending a healing retreat. We talked about trauma, about father wounds, much deeper conversations than intended for a normal first date. We talked so much that by the time Thomas looked at his watch, he realized we'd missed the show.

"I'm not upset about missing the concert. This is better," he smiled. "Want to take our conversation somewhere else? On a walk, maybe?"

"Yeah. There's a park across the street we can stroll in together."

I put my jacket back into my car and grabbed a light sweater. Thomas quickly scanned the inside of it and notices the car seats.

"You have kids?" he asked. I remembered then that his profile said he was 26 and a Virgo. Meaning he just turned 26 because it was early September.

"I do. I have two boys."

To my surprise, he didn't act stressed out or panic. Instead, he smiled.

"I love kids. Tell me all about them," he said.

Any mother knows that gushing about her kids is one of our favorite things to do.

I followed Thomas to a park bench, and we talked about my life as a mom.

"That doesn't bother you?" I asked.

"About you being a mom? Not at all. My friends are starting to have families of their own, my siblings are starting their families and someday, I'd like to have children, too. So, no. I don't care that you're a mom. I think it's beautiful. A mother's job is impossible. Yet not only do you do it, it sounds like you do an amazing job, among everything else that you do."

The sun started to set, and the sky quickly fell into night. Thomas and I could've talked for hours but it was getting late. However, I had an idea to keep the night going.

"What if we walked that trail in the woods?" I pointed to the dark wooded trail to our left.

"Right now? But it's dark," he said.

"I know. I think it sounds… like an adventure. Want to?"

Thomas stood up and extended his hand out to mine.

"Yes. We're a little crazy for it, but let's see where it takes us."

And just like that, with Thomas's hand in mine, we entered a dark moonlit forest trail. We walked, laughed, and talked about anything and everything. There was not a single awkward pause. We walked across a bridge over a small river, the moon illuminating our faces through the trees.

"I'd be insane if I missed the opportunity to kiss you right now." He looked at me then.

I nodded and smiled as he pulled my waist in to kiss me. Fireworks may not be going off outside of our bodies, but I could feel them exploding internally. This kiss was magic and the scene was set for the movies. Thomas was sweeping me off my feet, unexpectedly so.

We walked in the dark forest hand-in-hand for a while longer until the trail ended, and then he walked me back to my car.

"It was nice meeting you," he said. "I had a great time."

He kissed me again as we leaned against the car.

"You can come over if you want. I know you work early, but it would be nice to spend more time with you."

He smiled. "I'd like that."

When he got to my house, he walked to my bookshelf and started naming off books he'd read and shared a little about which ones he was reading. Thomas was smart, and that was always a turn on.

Before you know it, I was wrapped around his waist, breathing him into a million fast passionate kisses. To be honest, Thomas didn't seem like the one-night stand kind of guy, in fact, he seemed quite timid, but we made it to my bed and an unstoppable force quickly came over us. In a hot surge of passion, he removed my clothes and began to use his mouth and hands in ways that forced bursts of air out of my mouth hard and fast. And when he was inside of me, he was gentle. Thomas didn't just try to get it over with and move on, instead, he stared into me with those golden eyes and made love to me gently. His sweat was pouring down my chest and when he flipped me over, I could feel him dripping onto my back. I was so full of him that it nearly took my breath away with each stroke.

*This man. This huge young man.*

When he was finished, he pulled me in close to hold me. In his big arms, even as a man I just met, I felt safe. He kissed my shoulder and asked to play a song.

"Do you know this song?" he asked.

Harvest Moon started to play on the speaker softly. Chills covered my arms and I swallowed hard.

"Yeah. I know this song." It was the same song I listened to when I sobbed into the carpet every night after Wil passed away. It was the number one song that made me think of him.

"It's one of my favorites. I can play it for you sometime. I play guitar and I sing. I'm not the best at either, but this song is one I enjoy quite a bit."

I choked back tears as I lay there in Thomas's arms. Closing my eyes and missing Wil while simultaneously feeling grateful to be held by someone like Thomas. I wasn't sure if I'd ever see Thomas again, since he was only in town for the night and lived in Iowa. But this was a night I could never forget.

The next morning I was in the middle of getting a manicure when I got a text from him.

**Thomas:** *What do you think about this coffee shop? Commonwealth? Is it any good?*

**Me:** *It's one of my favorites.*

**Thomas:** *Can you meet me here? I only have two hours, but I'd* *like to see you before I fly back home.*

**Me:** *I'll see you there when I leave the nail salon.*

I told the nail tech to skip the polish.

"Sorry, I suddenly have a date with this gorgeous man I met last night. I need to go."

I raced to the coffee shop that was luckily right around the corner, so I didn't miss another minute. I wanted to see him one last time.

When I walked in, he was in his business clothes, groomed, professional and incredibly attractive. I imagined his sweat dripping down my back and flashed a flirty smile.

"Order whatever you want. It's on me," he said.

"Thank you." I sat across from him, taking him in. "You know, I wasn't sure I'd ever see you again."

"I had to see you before I left. Last night was amazing."

I winked. "Oh, was it?"

He blushed. "Not because of that. I mean, yes. That was nice, but even if that didn't happen, it was perfect as it was up until then. Definitely unforgettable."

Over brunch in the short amount of time we had, he held my hand, and we talked about life, family, everything. With Thomas, it was easy and natural. All of it.

When it was time to leave, still with his hand in mine, he kissed me.

"I'm glad we met," he said.

"Me, too." I smiled. "Maybe we'll meet again.

He smiled back and drove off.

If this was anything significant, it was a reminder to not give up. This man lit me up. And I hadn't felt that since meeting Will at Whole Foods. At first, Will and I ran on all four cylinders, until he dropped all emotion, and then we were only running on three. Mason, I ran on three cylinders, missing the mental connection. But Thomas? It was all four, and it was instant. I knew that feeling. That spark. That "x" factor. It was chemistry, compatibility, and divine timing. A fluke chance that happens when you are fully surrendered and not necessarily looking for anything at all. That's always when it finds you. When you least expect it.

A TEXT LIT up my phone the next day.

> **Thomas:** Is it bad that I can't stop thinking about Thursday night?
>
> **Me:** If it's wrong, I don't wanna be right. I can't either.

From here on out, we talked every day. For hours. I'd been here before. Six-year age gap. Seven hours apart by car, one hour by flight. Of course, my mind was terrified this was another Mason situation. Another "almost there, but not quite." *What if he never wants to leave his state? What if he says he can't do a long-distance thing? What if he doesn't want to close the gap in distance? What if having two kids is too much for him? What if my baggage is too much?*

Something in me felt different this time. I didn't feel anxious anymore about the "what if's." I was at peace with everything working out the way that it was supposed to. I felt safe to trust the process and accept all that is right here and now. An even more positive thought came over me. *What if it worked out? What if he did end up moving here? What if this isn't too good to be true? What if Thomas is what I was praying for all along? What if he is my soulmate?* I knew I would survive any outcome, and even more than that, I just knew it all would work out. I felt it in my bones. If this wasn't "it," I would be okay. And if it was, I would be ready. I was finally ready for love again. If it had arrived with warm, ready, welcoming, and open arms, I was ready to fully receive it.

MASON CAME BACK, again, just as I met Thomas. A week after I met him to be exact. They a*lways* come back. But after a month apart I realized I can't run on three cylinders ever again. After running on all four, seeing how easy and natural it all could be. Having that feeling when I was holding his hand, like *wow, here you are. You're finally here, I have waited for you.* But only knowing him one night, it felt crazy. Feeling that otherworldly connection with Thomas on night one confirmed this was exactly what I was looking for. Though Mason and I had a beautiful connection, he wasn't the one for me. I wasn't the one for him. Mason was the fork in the road, a direction change. He was the piece of driftwood reminding me how close I was. I didn't know it would only be a month after him that I'd soon hold something new in my hand, that Thomas would find me, and we would begin a brand-new chapter together, no matter how long or short it would be. But he did and I was ready to start writing it anyway.

WILL ALSO POPPED back in. He always knew when I was moving on. I swear he could feel it. Like men have some sort of sixth sense when they're past romantic partner is not thinking of them anymore. He sent me a voice note after weeks of saying not a word. His voice note was buttery smooth, seductive, sweet, and enticing. But I didn't forget that he hadn't replied to my last text in over two weeks. I hadn't forgotten all the times he left my messages unread. I hadn't forgotten the abandonment, the tears, the rejection, and the heartbreak. In the past, I was always unconditional, welcome, and forgiving. He would hurt me, and I would brush off the pain and hide the wound like it never happened. The wounds were always open, just covered up. I got so used to the pain with him, it felt so normal that I had accepted it. Though I had never made peace with it, I was learning how to live bleeding wide open for someone who was willing to drain me dry. Much like I did in my marriage, I woke up one day and felt stronger. And when I peeled back the bandage on the wound I'd kept covering up, I realized it was finally a scar. I was still reminded of the hurt, but it didn't hurt anymore. I had layers of tough tissue that had been building over time, without me knowing. I wanted to be angry at him, but it never lasted long. Instead, I found myself sitting alone and crying in my car, praying for everyone who had ever hurt me, and that included him. Asking God to show him more love, more peace, more grace. Knowing deep down, he didn't want to be this way, even if he was this way. But I also knew it wasn't my problem to solve. He was who he was. And who he was, wasn't who I needed him to be. And as sad as it is, who I was, wasn't who he wanted.

## Sedona Awakenings

FOR FOUR YEARS, I felt the intuitive nudge to travel to Sedona, Arizona. Even though I was married to an airline pilot and had free travel benefits and often expressed this desire to make it there, it never happened. It happened once I got divorced of course, along with everything else I asked for. Looking back, that is exactly what the universe had intended for me all along. During the last week of summer in September of 2023, I landed with my best friend in a beautiful rental home nestled in the red rocks with the most stunning scenic views. If we were being honest, the scene was set for romance, and that's what we both needed. To romance ourselves. To love ourselves, pour into our own cups, reclaim, restore, recharge, and refresh our own energy. We are moms after all. Moms always need a good reason to relax, and Sedona felt like just the place.

For every year that I didn't make it to Sedona, I researched as much as possible as I prepared for my trip. By the time the plane landed, we had an entire excel spreadsheet itinerary full of things to do, places to see and food to eat. I didn't know when I'd make it there, but I knew I eventually would. I felt some sort of magnetic pull towards Sedona. There was something about that place that was calling me. Sedona is famously known for its healing vortex energy and energetic portals that are said to have metaphysical powers. So we decided to take full advantage. Audri booked sunrise vortex yoga, planned a daring off roading jeep safari-style tour through the red rocks, made a list of the best restaurants to visit and cool attractions to see.

"I have a feeling you're getting a tattoo when we get there," Audri said to me on the airplane down. Her Pisces intuition is always bang on. She just *knows* sometimes.

"Really? I wasn't planning on it. But now that you mention it—I think I will."

It felt like a sign. I love when the universe takes me by surprise. When we land, I'm getting a tattoo. Just decided. Just now. Just because. I live for that spontaneous thrill. I adore that rush of the unknown unfolding in a new and exciting way.

We landed and made our way to Scottsdale for brunch first. It was the best damn brunch I had ever had. We ordered mimosas and every bite of this meal felt holy. The bacon was so good I ordered extra "road bacon" for the trip from Scottsdale to Sedona. The waiter was cute and flirty, and I was having a ball. There I was in sunny Arizona, not a cloud in the sky, on another trip with my best friend, laughing so hard we could hardly breathe. And it had only just begun.

And, as she suspected, I stumbled into a tattoo parlor just a few doors down. The familiar buzzing brought me back to Texas, when I got my spontaneous tattoo there with a girl named Ashley I met on Instagram. And now here I am, etching another memory onto my body. This time I got a tiny lightning bolt on my left inner forearm.

"It feels like symbolism," Audri said.

"Yeah? Like what?"

"It feels like the symbol of your restoration and reclamation of your power since you left your marriage."

Oh. That was deep, but I felt that. I couldn't disagree. Sometimes we get the signs we were never looking for or asking for, and they show up right when we need them.

My favorite playlist was on and we were listening on full blast as we made our way into picturesque Sedona. Moments like this will forever be burned in my brain. Core memories being made with my best friend in real time. The way her face lit up when she smiled at me being my goofy, silly self. The way we sang and danced and laughed. The way she kind of hated always driving everywhere but she also requested it. And the four-second argument we had where we calmly dispute it after, because travel can bring out the best and worst in a person. But there was no one else I'd rather be here with than her. I'm glad my shitty ex-husband never took me. The dude would've been the ultimate buzzkill. Sometimes, a trip is best taken with your platonic soulmate. And Audri is mine.

The place we rented was gorgeous. Outside, there was a telescope for stargazing, hammocks, onsite trails for hiking, and a meditation space with prayer flags and a tiny ceramic buddha for good measure. Just to our left in plain view was the infamous Chapel of the Hill. We swore that the presence of God in this place was palpable. The vibes were immaculate, and the energy was so intense, every emotion was dialed all the way up. We couldn't stop laughing. Not just a regular laugh, the kind of deep belly laugh that sent tears streaming down our cheeks and had us crossing our legs, so we didn't pee our pants. We felt stoned, but we weren't. Well, we weren't until we were. We did stop at a dispensary, and I tried my first edible. I got so high that I started reading the birth charts of everyone we knew. I did that until I started feeling like I was inside of a spaceship, got spooked and forced myself to sleep. Edibles are not for everyone. Especially when you eat two because you didn't feel anything after the first one. Lesson learned, clearly.

AFTER VORTEX SUNRISE yoga the following morning, we made our way into town.

"Let's see an energy healer," Audri said. And so we did.

When I walked in, the woman began weeping.

"I'm sorry, this hasn't happened in over twenty years. It's just, your energy is so powerful and overwhelming, in a truly beautiful way. It's an honor to stand before you. And just so you know, these tears are not my own, I can tell they are tears of the ones who have wronged you. You have been called here to Sedona for a long time. Your ancestors are telling me they brought you here to cleanse you energetically, to break you apart and put you back together. The right way. Without cracks or missing pieces. You're finally ready now. You're ready to be the woman God intended."

The tears fell from my eyes then. I hadn't even spoken a word yet. It still brings me chills to think about. For an hour she performed an energetic surgery, removed energetic blockages, and performed a reiki healing on me and my spirit. She warned me of "the haters" coming my way and encouraged me to toughen up for when my time came to shine before the world.

"You have big dreams. And every last one of them is coming true. Get ready."

I left feeling whole and complete. A somber calm had come over me. When Audri walked out, I could see it on her face, that she, too, had spiritually awoken to a new self. Together, we elevated to a place and from here, there was only the way forwards and upwards.

We sat on a bench in silence, soaking in the lessons and the energy. Finally, we went back home to release more tears, meditate, journal and rest. When we came back into town, Audri suggested seeing a psychic. I waited for her as she went in and after, Audri confirmed that she was indeed spot on with everything she said. It was my turn, but I opted out. There were things

I knew internally that I didn't want to hear. I had just met Thomas and I didn't want the psychic to tell me how things were going to go. Deep down, I felt like I already knew. I wanted to bask in the present and enjoy the unknown ride ahead. That's what life is all about.

Maybe you might not believe in practices like this, maybe there's nothing to it. Or maybe there is. I was starting to believe there was, after communicating with the psychic medium on my birthday. She knew I was moving before I did. She also predicted that when I met the man I'd end up with, the number 8 would be significant. That he would have brown eyes, brown hair, and a beard. He would be an observer yet playful with a childlike energy. Very intelligent and have an easy smile. She also mentioned he would have a G in his last name. Oddly enough, that sounded like Will. Whole Foods man himself. Eight-year age gap. G smackdab in his last name. Easy smile. Intelligent. Playful. Young. Brown eyes, brown hair, beard. They say when you know, you know. Well, I had that feeling. But I fought it. I didn't want it in the way it showed up. I hoped I'd meet someone on the 8th month, or the 8th day, or even 8 weeks after talking to her. I never expected it to be someone 8 years younger.

Since signs were abundant for me, I decided to ask the universe for another one. I asked to see a sign of a shooting star if I had already met my soulmate while I was in Sedona. I asked for it to be so clear and obvious that Audri and I would both see it. We saw a shooting star less than twenty minutes later and thought for sure we were seeing things. It wasn't *that* obvious, we said. After all, we had just taken an edible or two. Nothing could be trusted. Then, on the way to the airport home before sunrise, we saw another one and looked at each other, because we knew. I had my sign. But who was it?

# Never Settle

I HAVE THIS new confidence within me now that knows no matter what, I will never settle in a relationship with a man ever again. If being single for over a year taught me anything, it taught me that there will always be a young, hot, DTF man with abs and a few spare inches that will pick me up in a cocktail dress and take me out to treat me like a princess for a night if my man won't. It doesn't matter if I am divorced, have children or if I'm in my 30's, 40's or 50's, there will always be a man who wants to if your man won't. It doesn't matter if you've had children, if you think your mom pouch or your tiger stripes aren't sexy, because I am willing to put money down that there is a young hot man that thinks you're a smoke show. He will take you just as you are. And not only that, he is also willing and eager to please you, spoil you and impress you, ma'am. Karma, as I've learned, is a young hot man that feeds you fresh fruit, plays with your hair and makes your body shake. Ladies—don't be afraid to remind your man if he starts forgetting your value, stops taking you out or starts getting lazy. Because if he won't, sweetheart, someone else will. In the dating world, women have thirty times the options that men have. When we're single, we could have a different man every night of the week doing things for us. It sounds lofty, but it's true. It is slim pickings out there for most men. And when he comes across a good one, it's no wonder he gets down on a knee quick. Because you are the best thing he will ever have. But women? Most of us don't know our worth. Because if we did, we wouldn't settle. Ever. And here's your reminder in case you forgot.

# Distance Makes the Heart Stop

AFTER JUST A few weeks of talking and FaceTime, Thomas booked another flight to Michigan. He had intentionally set his client meetings in Grand Rapids, just so we could spend a few days together. The plan was for me to stay with him at the hotel and when he was out of his meetings, we'd go on cute dates and spend more quality time with each other.

"My friends are super excited about this, by the way. They're really happy for me."

"That means you told them about me?" I gushed.

"Absolutely. I can't seem to stop talking about you. About us. About this."

"Really? You know I'm smiling right now, right?"

"Yes, really. I may have just sent a photo of you to my best friend and his fiancé in the group chat two hours ago. To which they replied, 'She's hot. We love this for you!'"

All signs pointed to positive in my book. This was good news.

IT WAS TIME to pack my outfits for the three days I'd have with Thomas. But unlike the anxiety I felt before picking my outfits out before my first date with Will, I felt like I was finally loving who I was and the skin I was in. I was confident with the new wardrobe I had in my closet, and even more, I felt like what I had was already good enough. Though I did buy a cute skirt and knee-high fall boots, just to elevate the date for my own pleasure.

I didn't feel like I had to dress younger, look a certain way to try and be someone I wasn't or try to impress him. Thomas was already impressed. He knew about my trauma, my baggage, my life, and he couldn't wait to catch a flight to simply hold my hand and cuddle me. We started our first date out with vulnerability, honesty, authenticity and holding absolutely nothing back. It was a beautiful foundation for a healthy relationship to flourish. The more we got to know each other, the more it made sense. We seemed perfect for each other. He was grounded and calm. He complimented my lifestyle. Our values, lifestyle and belief systems aligned. Everything seemed to somehow make sense. This was still basically a stranger, and yet, we felt like we knew each other nothing short of five years. We just made sense. So, we went with it.

At night, Thomas always played guitar for me over FaceTime and would sing me folky love songs with his smooth, smoky deep voice before I fell asleep. *This feels too good to be true,* I'd remind myself. Surely, there must be something wrong. Aside from Mason, I hadn't really felt this way about someone since meeting Will. Was it the same with either of them as it was with Will? Not exactly, but I finally felt like for once I was moving in the right direction of moving on, even if I hadn't fully recovered. I was hopeful that the heartbreak and the memories of him would all soon be distant ones. If I couldn't have the one man I wanted, I was coming to terms with that fact and accepting it. Thomas was attempting to cover the Will-sized hole in my heart and this time I wasn't going to stop him. It felt nice to have a connection with someone again.

I PICKED THOMAS up from the airport and jumped in his arms at arrivals. Something about being in his big strong arms just felt right at that moment. We made our way to the hotel and when we got in, he poured us two glasses of red wine and we talked as he rubbed my feet. He told me about his dad's brain tumor and the family issues he was having. Together, we had built deep intimacy and an emotional connection that I didn't think I'd find with someone else other than the one I had with Mason. And when we were physically intimate, Thomas was slow, gentle, and intentional. He made love to me and would pleasure me repeatedly. We hardly left bed and we rarely wore clothes the entire time.

"Yeah, it's fun having sex with a hot girl. But it's even more fun to bring her pleasure."

And that he did.

In the morning, I'd roll over and Thomas would immediately find himself inside of me. It was a magnetic sexual attraction. Our bodies were big fans of each other. From there, we'd find ourselves in the shower together. Thomas, being 6'4, would playfully adjust the shower head and splash me. He was cute, fun, and funny. *I could get used to this.* He looked at me then.

"Can I wash you?"

I gave him a soft smile and nodded.

He took the washcloth and sudded it up before slowly tracing it over my body. His touch was delicate and safe. With Thomas, I felt safe in every way. He got on his knees then and washed my feet. Thomas was adoring me and my body in one of the most beautiful ways I'd ever experienced. This was an act I'd read about in romance books, and I'd seen in rom-coms, but here he was, on his knees taking care of me in real life.

"Can I wash your hair?" I asked him. Water flowed down his body face as he looked up at me and nodded.

I lathered shampoo in my palms and massaged it into his scalp. He leaned his body and head into my stomach and wrapped his arms around me. At this moment, I was adoring him right back. Showing the most pure, gentle, and loving affection for him in return. If I'm honest, this moment between us was so beautiful it almost brought me to tears. How could two strangers connect like this? I found myself feeling my heart open for him in that hotel shower. Maybe Thomas was the person I'd been praying for.

Later that afternoon, I met up with my Audri while Thomas was in his meetings since she also lived in Grand Rapids. We had lunch together and I gushed all about him. And the sex. Clearly, I had a post-orgasmic glow all over my face.

"I love this for you," she said. "I will say though. I had the weirdest dream the other night about you. You were at my house and Will was calling you about car insurance rates and asking which one you preferred. You guys were married in my dream. It was so odd, but it felt so real."

Funny for her to mention him because she had sort of hated him this whole time. In the car on my way to Audri's, I asked God to deliver a sign about Thomas. If he wasn't it, I asked Him to let it be obvious and clear. I needed to know because I couldn't take another "almost relationship." I was ready for the real deal, and I wasn't settling for anything less. Before I left Audri's we made plans for her husband, Thomas, and I to have a double date.

"You know hubs is not thrilled about going, but hey, we'll make the most of it," she joked. But I knew it was true. Why would a prestigious doctor and father or two in his 30s want to waste a night out with a loose cannon of a single woman casually dating a 26-year-old? It seemed like it was going to be an epic fail. Until it wasn't. Until Thomas and my best friend's husband really hit it off. We had the best night on our double date. Thomas mentioned seeing them again in the future and us planning trips together. I could see it then. Thomas moving to Grand Rapids and us being together.

Everything was great until when we got back to the hotel room, my cremation necklace with Wil's ashes that his grandmother gave me fell off my neck. My jaw dropped and so did Thomas'. It didn't make sense, it had never done that before. It was screwed on tight and the only way it could've fallen off is to literally unscrew it. How it fell off is a mystery, but when I saw it, I knew. Wil was communicating with me. I asked for a sign about him hours before, and I got it. This was not my man, and Wil showed me immediately. And even though everything was seemingly going well and felt promising, there were other subtle signs that maybe Thomas wouldn't be it. Like when I'd talk about my kids, he'd change the subject. And when we would walk together, he would walk ahead of me. Research shows that when a man sees you as a romantic match, he matches your pace. Thomas didn't. He raced ahead of me everywhere. Crossed the street without me. Just like my ex-husband. I knew it wouldn't be long before this was over. And I was right. A few days later we ended it, for all the reasons I thought.

"Thomas, I like you. But I have to be honest. I'm in my intentional dating era and I cannot do another situationship. If you don't honestly see this going anywhere, please tell me."

"Wow, I really did not want to have this conversation," he said admittedly. His voice choked. And that was when I knew.

"This is really hard for me to say, because you are an amazing person. You're beautiful and I adore so many things about you and love how I feel when we talk and when we're together. But I have to be honest, I have tried other long-distance relationships and they just don't work well for me. I wouldn't be able to move to Michigan for at least another year and that makes it a challenge as it is. And also, as amazing as your kids sound, I think being a father is one of the most impossible jobs on the planet. And while I'm excited to someday have the opportunity, I know it's not the journey I'm ready for at this very moment."

"I see." I swallowed down a few tears.

"I hate this because usually when a relationship ends, it feels like it's supposed to. But Brittany, this doesn't feel right at all. This doesn't feel like a natural ending. I don't want us to stop, but if I'm honoring and respecting you, that's exactly what we should do. But believe me when I say, I hate this. I will miss you. And I want nothing but the best for you. And I wish so badly that it could've been me for you."

So, I turned the Thomas chapter closed and accepted my fate. Even if I still didn't fully know what that fate was yet.

# An Open Love Letter to Men

I REALIZE AS I am writing this, that every man that has been in my life to date has wildly disappointed me. In that disappointment, I still have not lost hope. To the outside world, I should probably give up already. I should've stayed angry at men, believed all the patterns I'd been shown, and I should've sworn them all off by now. I should've agreed with the logic that all men are terrible, and they always let me down. Instead, I decided to test a new theory. What if I changed my lens? What if I decided that all men didn't suck? What if my past experiences were only because I didn't yet know how to identify a safe man because I hadn't yet experienced one, not because they didn't exist?

Just because I've never tasted New York Style Pizza or seen the Egyptian pyramids doesn't mean they aren't real. What would happen if I opened myself up to the possibility that they do exist? There are good men, and not just a few rare ones. What if I opened myself up to the possibility the universe has many and they're in plain sight? What if I changed the way I viewed men? If, instead of searching for red flags for how they are going to fail me, like the rest of them did, that I look for the green flags instead. What if I decided to appreciate and love men for all that they are? What would happen if I respected men and found them deeply loveable down to their core?

It was an experiment. When I made that shift, I began to radically appreciate the wonderful things about them. Like, the way the good ones have the innate desire to provide for their loved ones and keep them safe. How they can solve problems seemingly without effort. How their bodies are built naturally stronger than mine, but when I see a gentleman holding space for my emotions, it's magic. I remained open to receive the divine gifts a good man had to offer. To be in love with the masculine energy that is a "real man." To see men as beautiful and safe beings of light and love. Even if I never experienced it in its full expression, I had received many glimmers of it.

When Mason was visiting, he saw small problems in my home and fixed them with ease. He took me to Home Depot to buy my first set of tools. He hammered in rogue nails, hung up a couple sets of blinds for me and built my fire pit. When we walked, he walked on the right side of the sidewalk to keep me safe, and he walked at my pace. He wiped tears he didn't cause, and he held space for my emotions. When I suggested therapy for his grief, he booked his own appointment and he began to go religiously every week. He listened and really heard me. He saw my flaws and loved them anyway. He wanted to be a better person for his own growth and healing, but also to be better for others. Mason showed me many glimmers, and, in many ways, he set a standard for what I know I deserve.

Thomas showed me the depth of a man. He showed me how a man can be emotionally deep, spiritually connected, mentally strong and physically in sync with a person. Thomas was a close glimmer that what I desire is out there, that there is a man who fires me up on all four cylinders, even if he wasn't mine to keep. He showed me men can be smart and strong, yet soft and romantic when they need to. A man could be playful and fun, but also driven and focused. That a man can hold you in his arms when you're broken, with his warm and tender heart, and he can help heal you. My problems seemed to melt away when the man had good and honest energy. Thomas did and that gave me hope.

If Will was a glimmer, if that's all that he was, he showed me the true longing of my soul. He was the archetype almost exactly of the man I wanted, the avatar of my dream man. But he was also a mirror of all my flaws and all of my strengths. He held a mirror to everything I loved and everything I hated about myself. He triggered me into becoming my best self. He inspired me to think deeper, to work harder, to raise the bar and raise my standards. He showed me that it's okay to transform repeatedly. That I am still "growing up" and evolving into who I'm really meant to be. He showed me fate, divine timing, and spirituality in a way I never thought I'd experience. If there was such a thing as a soulmate or twin flame, Will showed me that he was one of mine. Even if I couldn't explain why. Maybe you don't keep a soulmate or a twin flame, but they do teach you lessons to carry with you for a lifetime and beyond. I will carry his with me for just as long.

As a mother of sons, I have had to take a very close look at masculinity and men. From birth to toddlerhood and into adolescence. I've seen men and their inner child. I've seen their core desires. I've seen their needs. I've seen their struggles. I've seen the pressure the world puts on them to be superhuman and how their biology triggers specific reactions out of them, some better and some for the worst. Some of these are innately beautiful. I chose to focus on those qualities of masculinity.

For me to attract a good man, I knew it started first within the wounded little girl living inside of me. Shifting the narrative that, because men have hurt me, that all men will hurt me. I decided to unsubscribe to that narrative and trust that what is meant for me will find me, but it will never find me if I have an attitude of lack and negativity. If we are a magnet for our desires, then I needed to learn how to heal the hurt little girl, heal my masculine wounds to become a match for the man I was calling in. If I wanted a healthy, safe, and healed man, I had to find emotional health, safety and healing within myself. Once I realized that the quality of men I was attracting had more to do with the work I was avoiding internally, everything else made more sense. I stopped being the victim to my circumstances and became my own knight in shining armor. No one's coming to save you. We must do the saving first. And once we do, that knight has better odds of appearing.

## One Year of Will

NOT EVERYONE FOLLOWS the phases of the moon, but I do. Maybe it's my red flag, my toxic trait, but I find astrology to be wildly interesting. I did go to space camp as a kid, what do you expect? I'm an intergalactic woman that is deeply connected to the stars. When I tell you the energy around eclipse season was intense, I mean it. For those who believe or follow astrology, the eclipses are symbolic and energetic transmissions into new timelines. They are a time of destiny and fated connections. They're a time of people and things either being making their way into your life or being phased out. You trust who and whatever was phased out was meant to fade away out of your life for a divine reason. Those who make their way in? There's some "meant to be" aspect to that energy.

Even though we hadn't talked in a while, I was feeling Will's energy so intensely. I even had to call my friend Natalia to talk to her about it.

"I just can't shake this connection with him, No one else compares. I feel his energy even when he's not around." When we hung up, I found myself on my knees, begging God again for a sign. I needed to know what to do. *What was the point of him? What did any of this mean? What do I do with the feelings I have for him?* I needed to know if he was supposed to be in my life or not. Or if I was supposed to move on for good. We'd always found our way back. But why? Within twenty minutes of that prayer, he texted me. As if I wasn't feeling confused enough.

**Me:** *I knew you would text me, today.*

**Will:** *You're a sorceress.*

**Me:** *That's old news.*

**Me:** *I have an idea.*

**Will:** *What?*

**Me:** *Come over*

**Will:** *Ahh… is that a good idea?*

Was it my best idea that I've ever had? No. But I was still craving him. If there's something I knew about him by now, he couldn't say no to me either. We were each other's weakness.

He showed up after dark, as always. He made himself cozy on my couch and I sat there next to him, burning alive from our sexual chemistry. There was always this push and pull energy. This tension we liked to build. Usually, it was both of us acting aloof as if we were not about to ruin each other's bodies. It was this sense of hiding the animalistic urge to consume each other wholly and completely that made it exciting. Sometimes it felt as though our desire for each other was so intense, it was almost awkward, because how can you act normal when you crave the taste of the person sitting next to you? The eye contact was piercing, and everything buzzed around me when he was by my side. And it didn't take long for our bodies to connect in other ways. Before you know it, Will made his way inside of me. This time, he made it clear that we were making love. He was intentional, slow, passionate. His eyes were locked with mine, and before each new stroke, his lips parted as he moaned out soft hums of pleasure. While our eyes were locked, that euphoric feeling took over. A full body cosmic bliss. I could see it in his eyes, he felt it, too.

A whisper escaped my mouth. "This…is different." I said,

staring into his soul.

He was softly crashing into my entire existence, and time and space and reality melted into the background. In this moment, we were in another dimension.

"You're trouble," he said, trying not to lose control while he was inside of me. I could tell he was feeling the euphoria, too. It was a feeling I could hardly describe because I'd only ever felt it with him, and it felt almost too holy to speak about.

"I want to come together like we did that one time."

He remembered. We had felt this before. While he would often avoid this tantric sex with me sometimes for the sake of avoiding deeper feelings and vulnerability, it was clear that all bets were off. He wanted all of me, which included rubbing his soul against mine. This feeling we created together was magic and it was only accessible with each other. No one else could replicate this feeling. I was confident in that. Whether we ever wanted to admit it, there was some sort of energetic continuum that existed when we were together.

Afterwards, Will surprised me. He also was … different. He was gentle and attentive in all the ways he was in the beginning. In the ways that made fall for him. Instead of pushing me away for space, he stayed to snuggle. He reached for deeper connection and conversation. He made us warm tea, fetched me four different kinds of snacks and fed them to me while naked in bed. He fell asleep in my arms with my head on his chest and kissed me with passion. He smiled and stared into my soul. Before he left, he even took my trash out. *Who the hell is this and what happened to the Will I was trying to hate?*

This man could no longer hide his feelings. They weren't going anywhere. They were only growing stronger. Will and I always felt like fate, and it felt like fate was hitting us right in the face. It was time. Were we doing this? Would we surrender?

What would happen next? Forces outside of our control brought us together, and after a year, that continued to be the case. We couldn't seem to fight it anymore.

*Two weeks later*

THEN, HE IGNORED my text for two days and I finally broke. I just couldn't do it. I couldn't live with these feelings building anymore. I needed to finally tell him everything. No more bottling up. No more *not* sending him the text. I was ready to pour my heart out and express it all. The good, the bad, the ugly. What did I have to lose? Nothing. So, I sent him a couple of three minute voice texts.

The summary was—*you have made me feel terribly unseen, unheard and disrespected over the last year. I don't deserve it. If you care, show it. If you don't, I'm begging you to leave me alone. Either be in my life fully, add value, be here or stay away and stay out. I don't have time or room or space for half-hearted lukewarm people.*

This time he responded. Not just any response. He knew it was time to show up. He sent me paragraph after paragraph, vying for a spot still in my life. Fighting for the connection instead of throwing it away. Choosing to have the difficult conversations over ignoring it like he did in the past.

"Let's talk in person. I want to fix this."

He arrived at my house at eight P.M. on a Sunday night. He was wearing a hoodie that had a heart with boxing gloves, and a brain with boxing gloves. Slight symbolism over his head and his heart fighting. He sat on my couch and had that look in his eyes, all knowing. A look of failure and a look of surrender. He had tried as long as he could to avoid this very conversation. This very connection that kept showing up.

"You know why you're here, right?"

"Because you asked me over."

"No. Because you had a choice to show up and care about me or to not and leave me alone."

"That's true," he said, looking down and then back up at me. "Well, I'm here, aren't I?"

I nodded. "You've really hurt me, you know. I've been so mad at you."

"I know you have. I understand. But I also want to understand what you expect and what I can do to prevent this from happening again. I don't want you to be upset with me."

For two and a half hours, I shared the many ways he'd hurt me and what I needed going forward. He listened. I set boundaries. He agreed. I shared my true feelings that I kept hidden all this time. To my surprise, he confessed his, too.

"I've been scared to get closer to you and your life, unsure how to appropriately show up for you when we've been avoiding anything serious. Feelings inevitably grow and we find ourselves back at the start. In too deep and I'm afraid to get there again and we both get hurt," he said. "I don't think I'm good for you, and I don't think you're good for me."

"Really? Why? What do you mean?"

"It's not that I don't think we are compatible. Because we are."

"You think so?"

"Yes. We are extremely compatible. It's just the other things we've already talked about. I can't give you what you need, and I have certain preferences.

"Like what?"

"Brittany. You have two kids; you are divorced, and you are eight years older than me. I prefer to be with someone my age, without kids. I think that's what is best for me."

I nodded and collected myself. "And what? You think I chose

this? You think I sat down one day and prayed for a man eight years younger than me to waltz into my life and change it forever? You think I asked God for this specifically? Instead of a man my age or even a little closer to it? You think a 24-year-old that lives with his parents was on my wish list?" I laughed and shook my head.

"What is it about me then, why me? Why do you like me more than everyone else?"

"You really want to know?"

"Yes, I do."

"You sure?"

"Yes."

"I don't know, Will. I can't explain it."

"Try."

What I wanted to say, I didn't. I wanted to say that I knew it was real *because* I couldn't explain it or put it into words. *It just was.* When it's real, logic disappears and rationale is irrelevant. It's real when it's heart over head.

"Because no one looks at me the way you do, Will. No one touches me like you. No one fucks me like you. Because I don't feel *this* with anyone else." I grabbed his hands then and held them in mine.

"Explain *this* with words and not feelings."

"I can't because it's a feeling. It's a feeling I can't describe."

"Try."

He looked into my eyes, staring into my soul as he always does.

"That. You feel that?" I ran my thumb over the top of his soft hand then. "*This.* Even the way your hand feels is different. It all feels different. I have looked a million people in the eyes and not one of them sets me on fire the way that you do. This is different. You know it is."

He looked away, collecting thoughts to himself. He nodded.

"I agree. It is," he said. "Do I think you're my soulmate?"

My heart dropped as I wait for what he says next.

"Yeah," he continued. "I do."

My eyes widened.

"So, I'm not crazy?" I asked. "What I've been feeling isn't crazy? You feel the same way?"

"But," he said. "I think maybe it's just an eighty to ninety percent soulmate. Because I think my soulmate is likely my age."

"Will. I don't think you get to pick a soulmate. I mean, clearly, this thing picked us. We had no control over this. It just happened. By fate."

"I think fate isn't real. I believe in free will."

"So, running away from fate and calling it free will?" The irony in the words here were not missed by me. *Free Will. Running away.*

"I think having preferences is okay and we shouldn't settle."

"You think you'd be settling with me?"

"Not in that way. It's just… this isn't what I had planned for myself."

"Me either, Will." I found myself cradled in his arms by a force outside of my control. He held me tight.

"What do we do, then?"

"Why does it feel so much better with us?" he asked. "Do you think sex feels better with someone you love?"

"Of course, it does."

"So why does it feel so much better with us?"

I looked at him then.

"What if this is love? What if we are in love?"

"Yeah. What if it is," he wondered. "I've never been in love before. So, I don't know what it is exactly, you'd be the better judge."

"If it isn't full-blown love yet, it's definitely something. We have a very special connection. And if I'm honest, I have felt this way before. With the other Wil. And he passed away. I had my chance with him, and I didn't take it. I have to pay the bill of regret for the rest of my life." A serious gaze glossed over his face as he watched mine when I spoke his name again. My first love. The person that I didn't get to keep. The regret was painted over my face. The grief hung from my eyes. The haunted echoes of him escaped my throat.

"Do you think you're trying to re-create what you had with him, with us?"

"No. That's how I know it's real. Because I'm not trying at all. It's just happening. Just like it did with him." I looked in his eyes. "Will, I know you don't know this right now. But I've lived a little longer and I can tell you, a connection like this is rare. Rarer than you realize and understand."

He nodded. I can see it in his eyes. The fear of losing me, forever.

"We can stay in touch. It doesn't have to really end when we find someone else."

I choked back tears and swallowed them down.

"It doesn't work like that. It's not that simple. We would never see each other again. We wouldn't have *this* anymore."

"What would we do then?"

"You either let go fully and grieve it. Or you stay."

My head fell on his chest and he stroked my hair. I pulled back and looked at his face. Adoration and a look of love hung from his eyes. I ran my hands over his beard and straddled his lap. Tension built as we avoided the kiss that would set it all off again. My cheek caressed his tenderly, his warm breath covered my neck, our breathing pulled our lips together but instead of kissing, we let them linger there. Our foreheads pressed together, and his hands slid up the small of my back. He pulled me in closer. Finally, our mouths opened, and our tongues met. He drank me in, and I devoured all of him. Slowly, he pulled off my shirt, then my pants. I was wearing a red matching set to make a statement. Memorable. I didn't ever want him to forget this. Or to forget us.

"Mmm." He moaned. He slipped his fingers inside of me and opened me up.

"Let's go to your room." He carried me then. "Do you have a blindfold?'

"I have a scarf, why?"

"Get it. And the rope."

I handed him the scarf and the rope.

"Will, what do you have up your sleeve?" I said with a smirk. I was so wet I was overflowing, throbbing, aching for him.

"Come here. Get on your knees."

He blindfolded me, pressed me down on my back onto the mattress, and tied my wrists to the post of my bed.

"That shouldn't be too tight, but it might hurt if you pull your wrists too hard from the squirming."

My breathing heavied and goosebumps covered my body as I felt his lips trace up my legs, my inner thighs. I arched my back as they made their way up to my stomach, over my breasts and on my neck. He kissed me then and his tongue slid into my mouth at the same time his fingers slid into me. Blissful moans hummed from my throat. He brushed my body with the rope softly, teasing it over my nipples and down over my panties. He moved my panties to the side and began to lick me with his tongue. Just before I came, he stopped. I heard him taking off his pants, the jingle of his belt giving me every clue I needed. With his warm palm, he opened my legs and plunged himself gently into me. I instantly begin to shake. The pleasure was so overwhelming I could feel tears building up under the blindfold. My body was so full of euphoria, it didn't know what to do. I pulled my wrists tight against the post and felt his strokes building with intensity. As the energy built, his moaning escaped him more and more. "Oh my god," he said, as he forcefully pulled out and came all over my stomach. When he finished, he leaned in to kiss me and a sexy, playful laugh came out.

"Do you want to taste me?"

I nodded as he drew his dripping wet finger to my mouth.

"You taste so good," I said as he filled my mouth with his pleasure.

He removed the blindfold and the rope from my wrists and cleaned me off. He collapsed next to me, and we melted into each other as we listened to his orchestra playlist.

"This feels like a movie," he said.

"It does." It always had. Almost too perfect, too good to be true. Never felt real, but it was.

An hour passed before he was inside of me again. This time a fiery passion consumed him. Insatiable for each other, we found ourselves back in bed, back into bliss. I'd never experienced a desire for a human more. We simply could not get enough.

"What do we do now?" I asked, breathless on his bare chest. He smiled, looking into my eyes. I felt wide, pure, vulnerable, honest, open.

"We'll figure it out, okay?"

I nodded and planted a million kisses over his bearded face.

"Okay."

SOMETHING MUST'VE LANDED well, because two days later, he texted me up a storm. The night after that he hit me up after leaving the gym, and we talked for two hours on the phone.

Before we hung up, he tried nailing down plans to see me in a couple days, which would only be a week from when I saw him last. I was seeing and hearing from him more in the past week and half than I had in months. It was clear—he didn't want to mess this up. I told him to show up or get out, and he was showing up. I recalled something he said in a text before I suggested meeting up.

"We've had this conversation twice and there's something about that third time, I'm trying to avoid that at all costs." What is the age-old saying? Three strikes and you're out? That concept probably rang a very alarming bell for him. Act right or lose out on our relationship completely and totally.

It appeared that wasn't his intention this time around. I was so shocked about his new and improved behavior that I called my friends. Of course, Audri had enough of him, and she couldn't even hear the mention of his name. She had coined the term for him as Will Band-Aid. Because all he ever did was hurt me and cover up his own hurt. Usually, the Band-Aid was sex and sporadic attention, and she just wasn't buying any of it this time. The thing about Band-Aids is that you throw them out once the wound has healed. I was starting to feel foolish after all this time, but my friends Natalia and Claire seemed to still harbor some hope for him.

"Maybe he is finally coming around. Maybe this whole year helped him come to his senses and realize how great you guys are together. Maybe he just needed time to see that no one else compares. He's young, just be patient. Maybe he's changing. Maybe this is finally happening this time. Maybe everything will be different now," they said.

I agreed. Maybe it would. That Saturday night, we had an official plan. Will was taking me on a date. A real date. Exactly one year to the day when we met. It felt like a sign. This could be it for us. My heart was full and hopeful. A new beginning sounded perfect. And the timing did, too.

I put together a cute outfit I bought the week before. I had purged and donated my entire closet months ago and all my looks were fun, fresh and flirty. I slid on a royal blue and black plaid mini skirt, black bodysuit and my tall leather black platform boots. Paired it with a long black pea coat and my new Prada bag. The make-up was done for a night out, smoky eye, sheer plumping lip gloss, hair was short wavy and sassy, and of course, I felt like a million bucks. I wasn't the sad broken newly divorced single mom he met a year ago still in her Amazon.com mom underwear and nothing in her closet for a date. I wasn't that woman who was still in her cocoon waiting to spread her wings. I was a full-grown butterfly with sparkly wings, and a sexy mini skirt. I was a brand-new woman, with style and poise. I looked different. Felt different. Acted differently. I was stronger, more confident than that woman he met at the grocery store. I was better all-around. Emotionally. Spiritually. Physically. And mentally. I had put in the work, and I could literally see and feel the evolution I had made over the last year. No more miss nice girl. I had boundaries in place and a voice, and I was going to use it.

Two days before this, I slid in this guy's DMs, not realizing who he was. I saw a video of him on my explore page and dropped a quick line to shoot my shot. Shortly after I messaged him, I scrolled through his page and realized, *"Holy shit, this guy is famous! There's no way he will respond."* I shook my head and even laughed at myself to my friends for being so bold. I sent them his profile and said, "Just shot my shot with this guy. But JK, he's famous." Five minutes later, he replied to my message. Not only did he reply, he replied with his number and said to reach out when I was in town. *You've got to be fucking kidding me.* I FaceTimed my besties right away. HE GAVE ME HIS NUM-

BER! I couldn't believe it. He is a very well-known reality tv star and was a former NFL player. This couldn't be real. I decided to text him, just to see if he was being nice. When he replied to my text, I nearly collapsed.

On FaceTime with Claire, I did several victory laps in my backyard. HE TEXTED ME BACK! I HAVE A FAMOUS DUDE'S NUMBER!

"Hell yeah you do," she said. "And all the guys who fumbled you are going to feel so dumb when they hear about this." No pun intended with the NFL reference.

> **Audri:** Dude, what if you end up in paparazzi pics with him. This is no joke. He's always in the press. Can you imagine?

For a moment I pictured it. Me, fanning away the paparazzi while out being out to lunch with my handsome celebrity date. Hours before his text, I was just a single mom still in pajamas at three P.M. with a messy bun and unwashed hair. A year ago, I was the saddest woman I'd ever been. If you would've told me this was going to be my life this time last year when I was face down on my bedroom floor sobbing into the carpet, I wouldn't have believed you. But again, here I was, surprised and in awe of this new life. This life I was terrified of leaping into but was now happily soaring through.

> **Me:** I don't know if this will ever turn into anything romantic or turn into anything at all, but it gave me the confidence to kick a door down and French kiss the pope.

Audi and I both laughed, but it was true. I was confident. Confident that what was meant for me wouldn't miss me. I didn't know much of anything at this point. Everything was uncertain, but I was fully surrendering. I was exactly where I needed to be.

WILL SHOWED UP around eight P.M. for our date. He was wearing the same jacket he wore on the day we met, like I wouldn't notice. I noticed immediately. If I pointed it out, he would pretend like he didn't plan it, but by now I knew him too well. Deep down, he was a romantic softy and it was one of things I loved most about him. This move was intentional like so many of his other moves that he played off. He walked in and I realized I forgot something in my room.

"Wait a minute, I need something." When I walk back, I noticed a huge spider on the wall that made me scream and jump back.

"Holy shit!"

"What is it?" he asked, rushing to the scene.

"A spider. Can you save me?"

He laughed. "I can, but what if I crush it and a million babies come out and lay eggs all over your house."

"Will! Oh my god, don't say that! Please just kill it."

"Here, I got him," he said. "And I'll flush it, so no baby spiders get you, either."

"You saved my life. You're my hero. Thank you."

"Apparently you needed me around today for a variety of reasons. Do you have a lint roller?" he asked.

"No. I lost it in the divorce," I joked, but it was kind of true. I was pretty sure that was something I didn't realize I needed and left with my ex.

"Do you have tape? You have lint all over your jacket. I can't let you leave with your coat like that."

"Tape? Why?"

"Just hand me tape. Watch." I handed him a roll of tape. He wrapped it around his hand so the sticky part was on the outside.

"Come here," he said. I walked towards him. He patted my coat with his hand gently.

Down my arms, the back, and the front. He spun me around, looked at me and smirked proudly.

"There. All better now."

"That was actually genius. And super cute, by the way. Thank you." I looked at him and smiled back. Glimpses of his soft side kept me holding on for dear life. I knew there was a good boyfriend hiding somewhere. Every now and then, I saw it. When I did, my heart checked into the hopeful romantic hotel.

"Ready to go?" he asked.

I nodded and we headed out of the house.

He walked to the car and let himself in. I stood outside of the passenger door. He looked at me before popping back out.

"Everything okay?" he asked.

"You know, every man I've been on a date with has opened my car door for me. Every single one but you." All the time apart had me spoiled by the reality that there were good men out there. And the good men opened the car door for me before a date.

"I guess I didn't realize. It's not something I ever really do. Most of the time I'm meeting girls for dates at the place. I rarely pick anyone up." The ick shook through me. I hated imagining him on dates with other girls. I couldn't stand the thought of him with someone else.

"You're absolutely right, though. I should open the door for you." He got out and opened my door.

"Watch all extremities, ma'am."

"Gee, thanks. Way to make it weird, Will." I laughed.

"What?" he smiled, but deep down he knew I was no longer accepting anything average. What I realized this year as a single woman was that you teach people how to treat you, by what you do and do not accept. I decided that I was no longer accepting anything less than queen treatment from men. That included Will. My value had gone up over the last year, with tax and interest. The most dangerous woman to a man is a woman who knows her worth. I could tell he sensed this within me. A good woman and an easy woman are not the same woman. I was no longer easy to catch, or easy to keep. I was a dangerous woman now.

WE GOT TO the fancy cocktail bar in Birmingham, ironically the city he wanted to take me for our first date. I thought again about my evolution. When he first invited me to a date on this fancy side of town a year ago, not only did I not feel like I'd fit in, but I never would've imagined I'd live there a year later. Life was showing me a full circle moment in more than one way and it was hard to miss the signs.

At the modern upscale bar, we sat together. Designer furniture, plush velvet sofas, ornate light fixtures and elegant architecture set the scene. For a moment, it felt as though I was getting my wish come true. That I was getting him back. That we had made it back to "us" again. The silly, the sexy, the deeply connected us I'd missed and longed for this whole time.

"You know," he said, taking a sip from his water, "All this time I'd found a million reasons why this could never work. But when we're out together, and I can just relax and be myself, and everything flows and feels easy and natural with us. I can see how it actually could work."

I tried my best to hide my feelings, but my whole body melted.

"I know, this is what I've been saying all along. We are different. This *is* different."

"You haven't noticed this, but all the guys in this place have been checking you out."

"You're right. I'm just loving being here with you." I smiled then. "They aren't my type anyway."

"Yeah? What is your type?" he asked.

"You." I looked into his eyes. He looked back at me. I said it again. "You are."

He laughed and fought a smile. "I'm serious though, what do you look for in a guy. Like, appearance wise. What do you find attractive?"

"You."

He smiled and his eyes softened. "Okay, but what about other people? Other guys?"

"Someone who looks like you." I said. "I'm looking for you in everyone."

My hand made its way to his thigh, like old times, without effort. "Sorry, I didn't realize I was touching you like that. I can stop."

"No, no. It's okay."

I knew we weren't fully sure of where we were and it was unclear where we were going.

"I don't want to make it awkward. My body is just drawn to yours in such a way. Like a magnet or something."

"It's always been that way, though. Almost for a whole year."

He remembered.

"Yeah, almost to the day. You know, I know the date we met because I wrote about you in my journal that day."

"You did?" he aseds in shock. "What was the date?"

"November 21st."

"Man. What a year," he said, shaking his head in disbelief.

"What a year is right. It was supposed to be a one-night thing. But here we are."

The rest of the night he told me how terrible it had been trying to date, especially women his age. All of me died when I pictured him giving them the attention I painfully desired, on the dates in cute places that I would've given anything for, him putting his best foot forward, trying to do the most to impress anyone else but me. Him, doing all the right things for the wrong people. I thought back to the sunset photo I wanted and never got. And how easily it was for him to give that to someone else, someone who didn't want him. Someone who rejected him. Someone he fought for. That was never me. It was never me.

"These girls don't get it. They see you as just an option. A person on a huge waiting list, so easy to replace. No one really wants to genuinely *date* anymore. There's such a false sense of having so many options, no one wants to pick one anymore like they used to."

If he wasn't calling the kettle black right now, I didn't know what else he was doing. This felt so tone deaf I could hardly stand it.

"Is that right?" I said with noticeable sarcasm. Knowing he'd used me as a placeholder due to a sense of having so many options, that he could just find someone else, anyone else but the girl in front of him. The girl he didn't want because I wasn't the one that met his preferences.

You could lead a blind horse to water, but you can't make him drink. It didn't matter how many times I tried to get him to see what was in front of him, he wouldn't see it if he didn't want to see it. And so far, he hadn't.

"It's not like it was when you met your ex-husband. Whom you likely met in person organically before dating apps. It's rare to run into someone in a natural setting and meet them in person."

My face drew a blank. My eyes and voice lowered. "We met in person, Will." I shook my head then. I couldn't hide the frustration about his blatant ignorance.

"I know. That's super rare. It just doesn't really happen like that anymore."

It felt like screaming into the ear of someone who was asleep but refusing to wake up. I wish so badly he knew how this made me feel inside. The bitterness was building. And the fog was lifting. Maybe it'd been clear this whole time, but I couldn't see it. It was never me for him even if it was always him for me. He didn't want me how I wanted him.

Nevertheless, the connection still burned bright through the rest of the night. The chemistry was alive and clearly, we were still compatible. As always, we talked and talked and talked. Big talk, about our dreams.

"You know, I have been sitting on a few ideas for a while. I think we'd make great business partners."

"Oh really?"

"Yeah, I do actually."

"You don't find me... or the work I do... off-putting?" My ex-husband had made me feel so foolish for having a social media platform, for sharing content, for the creative work I did. It behooved me to feel a shred of his approval, let alone acceptance and the potential for collaboration from someone else, let alone a man. And not just any man, the man I desired over anyone else.

He knit his brows together and looked at me confused.

"Why would I find you or your work off-putting?"

I shrugged, knowing why but not willing to say it out loud.

"I think the work you do is really cool, and I admire what you've built for yourself. I have some content ideas for you. We could even work on things together. I could podcast with you on your show. We could riff. And I think we could make money together pretty easily and think we'd be a great team."

Could someone shake him for me? Could someone wake this man up? He saw the potential of us, it was obvious. And it was clear, he wanted me in his life. Likely long term if he wanted to be in business with me, but maybe not in the ways I was seeking. I entertained the idea and I pictured it. Being a power couple without being a couple. Having him in every way other than the very way I wanted. To be mine. All mine. He wanted to be half invested in my life and halfway out the door just in case. He didn't want to leave it fully, but he also didn't make it obvious in what capacity wanted to stay, just that he wanted to. Sometimes he'd say friends, other times he'd say we were romantically connected. As each month passed, confusion continued to grow.

"You want to do business with me? And what do we say? Who are you to me?"

"I'm… Whole Foods Man. Your followers know who I am. They probably remember the photos of us from the beginning of the year when you shared me to your stories." He was right. They did and they still asked about him. He was the only guy I shared about so far. "We can even talk about dating, how we met, all kinds of things."

"So, you want people to know who you are?"

"Yeah, why not? You can show my face in the video, say my full name. I'm fine with it."

"But won't that ruin your dating prospects. What if other girls stumble upon our content or listen to our podcast episode?"

He shrugged. "I don't know. I guess I'd cross that bridge when it came."

"Fascinating. And what if we crush it together? Then what."

"I'll spoil you with something to celebrate. Maybe a new bag. Girls like bags."

"We do. This is true. This is also super random, Will. We go from not talking, to talking again, to you wanting to do business together. You're a wild card."

"I am," he said. He looked at the time on his phone, then leaned into me and lowers his voice and whispers a seductive, suggestive tone. "It's getting late. And I think if we want to do what we do best and have enough time to make it count, we should probably head back to your house soon." He looked into my eyes then and bit his lip a little. "Yeah? Do you want that?"

A surge of heat pulsed below. *Fuck.*

"Of course I do."

I couldn't help but think about how sexy we looked together. I uncrossed my legs and his hand rested on my bare knee. There was nothing more I loved than PDA and flirting at a sexy cocktail bar. Especially with him.

Will headed to pay the bill and on the way up to the waitress, a well-dressed man stopped me.

"Miss, I saw you across the bar. There's something radiant about you. You stand out from the crowd. And look, I'm married." He shows me the gold band around his finger. "This isn't me being disrespectful. I just thought you needed to know. You are a beautiful woman; you carry yourself very well and you look chic in that outfit." He shook my hand and asked for my name.

Just then, Will walked up.

"Oh, are you two together?" he asked.

I looked at Will then. "Yes. This is my boyfriend." I don't know why I said it, but I did. He didn't object.

The man reached his hand out to Will to shake. "Wow, you are a lucky man. Look at her. She is stunning. You have a good woman right here."

We walked out of the bar together.

"That's the first time you've ever called me that. Boyfriend."

"Yeah, well. It just slipped out. I don't know." I shrugged it off. Just then, I remembered how Thomas didn't match my pace when we were walking. I recalled every time I was with my ex-husband, he never matched my paced either, even from the beginning. He'd always walked ahead of me. Every other man I'd been dating over the past year didn't match my walking pace, either But Will? He did, and he did it from the very beginning and every time after, and I noticed he was doing it now. I tried to trip him up to see if maybe it was a coincidence. As I started walking faster, so did he. When I slowed down, he did, too. The ultimate test was seeing how we'd cross the street. Would he fly right on by without me like Thomas and the others did? Or would he hold out his arm and guide me across as he always did. The thing is, I wanted a reason to not like him anymore. I wanted him to fail these little tests so I could validate that he didn't have feelings for me romantically and that it was over. But as we we were about to cross the street, he extended his arm out for me to hold, keeping me safe while matching my every step. *Damn it. Damn you, science.* And when we got to the car, he opened my door for me, remembering about how I'd asked for him to do that before.

When we got into my house, he propped me up on the kitchen counter. He opened my legs and I wrapped them around his waist. He pulled my body into his and kissed me as if he'd waited centuries to press his lips on mine. And when he did, all of me surrendered into him. His hand squeezed into my thigh as he breathed me in deeper and deeper. My head fell back.

"Give me that neck," he said. Will devoured me always in all ways. He unzipped my skirt and slid it down to the kitchen floor, I wrapped my legs around his waist again and my arms around my neck. He lifted me up and carried me to my bed.

"Do you still have that glass dildo you told me about?"

"I do. Why?" I asked as he slid off my panties.

"Because I'm going to need it. I've been thinking about using it on you as I go down on you all week."

I opened the drawer next to my bed and handed it to him.

"Lay back and relax," he said. I inhaled and exhaled deeply. My body melted into my mattress as he did what he did best with his mouth. Slowly he drew it in and out of me as his tongue pressed against my holy spots. My body arched in euphoric bliss as he sent me over the edge. I covered my face with my pillow and moan out screams of pleasure as I climaxed. When he was finished, he removed the rest of his clothes and pushed himself inside of me, to give me more and to take all of me. As we were intimate, thoughts entered my head of him with other women. A jealousy consumed me and suddenly I felt my body tense and tighten. So much so, that him being inside of me nearly hurt for the first time ever.

"Can we stop for a second?"

He stopped. "What's wrong? Are you okay?"

"I don't know. I'm just... in my head." I adjusted my body and looked at him. "Can you tell me something?" I asked.

"Yes, what?" His face softened.

"Can you tell me I'm safe? I need to know that right now because my body and mind are feeling disconnected and I'm not able to be in the moment right now."

He nodded. "It's okay, you can relax." He leaned in to kiss me as I put him back inside of me.

"I've got you," he whispered in my ear as he flipped me over gently to my stomach. "It's okay, I've got you." My body and my mind unwound with his voice, reassuring and kind. We made love and it was as beautiful as it always was. I felt him in my soul. I felt him everywhere.

Afterwards, he made us tea and brought snacks to bed. We threw popcorn in each other's mouth playfully, still naked. Then, we ended up where we always do. Lying together in each other's arms, snuggled up tight. Laughing, kissing, and listening to music. Not once in the year I'd known him did we ever need to turn the TV on. We never had to. We were so wrapped up into each other's presence, that was always amusing enough.

"Okay, one more Frank Ocean song and I'm leaving."

I looked at the time. "It's three A.M. Why not just stay the night?"

"I thought we've been over this. I can't stay. You know that. It complicates everything."

"But you also said you wanted to."

"But I won't."

"Ever? As in *never*?" I asked.

"Ever as in forever."

"Forever? Will, that's a long time… do you mean that?"

"Yes. Never ever. Forever."

I got up then and put my clothes on quickly. I felt naked in every way and the feeling was unbearable.

"Yeah, you should leave."

"Well, I can wait for the song to end. And maybe another one after that."

"Not necessary. Just go."

"What's happening?" he asked.

"Will, I want you to stay. You know that. And you never do. And it's disappointing. It makes me sad."

"Are we doing this again?" he asked.

I walked into the kitchen to get some water. He followed.

I sat in the barstool chair as he faced me across the counter.

"Will, I thought things would be different. I don't know why it has to be this way. Is it because you're worried about what other people will think?"

"No. I'm worried about the thoughts in my head and those voices and what I think. And what I think is that I don't want this. I still don't want to be with you."

"Ever? Not just right now… but ever?"

"Ever," he said quickly. It cut deeply on the way out. I could feel this word ripping me apart.

"Ever. Wow." I said, the words choking me. "I guess all this time I thought maybe you were fighting feelings for me, but were afraid to follow them. But I guess…" I swallowed the lump collecting in my throat. "I guess I was wrong."

"I see that. This has happened before. You thought something that wasn't really happening. I told you from the beginning, I didn't want a relationship with you, and I still don't. And I never will."

"So, I've been living in a fantasy land in my head since then. None of this was real?"

He stared at me.

"I don't know what you want me to say. I don't want to be with you. But I don't want to be without you. Can't we find some way to stay in each other's lives?"

"So what? You can have your cake and eat it, too?" I said, shaking my head. "No thanks, this has hurt long enough."

"It's not even the age thing as it is the fact that you have kids," he said.

This came as a shock, in the way he'd always seemed to admire my role as a mother and expressed concern and interest in my kids, maybe I saw things differently in my head. Though in hindsight, I guess it's not a surprise.

"I'm not ready to be a stepdad."

"You wouldn't have to be until you felt ready. We could take our time easing into the bigger things. It could just be us, like it has, for a while. If and when the time comes."

"What happens when it comes? All of a sudden, I go from zero kids to having two. My fatherhood experience wouldn't be what I always imagined for myself. I'd jump right into a situation helping you raise them. And for one, I'm not ready for that at this age. And two, I don't know if I ever want to be a stepfather, period. Again, it's not something I wanted for myself. And I just can't picture it."

"Maybe you could've *asked me* what I pictured for that role. They *have* a father, what they *don't have* is a good example of a good man. They don't have an example of what love between two people looks like, an example of how a man treats a woman." I swallowed down the building tears. "My oldest looked at me a month or so ago and said, 'Mom, I think I want you to find someone in the way that dad found his girlfriend. Because what happens if you're sick and I'm not there to take care of you. You're all alone, you need someone.'" A tear fell onto my cheek.

"He's right, Will. I do want someone to eventually help take care of me. I want a partner in this life to care about me. And I want to take care of him, too."

His eyes fill with wetness, but he swallowed and looked away.

"Will. What about what I'm saying makes you sad? I can see you feeling emotional."

"I'm not. I'm holding back a yawn and it's making my eyes water, I'm tired."

"Will. It's okay to have feelings. I'm not going to judge you. I just want to know how you're feeling."

He cleared his throat. "I'm fine. I'm just having a hard time hearing that."

"Why?"

"Because your kids deserve a good stepdad. And I know they're amazing kids because they're yours. But they aren't mine. What if they never felt like mine?"

"Maybe they would eventually. Especially if you loved me. You'd love everything that came along with me. Including them. That's just how it goes."

"But I'm not in love."

"You haven't given us a fair chance at it. You haven't even allowed us to fall in love. We've always stopped it right before it happened. Things would be different if we just let the love part happen. Naturally. Instead of fighting it."

"I'm not fighting it. I'm making a choice. I'm choosing not to. Because I can't. I don't want to."

"Okay." I said. "I hear you loud and clear. That's the last of it from me, Will. I'm not convincing you anymore to see what I see. You don't. And I won't beg for you to see it. I believe you. You say you don't want me; I believe you. It took me a year to believe you, but I do now. And that's okay. I accept it."

"Well, wait a minute. Because I do want you. I want you in my life."

"Not a good idea, Will."

"Why? Who says? Who says we can't stay friends?"

"Friends?" I laughed, but all I wanted to do was cry. "We've never been friends and we never will. You know this."

"So what, you're just disposing me. Discarding me? Like I never existed?"

"I never said that. That's not what's happening here."

"Then don't cut me out of your life."

I looked at the time. Somehow two hours had passed while we talked. It was clear to me that he wanted to fight for me, that he didn't want me to leave his life, but he was not doing enough to make me stay.

"Will. I can't keep you in it."

"Why?" his eyes filled again.

"Because as long as I see that face, as long as you're around, you will always be my first choice. You will always be the one I want. And I don't want just *part* of you. I want all of you. And I will always want all of you. I will never be satisfied with anything less. I will always want you, Will. And keeping you around would ruin me even more than it already has." I looked away. "When I met you at Whole Foods, I was figuratively starving. And when I saw you, I saw the most beautiful cake. Decorated exactly the way I'd imagined. It looked too good to be true. And then I got the try the frosting and it was delicious. And eventually, I tried crumbs of it. And it was instantly my favorite flavor. And anytime I was around this cake, I wanted more. I wanted the whole damn thing, but sometimes I'd tell myself I'd be happy with even a little slice. And I waited and waited an entire year for even a slice, and it never came. So, I tried other cakes, some cakes gave me big slices right away, and some gave me the whole thing in one sitting. But none of them tasted like the one I got at Whole Foods. None of them were you. And all I want is you. I want that entire cake to myself. And I don't want to share, okay? I want it all to myself. I don't want to share you anymore. I never wanted to, and I still don't. So, I'm sorry. But I can't settle for crumbs when I'm still hungry for more. And being around you would be torture for me. I can't. It hurts."

"You know, after all this time, not once did I ever feel like this wasn't worth it. There was never even the smallest voice or intuition that would tell me to leave you alone. That sneaking in your old house, meeting up after the kids went to bed, the divorce, the age, the kids, all of it. Not once did I ever feel like I shouldn't do this. Not once have I felt like walking away from you, even after everything and how hard this has been. If anything, I had the opposite feeling." A few tears fell from his eyes as he looks at me. I'd never seen him cry before.

"Will. I'm not asking you to leave. I'm asking you to stay. I'm asking to keep you. But you won't. You don't want to be kept by me. What am I supposed to do?"

"It's not fair to expect me to be a stepdad. Is that what you choose for me at this point in my life? I'm asking seriously."

"I didn't choose any of this. I'm sorry. But is it fair for me to stay when it breaks my heart? None of this is fair. This isn't fair."

I watched as he stood across the counter from me. For the next few hours, we go back and forth. A sallow look glossed over him, empty and grief stricken. He begged to stay without commitment. I asked him to release the grip we had on each other if we couldn't fully do this.

"It's obvious I'm procrastinating," he said, looking at the clock. It was six in the morning and we'd gone in circles repeatedly, ultimately wanting the same thing in different circumstances. He didn't want to leave, and I wanted him to stay. "It's clear I'm buying time with you because I don't want to leave."

*Then don't.*

I didn't say it because I'd said it a million times in a million ways. But I was thinking it.

I walked over to him, put my arms around his neck. Tears still hung from his eyes. I knew he didn't want this to end. And I didn't either. But it couldn't stay like this. It wasn't fair for either of us.

I whispered in his ear. "I'm sorry this happened to us. It's the saddest thing to ever happen to two people. It's heartbreaking."

Tears fell from my eyes on the shoulders of his coat. "I never wanted it to be this way. And I don't hate you, okay? I don't think you're a bad person. I understand you. I get you. It's okay. All of it. We will be okay."

He held me in his arms tightly as if he was afraid I'd disappear if he let go. I looked into his big brown eyes. Strangely, I saw him as a forty-year-old man looking back at me. And it was weird. Like somehow time wasn't the same. When I was with him, it all went by too fast. Age is just numbers, and nothing is linear. Like in Alice in Wonderland, something was wrong with the clocks. Somehow, being with him, we defied logic and time.

"You will be okay; I know you will. You'll achieve your wildest dreams. And I'll be the guy that walked away when I was too stuck in my head to do anything about it," he said.

"Oh, stop." I nudged him playfully.

"Maybe someday I will see things differently," he said.

I stared into his eyes again painfully. "Please don't say that." Those words would permanently plant seeds of hope in my brain and in my heart. I wondered then if I would always want him the way I did then. If he came back months or years later and did see things differently, I wondered what would happen. But I also knew holding onto hope is dangerous, especially when you're in the business of letting go and moving on. Acceptance is the final stage of grief. And though it hurt, I was finally arriving.

In the doorway, we held each other longer than we ever have.

"We've never been good at goodbyes." I said to him.

"Never." He held me tighter.

I pulled away to stare into him. Those interstellar eyes, cosmic and beautiful. I couldn't forget them in any lifetime.

"Have a goodnight, Will." He turned and looked at me. "And a good life."

I didn't say it, but I was thinking it.

*I love you.*

## Three for Three

CALL IT STUPID, call it crazy, or call it what is—I decided to rebound. I had three dates with three different men set up for three different days in a row. I could have had a new man for every day of the week if I wanted. I was trying to meet someone new as soon as possible, because if I couldn't be with the person I wanted to be with, I knew I needed to accept it and move on. So I put myself out there. It should've been no surprise to me that not a single date met my expectations. Instead, they all held a mirror to my inner world. The first one was with an entrepreneur who showed me what could happen if I slipped into old vices like drinking and not staying disciplined in my craft. He was not a match, but he was a mirror. We had so many similarities, it was uncanny. He even shared the same birthday as me and when we found that out, our jaws hit the floor. All we could do was talk about "the one that got away", it was clear our broken hearts still needed healing. And with discussing the pain our fathers left in our life, we realized that we were not a romantic match. Sometimes it's just you holding a mirror up to yourself. Life is funny like that. When you're awake, you'll see everything, and everyone is connected. Stranger than fiction.

The second date was with a single dad, my first attempt at dating men who also had children. He was cute, he was funny, and he was a Virgo. Triple threat of a good time. And honestly, he was fine, but he wasn't "it." He was a mirror to my core wounds and fears, as well. A divorced single parent and also had grown afraid of true intimacy, true connection, and commitment. His marriage ended poorly as mine did and he shared similar struggles in his day to day as me. With both dates, we ended with a hug and deeper understanding of the human condition and our own conditions that were calling for our attention. But on that second date, there were deeper layers uncovered within me. That after all these years, I was still holding on to guilt over Wil's death and having a hard time coping with it. The idea that I could've saved him if I chose him, and that if I chose him, he would still be alive. That because I didn't, maybe it was all my fault. I sat in that Mexican restaurant looking across from this man with tears in my eyes.

"Do you feel like it's all your fault?" he asked, empathy in his tone. His eyes were watery. "I'm sorry, I can feel the love and sadness you carry for him from here. It's palpable."

I nodded.

"To be honest, I'm still looking for him in everyone I meet." I swallowed my tears down hard. I couldn't possibly cry at another date. "And the only one who came close, who made me feel something, was the other Will. And that's not why I feel the way I do about him. Not because I'm comparing the two or trying to recreate what we shared. It was all just a happy chance. Serendipity."

So two out of two dates were no-go's, but they weren't failures if I was still learning lessons. I still had my third date with Nikolas to go. A 6'3" twenty-something cop who lived down the street. There was no long-distance drama to worry about. He knew I had kids and his response right away was "I'm not a child. I know what I want. It's someone like you. I'm not worried about that."

He showed up to my door and I can't lie to you, he was pretty damn hot. Tall, bearded, funny, great smile, smart and great style. He was wearing a sexy flannel, backwards hat, and vans. Definitely my style. And I loved how he didn't find my baggage to be too much and made it explicitly clear that he didn't want to engage in hookup culture. He was looking for a wife and wasn't interested in anything unless it was going somewhere serious. It was so refreshing compared to the other men that just wanted situationships without commitment and who weren't looking for genuine connection. Nikolas and I hit it off so well that we broke all our rules.

"I catch feelings too quickly and it messes me up," he said. "I don't even kiss on the first date."

One thing led to another and he had me on my knees with my skirt still on and pulled up, railing the dear life into me. When I say this man was packing a third leg, I kid you not. I could hardly breathe, I was so full. The sheer size and girth of this thing deserved a gold medal. Things in the bedroom were impressive and I thought I even saw a sliver of potential with him, until he asked to stay the night. Though all I ever wanted was Will to stay with me, I realized it was less the act and more about the quality time I wanted. I didn't know this guy too well, and he had just mentioned that his fatal flaw was that he fell too fast for people. He'd already broken his rule of not kissing on first dates. So I told him I had a busy day the next day and a lot of writing to do. He said he understood this more than anyone because his mom was a wildly successful romance author making nearly a million dollars a year in book sales, traveling, and touring the world thanks to the career she built as an author.

He asked to see me the next day. My knee jerk reaction was, *oh god, no*. I didn't really want to see him so soon after being with him all night. But I smiled as I let him out the door. "That sounds nice, I'll see you tomorrow."

All day, my stomach felt sick. I put my phone on to not disturb. I didn't want to text him or anyone. The last thing I wanted was to see this guy. Why? I wasn't sure, but I had a sneaking suspicion to was because he wasn't Will. My heart wasn't ready. Not yet at least.

Nevertheless, he came over with a bottle of wine dressed very cute and still very much attractive.

The more we got to know each other, though, the more aware I became of how incompatible we were. We had so little in common. To an alarming and almost hilarious degree. If I said I liked chocolate, he liked vanilla. If I said I loved music, he said he preferred the TV on. If I laughed at a joke, he was silent. Sometimes, opposites can attract, and it can be great. But it was clear this was not the "running on all four cylinders" relationship I was looking for.

I'm guessing he felt the same. During a terribly awkward game of Guess Who, he was overly competitive at trying to win, I think due to the nature of him being a cop. Then, my stupid sense of humor had me rolling on the floor laughing at my own jokes. I knew this was not the one. He ain't it. And that was okay. If I've learned anything so far about the people we meet, it was clear that he was a mirror to my career. He showed me what was possible with writing if I kept going and I didn't quit. He had perspective and told me, "You're still so young in your writing career, too. You're going to be so successful. My mom makes more money than anyone I know writing books. She's living her dream life. And I see you on your way doing the same thing. It's exciting." Nikolas showed me what my highest potential looked like. He also showed me how important it was for me to find a man who didn't tell me I was just a dreamer, that being a writer isn't a real job or real career, but to find a man who sees it exactly as he sees his mother. To value the life of a creative professional and their vocation. In the love department, he showed me that compatibility is just as important as chemistry. I was grateful for those lessons. Three for three in lessons, but not three for three in love. Just a few more pieces of driftwood made for passing through.

# A Love Like Oxygen

SHORTLY AFTER MY ex-husband and I got divorced, his lungs spontaneously collapsed. I'm no doctor, but I do know that our bodies keep score. The emotion that is stored mostly in the lungs? Grief. That's why you'll see the people who often smoke are the ones clinging to repressed and unexpressed grief. It felt like a metaphor of my love and what it feels like when someone loves you, truly and unconditionally. It feels like oxygen.

My love, like oxygen, was something that people like Will or like my ex-husband took for granted because it felt easy and free, because I'm unconditional with it. Like receiving oxygen every day. They know when they woke up, it was going to be there for them. They would have oxygen to breathe, and they didn't even think about it because, it was just as easy as breathing, it's fine and it's not complicated. Second nature. Always there. They might not even notice how deeply they had been loved, because when I am in love, loving comes to me as easy as breathing. Then my ex-husband's lungs collapsed. I'm not saying it's the cause, but it was a sign.

Maybe he didn't know I was his source of oxygen until I was gone. Maybe he didn't know how much life I gave him. He didn't know how much he needed me to breathe. He took me and my love for granted. He might not have felt my presence as powerfully over time, but my absence, like oxygen can and will be felt. Like oxygen, you don't know how great life is, because with me, it's just easy breathing, easy living, but when I'm gone, you will know it. I love powerfully, like the breath in your lungs, and when I'm gone, you feel it.

# Brewed Bonds

SOMETIMES I CAN be a bit reclusive. I can isolate myself and call it art. But something told me to get dressed, get out of my house and work at the coffee shop. Wouldn't you know it, I locked eyes with the hottest guy in the shop as I waited for my order. He was hard to miss, 6'4 to be exact and built like a fridge. He was a beast of a man, with brown eyes, brown hair, and a beard. All the things I love, as we know. He fit the avatar for physical attraction. I walked up to the counter and ordered an iced matcha latte and prayed that he one, didn't leave and two, kept the seat open next to him.

*Bingo.* He didn't leave. He was still sitting there. As I walked up to where he was sitting, a tall young slender blonde with a fancy coat sat near him, however, she left one seat open. Meaning I would have to be so bold to sit right next to him and ruin her attempt at flirting with him or give her a chance to steal him from me. So, what did I do? I did the bold thing. Was I nervous? Yep. Was I shaking a little bit? Also, yep. But what did I have to lose? Dating apps weren't working. Things with Will weren't happening. And I did think this man was pretty damn cute.

"Hey, do you know the Wi-Fi password? You look like the guy who would know it." I said to him.

He looked at me and flashes a killer smile.

"You're in luck. You asked the right coffee shop nerd. I have the majority of them memorized."

"You're so kind."

He leaned over a little. "Try 'blackcoffee or commonroast'" he said. We were at Common Wealth. The last time I was here, I was with Thomas.

"Ahh! It worked. Thank you."

"I'm Alek by the way." He looked at me with his beautiful brown eyes and extend his big hand to shake.

"Brittany."

"What are you working on today?" he asked.

"I'm a writer, so. I'm working on my book."

"A writer? Wow. That's more interesting than what I'm working on."

"Which is what?"

"I'm a giant nerd, so…" He shifted his laptop to show me the coding he was working on. "I'm in cybersecurity. I'm a hacker, but the good, protective kind."

He proceeded to passionately tell me all about it and I listened along. The conversation flowed naturally into dating, relationships and just about everything else. We talked for four hours straight. Time was flying without even realizing. He was also divorced and had been in his healing era, working on himself through therapy and mindset programs. We seemed to have a lot of surface level things in common.

"You're a writer, check this out. You'll love it," he said.

"What is it?"

He pulled up an app. "It's called Chat GPT, it's an AI automation scripting technology. A lot of marketing professionals use it to automate their emails, etc. But it can be used to storytelling."

"Oh, I'd never not actually write one of my own books. I love the mental stimulation of it all."

"You couldn't and you shouldn't, but I can," he smirked. "Watch this."

He began typing. "Here. I'll write our story by using AI technology."

"Oh really? What's our story called?" I flashed a flirty smile.

"I'll give it the story line and it'll create the title and write our story. You have to feed it a little plot, but it steers the outcome on its own."

He typed: *Tell us a story where two random strangers, a guy and a girl, meet at a countertop table in a café. They talked about life and struggles and became friends... fast...*

Within a matter of seconds, a story populated.

"Here it is. Our story is called '*Brewed Bonds*.'"

"Well, what happens? I need to know. Read me a bit of our story."

We both giggled as he read it out loud.

"I guess I'm Mark and you're Emily. But according to this... it says our story is..."

He cleared his throat and reads aloud:

*In a quaint little cafe nestled in the heart of the city, two seemingly unrelated lives were destined to intertwine. Mark, a software engineer with a penchant for coding, and Emily, a budding artist navigating the challenges of freelance work, found themselves standing side by side at the counter.*

*It was a chilly Tuesday morning, and as they waited for their respective orders, their eyes met in a moment of shared anticipation. Mark, a bit introverted but with a warm smile, decided to break the ice.*

*"Long day ahead?" he asked, noticing the bags under Emily's eyes.*

*She chuckled, "You have no idea. Deadlines and creative blocks seem to be conspiring against me."*

*Mark nodded understandingly, "I can relate. Tight project timelines and bugs that just won't disappear. It's a struggle."*

*Their conversation flowed effortlessly as they discovered the unexpected parallels in their lives. As they sipped their coffee, they delved deeper into their personal struggles and aspirations. Emily shared her passion for art and the constant battle with self-doubt, while Mark spoke of the pressure to meet high expectations in the fast-paced tech world.*

*The more they spoke, the more they realized how much they needed someone to confide in. In this chance encounter, they found an unspoken understanding and a shared camaraderie in the face of life's complexities.*

*Days turned into weeks, and Mark and Emily's friendship flourished. They became each other's sounding board, offering support and encouragement through the highs and lows of their respective journeys.*

*The cafe, once just a place to grab a quick coffee, became a symbol of their serendipitous connection. In the heart of the city's hustle and bustle, Mark and Emily discovered that a chance meeting could turn into a genuine friendship, proving that sometimes, the best stories unfold over a cup of coffee.*

"But wait. How did it know?" he said. We both laughed.

"Days turned into weeks?" I blushed and cover my smile. "Oh boy."

"AI is crazy. It just knows. It's predicting the future too now, apparently."

We both laughed and looked at the time. The hustle and bustle in the café was dying down.

"This has been so nice to meet you. Can I get your number?" He asked. "I'd love to see you again."

"Absolutely." I handed him my phone for him to plug in his information.

"Well, actually. What are you doing after this? Do you have big plans today?"

"I don't actually. I'm just heading to the gym after this. You?"

"I was also headed to the gym. My gym bag is in my truck," he laughed.

"You want to work out together?" I asked, joking mostly.

"Really? Honestly, I would if you'd be down for it."

"Alright then. Come with me. Why not?"

So, he did. And we worked out together for another distracted couple of hours. Of course, his gym outfit showed off his muscles. *He. Was. Hot.* Dripping sweat added a layer of sex appeal.

"Plans after this?" he asked.

"Not sure yet. Why?"

"I'd like to take you out on a proper date."

I smiled. "Yeah? I'd like that."

"Alright, give me an hour. I'll clean up and book a few different reservations. I have some cute ideas for us. Emily." He winked. The character from the AI generated story.

"I'll see you soon, Mark."

I RUSHED HOME to shower, shave and slip on something sexy yet classy. Tonight, it was a leather mini skirt and red high neck semi-cropped top with the knee-high heeled boots I wore on my date with Thomas. They felt like my good luck boots, and I thought I could use a little extra luck.

Alek arrives on time and he was clean cut and semi-formal. A snug fit button-up dress shirt that hugged his every muscle just right. A shirt like that makes you want to squeeze a man's chest with both hands. The man had taste. Expensive taste. He drove a brand-new luxury electric truck that just came out just last year. He was in tech, he's successful and it showed. He was also wearing a very fancy jacket which he would later tell me was over a thousand dollars with some animal skin from some unique animal that I'd later forget and that he bought in some country he traveled to for work that I wouldn't remember the name of. That part I'd remember. That what and the why always add up in my mind, but never the how.

"Wow. Look at you! You look stunning," he pulled me in for a hug.

"You think?" I ran my hands down my coat. "Thank you, mister." I used my soft flirty voice, pressing my red lips together. I'd busted out the red lipstick for this one. Who was this Emily girl and what did she do with Brittany?

Alek got the car door for me. *Already off to a good start. But will he pass the walking test?* I wondered.

We were on the way to the first restaurant when he told me he was nervous.

"I have butterflies," he said. It was rather cute, though deep down, I know that sometimes, as sweet as they sound, having butterflies might not always be a good thing. Sometimes, butterflies are our nervous systems telling us that something isn't right and that we're feeling activated. When we parked, I pulled out my meditation app and we meditated together.

"You know, it's really nice that I can just let my guard down and be myself with you. It's not like this with everyone. It's easy with you."

"I get told that a lot. I'm glad you feel that way with me. I'm a safe space." We both smiled and he helped me out of the car. "I am, too," he said.

As I stood next to him, I remembered this feeling. The same one I had next to Thomas who was the same height. It's an exhilarating feeling to be an entire foot shorter than a man. There's something sort of taboo about it, like it's not supposed to be like this. Like two misfits somehow made a match. And oddly, it works in some weird way. But the real test is still as follows—*will he pass the walking test?*

"The restaurant is this way, he says." He pointed to the left. The city was decorated for Christmas, and it was lit up beautifully. As we started walking, I noticed it. He was matching my pace. And better yet? He held my hand as we walked across the street. It was clear from this moment forward, I knew he had genuine intentions with me. And from that moment on, a slow leak of feelings within me would begin to spout off.

We arrived at the first destination. A trendy and upscale New-American bistro.

"I'm a foodie," he said, which is what anyone who likes nice things always says. I knew the kind. I was, after all, a fine dining server that used my tips and luxury wine bottle sales to help fund my college education. And ten years later, here I was on the other side of the table. He ordered a fancy first course meal and champagne.

"Cheers," I said, clinking my glass next to his. *Is this real life? What planet am I on?* Yesterday, this man was a total stranger. And today? I'd embarked on a twelve-hour date that even now didn't seem to be ending any time soon.

"To Mark and Emily," he said. "Should we ask Chat GPT what it thinks is next for us? Let's see if it gets the predictions right."

He pulled me in closer to me as he reveals the screen.

> *After a rigorous gym workout that left them invigorated, Mark and Emily decided to continue the positive momentum of their day. Sweaty but energized, they sat down in the gym's lounge area, sipping on protein shakes as they planned the rest of their evening.*
>
> *Considering their shared love for good food and the city's culinary scene, they chose a cozy Italian restaurant for dinner. Mark, a fan of bold flavors, looked forward to savoring a hearty Bolognese pasta, while Emily, with her penchant for vegetarian delights, opted for a flavorful eggplant Parmesan. Their choices reflected not only their gastronomic preferences but also their shared appreciation for diverse cuisines.*

*As they perused the menu, they decided to pair their meals with a bottle of red wine, a rich Malbec known for its velvety texture and notes of dark berries. The candlelit ambiance of the restaurant added a touch of intimacy to their dining experience, creating the perfect setting for more in-depth conversations.*

*Post-dinner, they embraced the festive spirit by heading to the city's Christmas tree viewing area. Surrounded by twinkling lights and the scent of pine, they marveled at the beautifully decorated trees, sharing stories of holiday traditions and childhood memories.*

*Mark and Emily's carefully planned evening was a delightful blend of culinary delights and festive cheer. The journey continued to unfold, now infused with the magic of the holiday season and the shared joy of exploring the city's cultural offerings.*

"Okay, but how does it even know that it's Christmas time?" I asked.

"It's a little spooky for sure," he said. He laughed with me. "I guess I'm getting the Malbec."

The rest of the evening was eerily similar to the AI story. The two of us ended up at a small jazz club downstairs for a craft cocktail, heavy flirting and some thigh squeezing. And after, he gave me his jacket and carried me to his car. The man was a romantic through and through. This was actually the first older man I'd connected with since dating. And when I say older, I mean he was only one year older than I was. It was new territory for me, but I was open-minded. We ended the night by leaving the bar with his jacket draped over my shoulder and a steamy make out in his truck. From there? Respectfully, he dropped me off back home.

"Can I bring you a cappuccino in the morning?" he asked.

I smiled and nodded. "Yes."

"Text me when you're awake and I'll deliver it."

THE NEXT MORNING, he did as he said. He brought me a cappuccino and then for the next month, we spent time together. We went to dinner dates, saw live music, he cooked for me, danced with me in my kitchen, brought me tea when I was sick, he held umbrellas over my head when it rained and when it came to physical intimacy, he was patient. The entire month, it never happened. Not because he wasn't attractive or that we weren't physically attracted to each other, but because he respected me, and I was learning how to respect myself. However, even though there were a lot of qualities to adore, something just wasn't right. The thing was, I liked him, and he was a lot of fun, but I just didn't feel that spark. Something was missing and deep down, I could sense this was also not my person to keep. On paper, he also had nearly everything on my list. My friends and even my family suggested giving him a chance, because it was clear that he was checking a lot of my boxes. But if I've learned anything so far, it's how pointless those boxes are if there isn't a genuine connection. I want the whole damn cake and with Alek it seemed possible, but I need to also be in love with the flavor. And I wasn't. It seemed to have all the right ingredients, but it still wasn't my favorite. And life as we know it is too damn short to eat shitty cake.

## The Secret to Letting Go

THE SECRET IS knowing that life will give you something better than what you gave up than whatever is asked of you to give up. That is where we find peace, truth, love and to become fearless in your pursuit of your most authentically aligned life.

"This or something better."

So, I walked away from Alek. Was he great? Sure. But he wasn't mine to keep and my soul knew it. I let him go, knowing I'd get something and someone meant for me. He was also not looking for a relationship and I was. In my time alone I learned there was no point in staying if you aren't on the same page, because staying in hopes of changing someone's mind will forever be a losing game. If it isn't a hell yes, it's a hell no.

At this point I knew many things to be true. And that is that letting go is never easy, but someone new or something better will always fill its place. Even if that is temporary. Even if it doesn't stay for long. It eventually keeps getting better and better. As Rumi says, attachment is the root of all suffering. Let it all go, free them, free yourself. And if it comes back to you, it's meant for you. But when it comes back again, it can only come back better than it was. And if it isn't, just know, you're on your way to something better. That's not to say to throw things or people away when they get hard. Of course, we must use our own discernment and intuition. I make such calls and decisions in life, but if you feel the nudge inside and you're brave enough to trust it, please know you'll be divinely guided with as many life rafts as you need. You'll never float alone long enough to drown. I don't believe the universe isn't that cruel. So, hold on. To every life raft you can until you make it past the shore to the other side. When you see the driftwood, like Aleks or Mason, learn to smile instead. Because it's a sign that you are not lost, you're on your way.

## Screw It All, We Ball

THE YEAR 2023 was jam packed, and I didn't think there was any more room for spontaneous excitement to be had before the end of it. Especially a few days before December closes out. But as the universe does, it has its way of completely surprising me.

If I was enjoying my final days single, I knew I must go out with a final bang. I was ringing in the new year the only way I knew how—saying hell yes to all the things that lit me up! A formal ball in a beautiful city with twinkling lights at a five-star hotel? It's an opportunity I wouldn't dream to miss. It was settled. I was going even if I didn't have a date, I was going alone. Who knows, maybe I'd find a babe to kiss at midnight on NYE, or maybe Will would show up to my door asking for a second chance. I was open to the many possibilities of the universe. Whatever it had in store would delight me, I knew this much to be true.

I arrived at the Daxton Hotel. The same bar I was last at with Will. Rumor has it that there's a golden horse art fixture here that is worth a million dollars. I remember telling him that, too. Being there without him on New Year's stung. Being here without anyone stung more. All my other friends had plans tonight, So I had two choices—sit at home and cry about being alone, or I act as if I was spending NYE with my soulmate, my life partner. And if that was the case, my soulmate would tell me to get that red dress on and take me to the Daxton for the NYE Ball. I decided to put that red dress on. The plan was to sit at the bar and have one glass of champagne. I was planning on people watching for a few laughs and heading home alone to eat my twelve grapes under the table by midnight. Something Tik Tok told me to do if I wanted to attract a romantic partner and call in twelve wishes. Worst case scenario? I choked on a grape, or nothing happened. Best case scenario? What if my twelve wishes came true? I placed twelve grapes into a zip-lock bag, stuffed them into my Prada purse, shimmied into a red dress, glided on some lipstick, and headed into a night of the unknown. Had I ever done anything like this in my life? The answer is no. But that old life got left behind along with my ex-husband and everything that came with him. It's still buried with my wedding ring somewhere in the dirt. I planted that old wedding ring into the ground and became a new woman. The result? A new life that demanded a much braver, bolder me. And that woman wasn't afraid to attend a formal ball alone.

I WAS STANDING near the bar when a woman got up and cleared a seat for me.

"That's prime real-estate," she said to me. "Best seat in the house. You're lucky."

And lucky I was. Twenty minutes later, I got a free VIP ticket into the Ball that cost hundreds of dollars to get into. How? I bumped shoulders and made small talk with the right people. And before I knew it, I was at the black-tie ball filled with beautiful women in gowns and yes, the men were attractive, wealthy, and abundant. But best of all? I made two new girl-friends who never left my side. It was a clear indicator that I needed more female friendships. I couldn't expect a man to fulfill all my social needs. The rest of the night I spent twirling and dancing the night away with my new friends. Having a dance off with a flamboyant and super-hot gay man. The time of my life was happening all around me in the most magnificent unforeseen way. And though there were plenty of men who wanted my attention, I was having more fun without it. I didn't need a man or his validation. Not this time. I was content and at peace perfectly on my own. And with the girls.

At midnight, I declined all requests for a New Year's kiss. Instead, I ate my twelve grapes alone under a table near the bar. I crouched down in my tiny dress and heels and said one wish per grape. I saved that kiss for the man I wished for tonight, the one that I was looking forward to kissing into the next new year. As with most things in my life, the night didn't go as expected. But if you ask me, I think it went better. Another life lesson for me to unfold in real time. Most often, the unknown is a wild ride, but it never lets you down. If this was how I brought in the new year, I couldn't wait to see what the new year brought me.

It's worth noting that through it all, I noticed something important was missing. Not a man or romantic partner, but the presence of quality female friendships. Sure, I have my long-distance besties, but if I was honest with myself, I wondered how much time I spent with random men on dating apps just to fill the void of loneliness where a genuine connection with female friends would fill that void with companionship.

The two things were not mutually exclusive. I could be single, and not be lonely. I could be excited for new love to enter my life, all while building a rich and full one that I love on my own. A shift had happened within me since that last talk with Will. It was hard to tell if it was heartbreak, healing, or both, but I was less interested in the male gaze and more interested in my own gaze on building a life that felt good without a man in it. Men have let me down time and time again, and while I still have faith in men to be great, I can say with my full chest that my female relationships have supported and helped me through it all. They don't do it in hopes to use my body or with an ulterior motive, they do it because they love me unconditionally, because I'm worthy and enough as I am. So, from that point forward, I vowed to forever nurture my female friendships. To tend to their gardens in the way they tend to mine, for I would have no roses to give a lover or even to myself if it wasn't for the women watering my garden on the days that I could not.

# New Year, New Chapter, New Us?

IT WAS STUPID to call him. Besides, it had been nearly three months since we last spoke. But there's something about a girl that doesn't drink often—if she has a glass or two, it's enough to make her do something crazy.

My hands trembled. My heart was beating two times too fast. But that champagne spoke to me loud and clear. *Just call him.* Maybe I shouldn't have listened to that voice, but I did.

Standing outside of the trendy bar next to the restaurant where Will and I had our first date, and I missed him. I scrolled through my contacts list and when it got to his name, I considered not calling for a second, and the next, my finger pressed the button to do it.

He didn't answer. *Of course not*, I thought to myself. From there, I called a taxi to take me home. In the car, a text lit up my phone a few moments later.

**Will:** *I saw you called.*

To my surprise, he responded. And fast.

**Me:** *Oops. I had a thought.*
**Me:** *Come over. It's important*
**Will:** *What's up*
**Me:** *You here?*
**Will:** *No*

**Me:** I want to talk

**Will:** About what

**Me:** Come over and I'll tell you

**Will:** You can tell me over text

**Me:** Oooo. Why?

**Will:** Because I'm not dropping what I'm doing at 1 in the morning to go somewhere and not know why

**Me:** It's a lot to type. It's important. I don't lie

**Will:** Are you injured?

**Me:** Why would I call you if I was injured? Haha No

**Will:** Then why do I need to come over

**Me:** Because I can't articulate in text. That's why I called. But face to face is best anyway

**Will:** What is this about

**Me:** We have a lot to catch up on tbh

**Will:** I don't think we do. Pretty sure you made it very clear you would never be speaking to me again

**Me:** Well…If you don't want to that's fine

**Will:** If you want to explain to me the context around why I'm being called repeatedly at midnight from someone that I've spent time moving on from then do so right now. I don't want to play guessing games

**Me:** I accidentally called you twice. But I hear you and I'm sorry if that rubbed you the wrong way

**Will:** You called. That's the point

**Me:** I don't want to hurt you. I'm sorry… just forget it. Impulsive sometimes

**Will:** If you don't want to text me I will call when I'm finished with my night

**Me:** I'd rather see you

**Will:** Not if you don't tell me what this is about. I don't need a whole novel but I'm not walking in blind

**Me:** It's not a bad situation I promise. Business mostly

**Will:** Why was that so hard? I'll call you in 30 mins

**Me:** Are you coming over? In person hits different

**Will:** When my night is over I will call you

I could feel his moody energy through the text.

**Me:** It's late so just lmk if you plan on coming over. I just got home. It won't take long, just stop by real quick. I've never once played games with you William John

**Will:** I'll be there in 15 minutes

Will was on his way and my heart at this point was racing. I fixed my makeup and waited on the sofa. I saw his headlights turn into the driveway and all of me sunk into the pit of my stomach. *He's here.*

"Hi."

I opened the door with a soft, half-buzzed smile. His face looked pained and hurt. But he was here.

*I called and he came.*

"What is this about?"

"I wanted to see you."

"What for?" his voice took on the same angry tone as his face.

"Are you mad? I can sense you're upset."

"Brittany, it's two in the morning."

"You didn't have to come. You could've said no. But you didn't."

He took a silent pause so long; you can hear the refrigerator hum behind him.

"Well, I'm here. So, what is it?"

"Honestly. I missed you." I said, shocked that I did. "You look good, by the way." He did. A black denim jacket, burgundy beanie and nice fitted dark jeans. He also looked thin. And grief hung from his face. The light I once saw in him had dulled. The sparkle in his eyes had disappeared. It was clear he was hurting. Or worse, that he was changing.

He nodded. "Thanks."

"I'm having a hard time speaking Will, you look so… upset. It's hard to cut through that."

"I'm not upset. I'm guarded. And it's late. I'm tired."

"Why did you come?"

"Because you called," he said. "And you said it was important."

He stood far away from me, as if he was afraid to be close to me again. Getting close to me hurt, but me leaving him hurt worse. I knew this by now.

He looked at me, and he really looked at me.

"Are you happy?" he asked.

"What do you mean?"

"I mean, are you happy?"

I paused for a moment and looked away.

"Are you?"

He replied quickly. "Yes."

"You don't look very happy."

He said nothing.

"Are you happy, Brittany?" he asked again.

"Yes." I responded. "I'm very happy."

We were doing our best at two things. Trying to move on as if we are happy without each other and trying to pretend.

"You seem lonely," he said.

He'd brought this up several times before. This concern for my loneliness.

"Aren't we all a little lonely?"

He softly nodded and examined me.

"I guess. But you seem lonelier."

"It's a chosen loneliness, for my peace. Not everyone deserves access to me. I don't spend time with just anyone. I'm not afraid to be alone, it's better than having company I don't enjoy. I enjoy my own company."

"Just thought I'd ask." He paused for a second.

"So, the last time we talked, you were upset with me," he said. "I felt like I had to say something I didn't want to say, just so you would…"

"So, I would do what?"

"I don't know. You just didn't seem to accept things as they were. Even though I said I didn't want a relationship. I still don't. With anyone."

"Really."

"I think I'm an open relationship kind of guy. You'd never be down for that."

It struck me as interesting.

"I actually don't know. I think I'd want you to myself for a while. Something about that turns me on. I'm pretty open to learning about most things. I had a very traditional relationship and marriage, and it didn't work. Who is to say what does work? I don't know what works; I'm still figuring that out. But I know what doesn't work."

He asked about my life and it comes up that I hadn't been intimate with anyone since him. That was months ago.

"Why not?" he asked.

"I'm done with hookup culture."

"But you love sex. Why not have it? Aren't there people you can find?"

"It's not like I can't. It's not like I don't have options. I could have a nine inch magnum crashing into my cervix right now, a line of guys every day. I don't want that anymore."

"Anymore?" his eyebrows knit together as a wave of visible jealousy came over him.

"Yes, Will. I had a lot of sex when we weren't "on". What was I supposed to do? But that wasn't fulfilling, so I'm not doing that anymore."

He looked at me and nodded.

"I've been seeing this girl on and off for a while. She doesn't live here, but when she was here over Christmas and every time she came back home, we had sex."

That clipped me like a bullet.

"I like having my options open. She does too. And it works. Would you be okay with a relationship like that?"

I pictured him inside of someone else and all of me died. My eyes were dead at the moment, too.

"No."

"See. So, what are we supposed to do?"

I looked at the clock. It was six in the morning again, and the same conversation in a different font. I felt less sad. More indifferent. Maybe this is what moving on was like. Maybe you needed to go back to the person that hurt you repeatedly until you finally learned. It's a lesson only you will learn when you're ready. We spun around and around on the subject before we gave up, again, with little to no resolve.

"So, what is it? What do you want to tell me?"

"I want to tell you about the memoir. I think it's important to talk about this. You know I write about you, and about us. Quite a bit. And I need your permission to keep your name or not. Last we spoke, you wanted to keep it in. But things have changed, and I'm almost done with it."

"Well." He thought for a minute. "If you use my name, I want to read it first before it's published. And if you don't, you can use whatever name and I don't need to read it first."

"You actually want to read it?" I asked.

"Yes. I told you that a while ago. I want to read it."

"I don't think I want you to read it before it's published."

"Why?"

"Because."

Because then he would know how I felt and what would happen then? It felt too vulnerable.

"Okay, if you don't use my name, I won't need to read it first."

"Deal."

"We'll talk about it another time," he walked to the door. "It's six in the morning and I'm exhausted. But I want to know what you decide to do."

"Okay. Good night."

"Good night."

He walked away frustrated and didn't look back. I closed the door feeling more broken than I did the last time. Every time we walked away from each other, it seemed we both continued to break. The truth is, I fell in love with him, and I hadn't gotten back up since. How would I tell him that? He wanted to read the memoir before it was published. But there was no way I could do that. Not after that night.

# The Seashell Theory

I DROVE THREE hours back to my cozy hometown to potentially close a six-figure deal on a piece of waterfront property. It's important to mention why I was here and what my intentions were. To acquire this home and make a boatload of money, no pun intended. At this rate, I was on track to have acquired three six-figure annual income producing assets in two months. I was on the fast track to making serious money in a very short amount of time. My whole drive to the West Michigan coast, nothing could bring me down. This home was about to be mine and I was going to scale my business to seven figures before I knew it. Not only would it help me feel more secure as single mother to have the security financially, it was also the kind of "fuck you" money I was after to show my ex-husband, his family and his friends just how capable I was without him. For every doubt they had about me, I wanted a handful of wins ready to fan out. If this was a game of bet against Brittany, I wanted to be the MVP with the best hand. And the only way I knew how to do that, was to play my hand myself.

The woman rushed me through the property and ultimately told me she wasn't interested in giving up her real estate in this location but was willing to show me the other property she had. To be honest, I wasn't, but I wanted to build the relationship in the event she would change her mind.

She looked at me and asked, "Why real estate? I thought you were an author?"

"I am, but I want to have more streams of income to put food on the table. I can't confidently say that my books can do that yet."

"How many properties do you have and how many do you want?"

"I have two so far. I was hoping to set up four to six more this year."

She nodded. "Why so many? A couple seems like plenty to handle."

"Honestly? I want to make more money than my ex-husband. To prove a point."

"Can I tell you a story? I've been at this game a long time and I've learned some things. Do you have a minute? I think it might help you."

"Of course."

"It's a story about a father and son on the beach. It's called the seashell theory. Have you heard of it?"

I shook my head no.

"There's a little boy and a father on the beach and they're collecting seashells. The little boy has his arms full of seashells, all kinds of beautiful seashells, all shapes and sizes and he's so happy, he says, 'Dad! Dad! Look at all these shells I collected from the beach.' His tiny arms are full of them. His father looked in amazement. 'Those shells are beautiful,' he said, and he could hold all of them in his arms all at once. But then, out in the distance, they see this great big giant beautiful shell. They both noticed it. The Dad says, 'Wow, that is a pretty amazing shell.' the boy says 'Dad! Dad! I really want that shell.' And the father says to him, 'Okay, go get the shell.' So the boy goes out, and as he opens his arms to reach for the big shell, all the little ones start slipping from his arm. He yells, 'Dad! I'm losing my shells! I'm losing my shells!' And the dad says, 'Well, do you want all these little shells or do you want that great big beautiful shell?'"

I wasn't sure where she was going with the story.

"What does that mean? Does that mean I should hold onto all these little things and not let that go for that one great big thing?"

"Brittany, What do you think your great big shell is in life? What is that one thing, that if you were to get it, you'd have to let go of all those little shells, but you would be so happy to let all of that go just to have that like one big, beautiful shell?"

I thought for a minute and not a minute longer.

"That would be my writing career. I would want my big shell to be the books that I write."

"That's what I thought," she said, "If I were you, I wouldn't worry about all these little shells. Go after that big shell. This real estate thing is important, but these are little shells in comparison to that big shell that I know you can reach for. I'm not saying these little shells won't be like stepping stones to some beautiful things to hold while you are on your way to your big shell, but don't busy yourself to have an arm full of small shells that might be blocking you from having the space to hold your big shell. You might not need as many small shells as you think, because that big shell might really be everything you thought and more.

Tears bubbled to the surface for us both. The seashell theory even applied to me and dating. All these little shells, like I'm holding onto these tiny relationships, hoping they come back, or that I'm afraid to let that all go in hopes to get my big shell—my person, my soulmate. What if I had to let go of all these little shells first?

I left without the keys to the destination I was headed in, but I was driving away with more than I ever knew I needed. Wisdom. The drive home, it hit me. *Write the books. Focus on the big shell. Don't bog yourself down with an arm full of small shells.*

A few miles up the road as I was driving back home, I looked up and I saw a billboard. On it, was a big shell, a logo for a gas station. A sign that read, "Big shell, Next Turn." Chills covered my body. I had my sign, loud and clear.

I remembered the second half of her shell story.

She said, "I've been married a long time and I've had lots of shells; I've even had a few big shells in my life. I hear what you're saying about your ex-husband, and it sounds to me that he knew all this time what you were capable of. It was as if he could see your big shell out in the distance and he knew, *this girl, she's gonna get that big shell and I don't have a shell like that waiting for me. I won't ever have a big shell like hers.* And he could never be happy for you because he knew he wanted a shell just like that but could never have it. So, if I give you any more advice, I will say to find someone who is happy for you that you found that shell. That will love and cherish your shell. That would be happy for you even if they didn't get to share it, because that's love, and you want someone who's gonna be proud of you and your shell. And you want someone who isn't jealous of your shell, who doesn't want to steal your shell or take your shell away. Someone who isn't angry with you for being able to get a shell that big because they're not capable of holding a shell like yours. You know, maybe your person is that someone who sees you getting a shell that large but would never look down on you for getting a shell like that, because they know that they're capable of getting their own big shell, or they're happy for you even if they aren't capable."

## Arriving to Shore

MY EX-HUSBAND WAS wrong about a lot of things, but when he told me no one would listen to my podcast and that I'd eventually quit, he was dead wrong. I'm a lot of things, but I'm not a liar, cheater, or a quitter. I am four years into podcasting and recently, I hosted an episode with a relationship psychologist. The podcast episode blew my whole world open. At first, we chatted about our divorces, dating and the experience of it all while still being parents, and then we talked about a lifestyle she participates in, which is called creative monogamy. I'm a very curious and open-minded person, but I had a lot of questions. And by the end of it, my head was spinning when I shared my relationship struggles, including the ones I was having with Will over the last year. I wanted professional advice. Her take on the whole thing?

"Treat other people the way they want to be treated." At first, I thought of myself. But then she said, "He wasn't wrong because he had boundaries, he stated his limits. It was you that never accepted it and it was you that was wrong."

She invited me into the discomfort of a new perspective. the one where maybe I wasn't a victim here. That maybe I had done this to myself for the sake of wanting to be chosen. I wanted him to choose me more than I was willing to accept where his feelings were at. As a result, it caused more pain than was necessary on both ends.

"Humans will always want the things someone won't give us.

It's classic Jungian research. The value of what you wanted from him went up because he wasn't available for it," she said. My eyes widened and my mouth fell open.

"Get very suspicious of your wants," she added. "Believe people when they tell you they aren't available for something. Believe it and move on."

"Wow," is all that I could utter. I shook my head. This whole time I tried hating him for the very thing he could have hated me for. Not accepting his choice and pushing him anyway.

"It's also a case of Lakonian theory there," she added. "Desire seeks desire. The thing we can't get is the thing we will want. The work there is to meet that need yourself first and see if you still want it."

It hit me. All this time I was reaching for driftwood, hoping for a sign that I was close to finding my person. But if this journey taught me anything, it's that driftwood isn't a person. It's a destination. An internal place you arrive to on your own. I had hoped that if I cracked myself open, another man would see me, choose me, and fill my voids. When all along, it was God and my own higher consciousness that cracked myself open and poured everything into me. All this time, I had a master list of the dream man I was manifesting. But now I see, I was not looking for my dream man. I was looking for myself. The woman who got lost and entangled in other people and their desires along the way. I was searching for someone who meditates, someone who journals, someone who's fit, someone who is kind and loyal and compassionate—and that person is me. *It was always me.* And when people didn't show up for me, it was because I was supposed to show up for myself. I was expecting to show up in other people because I wasn't ready, and I didn't know how to show up for myself yet. Instead, I was hoping that maybe *I* would arrive in the form of other men filling me up, that maybe, just maybe I would be whole and complete with their help, if someone chose me. But they weren't choosing me—because it was never about them. It was always a journey back home to me. *I had to choose me. It was always me.* Looking back, the signs were always there. How could I have missed them? The solo trip to the mountains, the twelve-hour solo hike in my hometown, my New Year's Eve alone—it was all just *me* beginning to come home to *myself.* I see it now. I finally see. With the help of many life rafts, ports, rip currents and little shells. I finally made it home. To myself.

# Leap Year

It was February 29th. Leap day. Maybe it was something cosmic, but I felt the shift. It all connected for me. I sent Will a voice text I never thought I'd send.

The one with me being the one apologizing.

"I was wrong. I see the whole situation differently. I have finally accepted it. I'm moving on. You don't need to respond, and everything is okay. You deserve all the good things. I want you to live such a good life. A happy life. Everything is okay."

I kept it brief and to the point. I just wanted us both to find peace. I didn't want the tension anymore. To my surprise, he sent a message back.

"I accept your apology and I believe I owe you an apology, too. At times I was impatient and angry with you, with this situation and with us. I'm sorry, too," he said.

I never thought we'd find ourselves here. I never thought I'd find *myself* here. But when you've had awakening after awakening, epiphany after epiphany, the dots finally begin to connect, and it all makes sense.

Am I disappointed that it wasn't Will and I in the end? I would be lying if I said no. More than anything I was hopeful that it would be. But as an adult woman, I realized that sometimes you don't get what you want because you deserve better. If I got what I wanted exactly when I wanted it, I would've received a young 23-year-old who still needed to find himself, and a broken woman who needed to do the same. Two lost and broken people can come together, but not without causing a lot of damage along the way, which is exactly what we were doing. It was clear that we needed to heal on our own path, whether that was coming back together in the future or simply back home to ourselves. I could remain sad that the relationship I wanted didn't pan out how and when I wanted to and simply write everyone else off as a waste of time. But I was choosing to see it differently. I fell in love, I made memories that would last a lifetime and it was all a journey worth falling for.

Part of this was an unintentional love story. I fell in love with a person, but most importantly, with myself. I don't consider any of it to be a loss. Love is the most powerful feeling of all. How lucky am I to even have had these experiences? I choose to remain in gratitude for the journey, regardless of the outcome. Eventually the wheel will turn in my favor, it always does.

WILL TAUGHT ME some of the most important lessons I'd ever learn in the window of time that he was in my life. But I also learned the big difference between love and attachment. Love without attachment says, "I want you to be happy." Love with attachment is "You need to make me happy." In love, you think about other people's happiness. In attachment, your approach is more selfish, and it tends to be about you and yours. Attachment happens when you see someone who makes you happy and you cling because you "need" them to make you happy. Real love is one that is unattached. If you love them, let them be. Let them all be, let them all go. Nothing is forever. The sooner we realize this, the better.

I do love Will. Unconditionally. Which is exactly why I had to let him go.

And I pray that he lives a happy, fulfilling life. Even if it's without me.

## The American Nightmare

TO SUM IT all up, Disney lied to me.
Marriage didn't give me my prince charming. Instead, I spent all of those years in a performative role as a wife that wasn't in alignment with my soul, then I listened to my inner compass and wound up a divorced single mom out in the wild. To my surprise, my knight in shining armor didn't come to rescue me after divorce, either. Yet another fantasy I was programmed to believe—that marriage was supposed to be the ultimate destination, and that without it, I wouldn't "make it." And even though divorce was an exit ramp, the only way society told me that I would "make it" was falling into the arms of another man. And while I deeply desire falling into the arms of a man that loves me, I know that for a relationship to be built on a sturdy foundation, it takes two whole people who have done the work on themselves, who have committed to their own growth journey independently. I can't expect even the arms of the strongest man to carry it all for me. It's my job, my responsibility to do the work and drop off my own burdens when the load gets heavier. And even more, I have learned that a relationship doesn't have to look traditional or like what we've been shown marriage is to be at all for it to add value to your life. Marriage is beautiful, but maybe it's not everything. At least not in the ways we've been taught. And maybe marriage and relationships can look any which way we want. Maybe we can build and create harmony in love to look entirely different, despite what we've been told. Maybe the

journey to love and fulfillment is not outside of ourselves after all. The journey to and through marriage is an ever evolving personal one, but it's one that we get to create however we choose. We get to write our own rules. And if we get honest with ourselves and our desires, we have the answers that hold the key to the life that feels the best. Not looks the best, but *feels* the best.

I can't tell you how to have a successful marriage or what one looks like. Mine failed by definition. But I can tell you that going forward, I will be writing my own rules with a partner and for my life independently. Because I have outgrown the old traditional paradigm and the way society has laid out relationships and family systems. Those antiquated rules and constructs that failed me and I know they've failed other women, too. From this point forward, I have the freedom to choose how my life and relationships look. And so do you. Life doesn't start or end without the presence of a man by your side. It starts and ends with you. It doesn't start or end on your wedding day, it starts when you come home to yourself. It doesn't start or end whether you have children or not, it starts when you love and nurture your own inner child. And before you choose someone else, or ask to be chosen, I hope you choose yourself.

# The End Is Just a New Beginning in Disguise

IF YOU WERE hoping for a happy ending, I have good news.

Because as fate would have it, I finally have the second half to my dream. The person I'd been waiting for. My soulmate. My person. My life partner. It all crashed into me hard and fast without warning. An all-consuming love, that again, that I never saw coming. But when it showed up, I knew. Everyone knew. This was it. The love story of my dreams had unfolded right before my eyes. Passion, bliss, out of this world romance and a love so deep it would make the ocean jealous.

I'm safe.

My heart is loved.

I am valued.

I am respected.

I am cherished.

I have made it to the shore. I swam across to the other side, with the help of other life rafts keeping me afloat along the way. And though I had to weather the storm alone and the ride was bumpy, I made it to my destination when the timing was right. I made it home.

*To myself.*

And funny enough, now that I made it, I can see that the light had been shining on the shoreline for me this whole time, but it was only when the waves were calm, and the storm had passed that I was able to continue to float out far enough in distance to see it.

Love, when it is real, is like a lighthouse. It's the compass leading you home through the darkest of storms. It's the stable building that's strong enough to brave harsh weather or powerful waves that crash into it, yet still, it stands there, shining tall and sturdy for you. All this time I was reaching for driftwood, searching for my missing piece. Yet, all along I had been guided by other forces at hand. I was always on my way there. Finding a home within myself and leaning on my lighthouses, the strong women in my life whom I couldn't' have made it to the other side without. A journey I never thought I'd have to make, but the journey I'd do all over again if I had to.

If I can leave you with anything I've learned, it's that you must trust that what you seek is seeking you and it always exists on the other side of fear. Even if that means you're being asked to give it all up and lose everything, trust that eventually it will all be replaced with things far better and more authentically aligned than you could ever imagine. I'm living proof. I hope you lose yourself to find it all.

# Acknowledgments

Is it normal to want to first thank everyone who ever hurt me? Because if I'm honest, this book would not have been possible without you. To the people who tried to cut me down, thank you for showing me that it is possible to grow on my own. To the people who left my side when I needed you most, thank you for showing me that I never actually needed you at all. To the people who refused to be a part of my life, thank you for removing yourself and showing me how to live without you.

To my mother, you are forever my queen and my lighthouse. I love you endlessly. To my girlfriends and to the strong and beautiful women in my life, I wouldn't be standing this tall and strong without you. To my editor, friend and mentor, Elle, thank you for holding me through this crazy writing journey. To my baby sister, thank you for all the silly memes and the endless phone calls to cheer me up about all these guys I dated post-divorce.

To my sweet boys, thank you for giving me a reason to keep on going when things felt hopeless and for meeting me with all your love and patience during one of the most difficult times we'll ever face together. Someday you will understand, and you will see why mom had to do all that she had to do. I hope you always know that your life and your happiness is worth fighting for.

To the BTR.org support group for women of abuse, thank you for being my lifeline while coaching me towards finding the strength to let go of a man and a life that was hurting me. To my kickass lawyer Kristen who fought hard for my freedom and to my therapist Tina who quite literally saved my life, thank you times infinity.

To Audri, for taking my hand and pulling me up from the mud and into a lotus flower. For shifting from friend to family. For reading and reviewing this book and hearing me yap about these men so many times you could probably recite these stories in your sleep. Thank you for your patience, understanding and love for me and all my causes.

To my ex-husbands new girl, God bless you for doing the lord's work. Here's hoping you don't have to endure half of what I did. To the men that didn't even make it in this book, what did you expect? LOL.

To my "Green Dot Gang"—AKA my private green circle Instagram stories crew, thank you all for being my beta readers and sounding board over the last couple years as I navigated the challenges and the humors of my new normal. Your support and love mean the world.

To Will, for being my muse while giving me something beautiful to experience and to write about. You helped make the story worth telling. I will cherish what we shared for all of my days.

To God and my angels above, thank you for the unconditional love, guidance, and support. For making miracles come true and blessing me through it all. Nothing is possible without you.

All of my love and gratitude. Thank you. Thank you. Thank you.

*BB*

Made in the USA
Middletown, DE
05 June 2024